Revision Guide

Cambridge IGCSE®

Geography

David Davies

CAMBRIDGE
UNIVERSITY PRESS

CAMBRIDGE
UNIVERSITY PRESS

University Printing House, Cambridge CB2 8BS, United Kingdom

One Liberty Plaza, 20th Floor, New York, NY 10006, USA

477 Williamstown Road, Port Melbourne, VIC 3207, Australia

4843/24, 2nd Floor, Ansari Road, Daryaganj, Delhi – 110002, India

79 Anson Road, #06–04/06, Singapore 079906

Cambridge University Press is part of the University of Cambridge.

It furthers the University's mission by disseminating knowledge in the pursuit of education, learning and research at the highest international levels of excellence.

Information on this title: education.cambridge.org

First published 2014
20 19 18 17 16 15 14 13 12 11 10 9 8 7 6

Printed in Great Britain by CPI Group (UK) Ltd, Croydon CRO 4YY

A catalogue record for this publication is available from the British Library

ISBN 978-1-107-67482-0 Paperback

Table of contents

Introduction *vi*

Theme 1: Population and settlement

1 Population dynamics ***3***

World population 3
Population density 4
The physical/natural factors 6
The human factors 8
Social factors 8
Population structure and the Demographic Transition Model 11
The problems of an ageing population 18
Migration 19
The impact of HIV/AIDS 25
Possible problems of growing population 26
Population control 26
Progress check 29
Examination style questions 29
Examination style questions for you to try 30

2 Settlement ***31***

Size, development and function of urban and rural settlements 31
Settlement hierarchies 34
Spheres of influence 35
Land-use zones of urban areas 36
The rural-urban fringe 39
Problems of urban areas in MEDCs and LEDCs 41
Impact of urbanisation on the environment 44
Progress check 45
Examination style questions 45
Examination style questions for you to try 46

Theme 2: The natural environment

3 Plate tectonics ***49***

The layers of the Earth 49
Types of plate boundary/margin 51
Earthquakes 52
Volcanoes 57

Tsunamis 61
Progress check 62
Examination style questions 62
Examination style questions for you to try 64

4 Weathering (Landforms and landscape processes) **65**

Weathering and erosion 65
Factors influencing the type and rate of weathering 66
Progress check 67
Examination style questions 68
Examination style questions for you to try 68

5 River processes (Landforms and landscape processes) **69**

River erosion, transportation and deposition 69
The landforms associated with the processes 71
Forms of river valleys 71
The building of dams on rivers 80
River flooding 81
Water resources 84
Progress check 85
Examination style questions 86
Examination style questions for you to try 86

6 Marine processes (Landforms and landscape processes) **_87_**

Coastal erosion, transportation and deposition 87
Features of coastal erosion 90
Features of coastal deposition 92
Coral reefs 93
Progress check 95
Examination style questions 95
Examination style questions for you to try 96

7 Weather, climate and natural vegetation **_97_**

Weather stations and the instruments used to measure the weather 97
Tropical rainforests 108
Tropical deserts 115
Progress check 119
Examination style questions 119
Examination style questions for you to try 120

Theme 3: Economic development and use of resources

8 Agricultural systems **_123_**

The classification of farming or agriculture 123
Commercial farming and subsistence farming 125
Food shortages and possible solutions 129

The use of irrigation 134
The problem of salination 135
Progress check 136
Examination style questions 136
Examination style questions for you to try 137

9 Industrial systems ***138***

Types of industry 138
Industry as a system 140
Factors affecting the location of industry 140
The changing location and nature of industry 143
Multinational or Transnational Companies (TNCs) 145
High technology or Hi tech industries 146
Progress check 150
Examination style questions 151
Examination style questions for you to try 152

10 Leisure activities and tourism ***153***

Tourism 153
The growth of leisure facilities and tourism 154
The advantages of tourism 155
The disadvantages of tourism 156
Case study – Tourism in Kenya 157
Sustainable tourism 161
National Parks 162
Progress check 163
Examination style questions 164
Examination style questions for you to try 165

11 Energy and water resources ***166***

Non-renewable and renewable energy resources 166
Development and siting of power stations 175
Water resources and the impact of water shortages 176
Increasing demand on Earth's resources 178
Progress check 179
Examination style questions 179
Examination style questions for you to try 180

Geographical skills for examination 181

Answers to questions 219

Index 232

Introduction

The purpose of this book is to help you revise for your Cambridge IGCSE Geography examination. The book covers the IGCSE Geography syllabus 0460. Revision and exam techniques play a major part in your level of success in an examination, so remember to start your revision well before the actual examination. Use several short sessions to help build up your knowledge of the subject over a period of time, so that you do not leave too little time to digest and understand the information.

Apart from reading through the text leave yourself time to attempt the questions. This is also a good method of revision and it allows you to do something practical rather than just reading. It may also be useful for you to make your own summary of the topics as you work through them – this can be done on postcard sized cards to allow you to quickly reference the information.

This Guide is divided into 11 sections which follow the order of the topics in the syllabus. At the end of each chapter, there are progress check questions to make sure that you have understood the main points covered by the topic. Following this, there are worked examples which look at probable answers to a question with appropriate comments. Finally, at the end of each topic, there are examination style questions for you to try which will further help you to prepare for examination. Some are from past exam papers and others are in the style of exam questions.

Cambridge International Examinations bears no responsibility for the example answers to questions taken from its past question papers which are contained in this publication.

Contents

The Examination-style questions, example answers marks awarded and comments in this book are written by the author.

Chapters 1 to 11 provide the information, knowledge and understanding from the content of the syllabus. The Geographical skills section includes the interpretation and analysis of geographical information and the application of graphical and other techniques. Chapter 10 covers the interpretation and analysis of geographical information and the application of graphical and other techniques.

The Inter-relationships between the natural environment and human activities are described throughout the first 5 chapters. The environmental risks and benefits, resource conservation and management involved in these systems, activities and resources are described in chapters 6 to 11. Chapter 11 provides preparation in the investigative skills needed for Paper 4 (Alternative to Coursework).

Cambridge IGCSE Geography assessment

All students will take Paper 1 and Paper 2 and then *either* carry out Coursework for Paper 3 *or* do the written Paper 4 – Alternative to Coursework. You should check the syllabus for the year that you are taking the paper for examination information and details of the individual papers.

Command words

All exam questions ask you precisely what they want a student to do and to answer. To make this as precise as possible they will use **command words** in their questions. Students must fully understand the meaning of these words in order to answer a question correctly. There are two very simple instructions to follow when doing the exam, i.e., **RTQ** and **ATQ** – **R**ead **T**he **Q**uestion and **A**nswer **T**he **Q**uestion. Unfortunately, many students do not do this, so learning the precise meaning of the Command Words used will help enormously in completing Geography examinations successfully. The examples of typical command words which could be used in an IGCSE Geography examinations are:

Annotate – You need to add labels, notes or short comments, usually to a diagram, map or photograph to describe or explain what is on the diagram.

Calculate – Work out a numerical answer. In general, your working should be shown, especially where two or more steps are involved. An example is to work out the Discharge of a River by multiplying two numbers – the Cross Sectional Area X Velocity.

Compare – Write about firstly what is similar and, secondly, what is different about two things. Be careful not to just describe the two things.

Complete – Add the remaining detail or details required to a diagram or sentence.

Contrast – Write about the differences between two things. Again, be careful not to just describe the two things.

Define or State the meaning of – Give the meaning or definition of a word or phrase or 'What is meant by the following term......?' This will be something like 'Hydraulic Action', 'Abrasion', 'Population density' or 'settlement hierarchy'.

Describe – Write what something is like or where it is. 'Describe' may be used for questions about the resources in the question paper (for example, describe the trend of a graph, the location of a settlement on a map, etc.). It may also be used when you need to describe something from memory (describe what a meander looks like, etc.). It is often used with other command words such as 'Name and Describe' (you will have to name a feature and say what it is like), or 'Describe and Explain' (you will have to say what it is like and give reasons for it).

Devise or Plan – You will need to produce something like a form or questionnaire.

Draw – This means 'Make a sketch of......' This word is often used with a labelled diagram (draw a diagram/illustration with written notes to identify its features).

Explain or 'Account for.....' or 'Give reasons for....' – You have to write about why something occurs or happens.

Giving your views or Comment on.... – Say what you think about something.

How... – In what way? To what extent? By what means/method? This word may be used with 'Show how...' (This means prove how or demonstrate how).

Identify – Pick out something from the information you have been given.

Illustrating your answer – You need to account for something by using specific examples or diagrams. (It is often used with a labelled diagram).

Insert or Label – Put on names or details on a diagram or map.

Justify – Say why you chose something or why you think in a certain way.

List – Identify and name a number of features.

Locate – Find where something is placed on a map or say where something is found on a map or mark it on a map or diagram.

Measure – This normally involves you measuring a distance on a map (make sure you use the scale correctly) or a value off a graph or diagram. You could use a ruler, or the straight edge of a piece of paper and then placing this along the scale line on the map or a ruler, to do this and once you have got a value double check it. This is a common mistake by pupils under exam conditions.

Name – Give the word or words by which a specific feature is known or to give examples which illustrate a particular feature.

Predict – Use your own knowledge and understanding of something to say what will happen in the future. This is often used to say what will happen when a waterfall or a cliff retreats (leaves a gorge or a wave cut platform – but you knew that anyway!).

Refer to... or With reference to.... – Write an answer which uses some of the ideas provided in a map/photograph/diagram, etc. or a case study.

State – Write down in brief detail. To refer to an aspect, or something about a particular feature by using short statement or by few words or by a single word.

Study – Look carefully at (usually one of the diagrams or figures in the question paper).

Suggest – Set down your ideas on or knowledge of something. This is often used with the word why (it needs you to give a statement or an explanation in which you refer to a particular feature or features).

Use... or Using the information provided.... – Base your answer on the information given on a map, graph or diagram – make sure that you use the information they give you and then expand on it with your own knowledge if they want you to.

With the help of information in... – Write an answer which uses some of the information provided as well as your own additional material.

What....? – This is used to form a question concerned with some ideas/details/factors.

What differences are shown between A and B? – Use comparative statements to describe the changes involved as A changes to B. Do not just describe what A is and then what B is, try to say what the differences between A and B are.

Where...? – At what place is something found? To what place is something going? From what place has something come from?

Why......? – For what cause or reason has something happened or formed?

The following is reproduced by permission of Cambridge International Examinations.

Syllabus Name and Code	Paper and Question Number	Month/Year	Page in book
Cambridge IGCSE Geography 0460	Paper 22 Fig 4	Nov 2011	Page 5 Figure 2
Cambridge IGCSE Geography 0460	Paper 12 Fig 1	Nov 2011	Page 12 Figure 3
Cambridge IGCSE Geography 0460	Paper 11 Fig 1	Nov 2011	Page 12 Figure 4
Cambridge IGCSE Geography 0460	Paper 23 Figs 8 and 9	Nov 2010	Page 23 Figures 5 (a and b)
Cambridge IGCSE Geography 0460	Paper 1 Fig 1	June 2009	Page 24 Figure 6
Cambridge IGCSE Geography 0460	Paper 2 Fig 7	Nov 2008	Page 24 Figure 7
Cambridge IGCSE Geography 0460	Paper 2 Fig 3	Nov 2002	Page 32 Figure 1
Cambridge IGCSE Geography 0460	Paper 11 Fig 2	Nov 2010	Page 34 Figure 2
Cambridge IGCSE Geography 0460	Paper 1 Fig 6	June 2008	Page 50 Figure 1
Cambridge IGCSE Geography 0460	Paper 21 Fig 7	Nov 2010	Page 60 Figure 2
Cambridge IGCSE Geography 0460	Paper 1 Fig 5	June 2003	Page 77 Figure 8
Cambridge IGCSE Geography 0460	Paper 13 Fig 5	Nov 2011	Page 89 Figure 3 (a)

Syllabus Name and Code	Paper and Question Number	Month/Year	Page in book
Cambridge IGCSE Geography 0460	Paper 13 Fig 5	Nov 2011	Page 90 Figure 3 (b)
Cambridge IGCSE Geography 0460	Paper 21 Fig 4	June 2010	Page 99 Figure 2
Cambridge IGCSE Geography 0460	Paper 21 Fig 4	June 2010	Page 101 Figure 3
Cambridge IGCSE Geography 0460	Paper 2 Table 3	June 2008	Page 101 Figure 3
Cambridge IGCSE Geography 0460	Paper 41 Fig 8	Nov 2011	Page 103 Figure 4
Cambridge IGCSE Geography 0460	Paper 2 Fig 1	Nov 2005	Page 105 Figure 5
Cambridge IGCSE Geography 0460	Paper 42 Fig 8	June 2010	Page 106 Figure 6
Cambridge IGCSE Geography 0460	Paper 1 Fig 5	Nov 2009	Page 108 Figure 7
Cambridge IGCSE Geography 0460	Paper 23 Fig 11	Nov 2011	Page 109 Figure 8
Cambridge IGCSE Geography 0460	Paper 2 Fig 6	June 2003	Page 110 Figure 9
Cambridge IGCSE Geography 0460	Paper 2 Fig 4	Nov 2003	Page 116 Figure 10
Cambridge IGCSE Geography 0460	Paper 23 Fig 6	June 2010	Page 129 Figure 1
Cambridge IGCSE Geography 0460	Paper 11 Fig 9	June 2011	Page 130 Figure 2
Cambridge IGCSE Geography 0460	Paper 23 Fig 5	June 2010	Page 139 Figure 1
Cambridge IGCSE Geography 0460	Paper 2 Fig 8	June 2008	Page 147 Figure 2
Cambridge IGCSE Geography 0460	Paper 1 Fig 10	June 2005	Page 176 Figure 1
Cambridge IGCSE Geography 0460	Paper 2 Q1 Fig 1	June 2006	Page 183 Figure 1
Cambridge IGCSE Geography 0460	Paper 2 Q1 Fig 2	June 2006	Page 186 Figure 2
Cambridge IGCSE Geography 0460	Paper 2 Q1 and 2 inc Fig 2	June 2003	Page 189 Figure 3
Cambridge IGCSE Geography 0460	Paper 1 Q1 Fig 1	June 2006	Page 190 Figures 4 and 5
Cambridge IGCSE Geography 0460	Paper 2 Q5 inc Fig 8	June 2003	Page 191 Figure 6
Cambridge IGCSE Geography 0460	Paper 2 Q6 inc Fig 5	Nov 2004	Page 192 Figure 7
Cambridge IGCSE Geography 0460	Paper 2 Q4 inc Figs 5 and 6	June 2006	Page 193 Figures 8 and 9
Cambridge IGCSE Geography 0460	Paper 2 Q2 inc Fig 2	June 2003	Page 194 Figure 10
Cambridge IGCSE Geography 0460	Paper 2 Q4 inc Fig 5	June 2003	Page 195 Figure 11
Cambridge IGCSE Geography 0460	Paper 2 Q4 Fig 3	June 2005	Page 195 Figure 12
Cambridge IGCSE Geography 0460	Paper 2 Q6 inc Fig 10	June 2003	Page 196 Figure 13
Cambridge IGCSE Geography 0460	Paper 2 Q5 (c) inc Fig 9	June 2003	Page 196 Figure 14
Cambridge IGCSE Geography 0460	Paper 2 Q6 inc Fig 6	June 2005	Page 197 Figure 15
Cambridge IGCSE Geography 0460	Paper 2 Q3 inc Fig 2	June 2005	Page 198 Figure 16
Cambridge IGCSE Geography 0460	Paper 1 Q2 inc Fig 3	June 2006	Page 199 Figure 17
Cambridge IGCSE Geography 0460	Paper 1 Q1 Fig 2	June 2006	Page 200 Figure 18
Cambridge IGCSE Geography 0460	Paper 1 Q2 (b) inc Fig 4	June 2006	Page 201 Figure 19 (a and b)
Cambridge IGCSE Geography 0460	Paper 4/43 Q1 Fig 3	Nov 2011	Page 205 Figure 20
Cambridge IGCSE Geography 0460	Paper 2 Fig 13	Nov 2002	Page 206 Figure 21 (a)
Cambridge IGCSE Geography 0460	Paper 4 Q2 Fig 9	Nov 2008	Page 208 Figure 22
Cambridge IGCSE Geography 0460	Paper 4 Q1 Table 1	Nov 2007	Page 210 Figure 23
Cambridge IGCSE Geography 0460	Paper 4 Q1 Fig 1	Nov 2007	Page 211 Figure 24
Cambridge IGCSE Geography 0460	Paper 4/41 Q2 Fig 8	Nov 2011	Page 214 Figure 25
Cambridge IGCSE Geography 0460	Paper 4 Q1 Fig 3	June 2007	Page 216 Figure 26
Cambridge IGCSE Geography 0460	Paper 4 Q2 Figs 7 and 8	June 2007	Page 217 Figure 27
Cambridge IGCSE Geography 0460	Paper 4 Q1 Table 2	Nov 2005	Page 218 Figure 28
Cambridge IGCSE Geography 0460	Paper 4 Q2 Fig 9	June 2008	Page 218 Figure 29

Theme 1:

Population and settlement

Chapter

1 Population dynamics

Learning Summary

In this chapter you will learn about:

- ***Factors influencing the density and distribution of population and migration***
- ***Reasons for rapid increase in the world's population in recent times***
- ***The main components influencing population growth***
- ***The relationship between population growth and resources and why problems may result in some areas***
- ***Contrasting patterns of population growth in different world areas***
- ***The consequences of different patterns of population growth***
- ***Reasons for different types of population structure***
- ***The major physical, economic and human influences on population density and population distribution***
- ***Reasons for population migrations***

World population

- The world's population in November 2012 was estimated to have passed 7 billion and this figure will continue to grow. However, the rate of growth of the world's population is slowing down – the rate of growth today has almost halved since reaching a peak growth rate of 2.2 % in 1963.
- World births have levelled off at about 134 million per year since the mid-1990s, and are expected to remain constant. However, deaths are only around 56 million per year, and are expected to increase to 90 million by the year 2050.
- Since births outnumber deaths, the world's population is expected to reach nearly 9 billion by the year 2042.
- Population projections/estimates are not always accurate. The graph that follows was used in the November 2002 Geography exam – have a look at the estimate/projection for 2013.

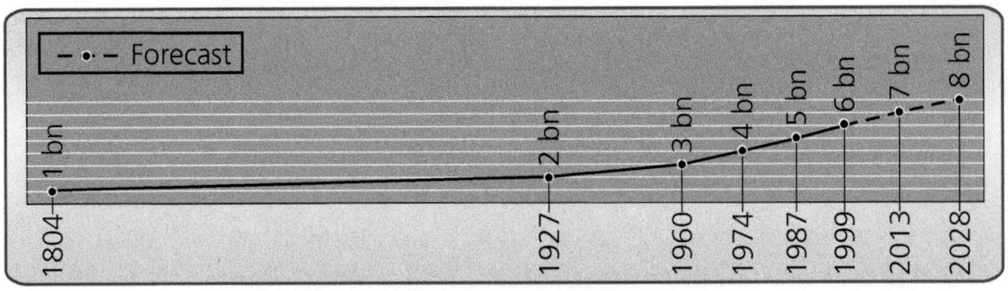

Figure 1 World population growth

Some important terms and their definitions

- ***Population distribution*** is a description of the spread of the human population across Earth. The distribution is very uneven – most of the world's population lives in only one third of the available land area.
- ***Population density*** is the number of people per unit of area usually per square kilometre. This may be calculated for a county, a city, a country, or the entire world. It is found by dividing the total population of a country or region by its land area (in square kms).
- ***Birth rate*** is the average number of live births for every 1000 people in a country.
- ***Death rate*** (Mortality rate) is the average number of deaths for every 1000 people in a country.
- The difference between the birth and death rates is either the ***natural increase*** or ***natural decrease***.
- The ***optimum population*** for a region or country is a level of population which is ecologically sustainable. It is linked to the ***carrying capacity*** of the region or country. If there are too many people the resources will be used up and problems will appear – in food supply and water for example. At this point, the carrying capacity will have been exceeded and living standards for many people will start to decline.
- At that point, a region or country is said to be over populated. Below this point a country can be said to be under populated. Therefore, the term ***overpopulation*** is used where the number of people exceeds the carrying capacity of an area, while the term ***under population*** is where the number of people is below the carrying capacity of an area.

Carrying capacity is the amount of resources in a country that can support the country's population.

Population density

Population density describes the number of people living in a given area, usually a km². It can be used on a variety of scales from continents, to countries to regions within a country. It is calculated by dividing the ***total population*** of one of these by the ***total area***.

On any population density map of the world it is possible to pick out areas that have high and low population densities. The areas with high population densities are in the following regions.

India and Bangladesh – along the Ganges river, the North China Plains, the China Sichuan Basin, the Nile river and its delta in Egypt, Southern Japan, Western Europe, the Indonesian island of Java, Central America (especially El Salvador, the Americas' most densely populated nation), and the United States' BosWash (the area between Boston and Washington in the NE of the USA) – an area where conurbations have grown and merged together creating a **megalopolis**.

The factors affecting population distribution and population density

The Earth's land surface is about 30 per cent of the total Earth's surface – the rest being water. However, only about 11 per cent of the land area is comfortably habitable by people. The factors can be divided into two groups – ***Physical (Natural)*** and **Human**.

- The ***physical (natural) factors*** are factors involving the natural environment and include climate, water supply, natural resources, relief, natural vegetation and soils.
- The ***human factors*** are factors that are a result of human activities and these may be economic, social (including cultural) or political. The economic factors include transport and money (sometimes called capital) to invest in industry. The social factors include housing, health care and education. The political factors include government investment in the infrastructure of an area such as in roads, railways, airports and sea ports, and land reclamation.

Figure 2 shows some areas of the world with high population densities. You may be given maps like this on a global, continental or country scale and be asked to describe the distribution of the variable shown on the map – in this case areas with a high population density. You should use the information on the map to identify the continents, the locations within the continents relative to the compass location and whether they are near to, or far from, the coast; as well as their location relative to the lines of latitude shown on the map.

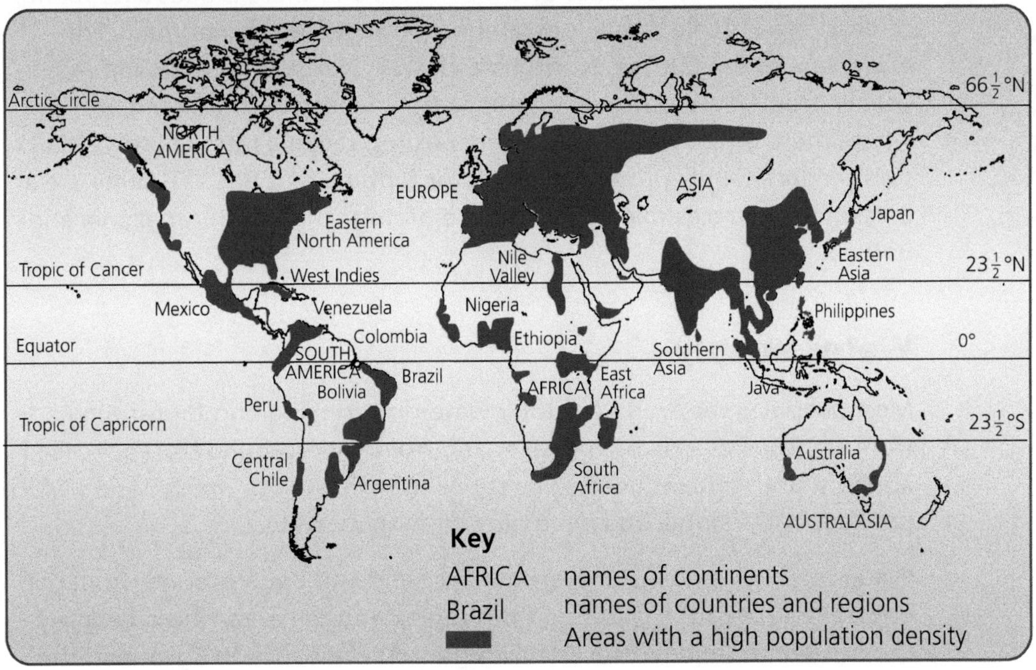

Figure 2

Cambridge 0460 Paper 22 Fig 4 Nov 2011

The physical/natural factors

Climate

There are 3 major climate zones covering the Earth – Polar, Temperate and Tropical.

People tend to avoid living in polar areas because of:

- the long periods of freezing temperatures in winter
- the very short growing seasons for plants.

These areas, therefore, have ***very low population densities*** and contain people who are traditional hunters and gatherers such as the Inuit of northern Canada, Alaska and Greenland. These people survive by hunting seals, fish and whales at sea and caribou (reindeer) on land.

Such cold climates can also be found in mountainous areas of the world, such as the Himalayas, Andes and Rockies. Again, these areas have very low population densities as well.

Other areas of low population density are the tropical deserts – the Sahara, Arabian central Australia, Atacama, Kalahari/Namib and South West USA – where the very high temperatures for much of the year and lack of rainfall combine to produce a very harsh living environment.

99 per cent of the Egyptian population of 81 million is found on just 4 per cent of the country's land area – the rest being desert!

Areas of ***high population density*** tend to be in, firstly, the temperate areas where there are no extremes of temperature and there is adequate rainfall to provide a reliable source of water for both people and farming. For example Western Europe, North Eastern USA, North East China and Japan. Certain tropical areas have high population density, such as Bangladesh, where there is year round high temperatures, reliable rainfall and fertile soils produce highly productive areas for farming, but not all – some are at present very inaccessible, such as the rainforests of Central Amazonia and Borneo.

Water supply

Most people in the world get their water for drinking and for farming from two sources – rivers and lakes and from underground storages called aquifers. Both sources need to be supplied with enough precipitation which provides both rainfall and meltwater from snow and ice.

Water can flow long distances, both overland and underground, from the original source of the water and this can extend the area where people can live. For example, the Nile flowing across the desert in Egypt and the Colorado in South West USA. Where there is a lack of reliable water supply population densities are normally low.

Soils

The fertility of the soil is very important in determining how productive an area will be for crops. The most fertile soils are mineral rich and well drained. These tend to be found in river floodplains and deltas and in areas of volcanic rocks – which tend to weather down into very fertile soils. Where water is available, either naturally or by irrigation, areas of fertile soil can support high population densities – such as the island of Java in Indonesia.

Conversely, upland areas with thin, rocky, infertile soils may have low population densities as they may only be used for the extensive farming of sheep, for example in North Wales in the UK and the High Atlas mountains in Morocco.

Relief (Topography)

The terms relief and topography are used to describe the height and shape of the land. Population densities tend to be lowest where land is high and steep and highest where land is low and gently sloping or flat. The high land found in the world's major mountain ranges tends to have lower temperatures, more frosts and higher rainfall, which often falls as snow.

Temperature drops at a rate of about 1°C for every 100 metres you go up in height.

High land also tends to have steeper slopes which are more difficult to farm (though this can be overcome by terracing – as in the rice terraces of Indonesia and southern China). As a result, most of the world's population tends to be found in the lower areas of the world – around the coastlines and on river floodplains and deltas.

Natural resources

The term ***natural resource***, in its broadest sense, applies to any natural resource from water and soil to wind and minerals. However, in Population Geography terms, it usually refers to minerals such as coal, oil and metallic minerals such as iron ore, bauxite (the natural ore from which aluminium is obtained), gold, silver, tin, copper, etc.

The Industrial Revolution in the nineteenth century saw a massive movement (migration) of people to the major coalfields of Western Europe, especially the UK and Germany, and the US. The coal provided fuel for major industries, like the iron and steel industries, which provided thousands of new jobs and had a huge impact on population densities in places like South Wales in the UK and the Ruhr in Germany.

The human factors

Economic factors

In today's world, economic factors are now extremely important in the location of industry which, in turn, provides jobs which affects where people live – i.e. population distribution.

The term ***cumulative causation*** is often used to describe this set of links – the fact that certain things will result (be caused) when a group of factors combine (accumulate) together.

One of the most important economic factors is transport. Where fast, efficient, reliable and cheap transport is available many industries will have an advantage as it will reduce their production costs and increase the area in which they can sell their products. A large modern port provides such a location, for example, Europort in the Netherlands, Singapore in South East Asia, Shanghai in China and New York in the US.

Motorways have a similar effect and attract industry. For example, the M4 corridor along the M4 motorway linking London and South Wales in the UK. These locations are often natural route centres on which other forms of transport, such as road, rail and air, converge. London and Paris are both good examples, as they are both at the centre of their country's road, rail and air networks.

Political factors

Political factors include government investment in the infrastructure of an area such as in roads, railways, airports and sea ports, and land reclamation.

National and regional governments, as well as the major ***Trading Blocs***, such as the European Union, have very important role in deciding where industry, jobs, roads, railways, air and sea ports, housing, hospitals and schools are located and therefore, on the distribution of population. For example, the siting of the new olympic facilities in old run down industrial areas in London in 2012 and Sydney in 2004.

Social factors

Social factors include housing, health care, education and cultural opportunities.

Areas of the world where many of these factors combine together can either be densely populated or sparsely populated. For example, the Sahara desert, which stretches across several countries of North Africa, is very sparsely populated because its climate is too hot and dry for people and animals to survive comfortably.

Its soils are too dry, sandy or rocky. It has a poor water supply. Lastly, the countries it runs through are all poor LEDC's whose governments do not have the money to invest in improving their infrastructure in transport, housing, education and health care or industrial development.

At the other extreme, the world's most densely populated country, Bangladesh, has rich, fertile soil. It has a hot wet climate with easy access to water supplies. All of this means that it is ideal for growing crops and can support a very large population on a relatively small area of land.

Sometimes large urban areas may grow up in areas which are otherwise sparsely populated. For example:

- Around an oasis in a desert
- Near rivers where they flow through arid desert areas
- Mining settlements on coal or iron ore fields, or the production of oil as in Kuwait
- Growth of tourist destinations and resorts such as Dubai in the UAE and Sharm El Sheikh in Egypt
- Market towns where the products of a large rural area can be brought to sell
- Route centres and the junctions of major highways often in openings or gaps in mountain and hill ranges – gap towns
- Towns of strategic importance controlling access to a region
- New towns created by government policies
- Dry areas in otherwise waterlogged marshy land
- A sheltered, fertile valley in a highland area.

The following list is a selection of countries which show the great variations in population density that exist around the world.

Countries ranked by population density – in people/km²

Country and Population	Area in km²	Population per km²
1. Monaco – 33 000	1.95	16 923
2. Singapore – 5 077 000	699	7 148
8. Maldives – 329 198	298	1 327
11. Bangladesh – 143 000 000	143 998	964
35. Japan – 128 000 000	377 873	348
31. India – 1 225 000 000	3 287 263	395
45. Philippines – 92 226 000	300 076	307
50. United Kingdom – 62 000 000	243 600	255
52. Pakistan – 178 000 000	803 940	222
61. Kuwait – 3 566 000	17 818	200
80. China – 1 349 000 000	9 596 961	140
86. Indonesia – 238 000 000	1 904 569	121
European Union – 494 070 000	4 422 773	112

Country and Population	Area in km²	Population per km²
120. Egypt – 81 850 000	1 001 449	81
169. South Africa – 51 000 000	1 221 037	41
179. USA – 313 000 000	9 629 091	32
223. Russia – 143 000 000	17 098 242	8
224. Canada – 33 740 000	9 984 670	3
230. Australia – 23 000 000	7 682 300	3
238. Greenland (Denmark) – 56 916	2 175 600	0.026
World Population – 7 000 000 000	148 940 000 km²	47

It also includes all continental and island land areas, including Antarctica.

Earth's population is 7 billion and its area is 510 million km². The worldwide human population density is, therefore, 7 billion ÷ 510 million = 13.7 per km², or 46.7 per km² – if only the Earth's land area of 149 million km² is taken into account. This density rises when the population grows.

Considering that over half of the Earth's land mass consists of areas inhospitable to human inhabitation, such as deserts and high mountains, and that population tends to cluster around seaports and fresh water sources, this number by itself does not give an accurate measurement or picture of human population density.

The most densely populated country is Monaco, with a population density of 16 923 people/km².

Macau, part of China, has the highest population density, with 541 000 people sharing an area of 29.2 km² – a population density of over 18 534 persons per km². Antarctica is 14 400 000 km² in area. With a population of roughly 1000, this results in a population density of 0.00007 people per km² (far below Greenland's density of 0.026). A peak summer population of 5000 results in an increase in density to about 0.00035!

The following list includes the top 10 countries by their population and the percentage of the total world population (to the nearest per cent).

1. China 1 349 000 000	20 per cent of total world population
2. India 1 225 460 000	17 per cent
3. USA 310 000 000	5 per cent
4. Indonesia 238 000 000	3 per cent
5. Brazil 196 000 000	3 per cent
6. Pakistan 178 000 000	2 per cent
7. Nigeria 158 000 000	2 per cent
8. Bangladesh 143 000 000	2 per cent
9. Russia 143 000 000	2 per cent
10. Japan 128 000 000	2 per cent
22. United Kingdom 62 000 000	1 per cent
136. Kuwait 3 566 000	0.042 per cent
214. Nauru 10 000	0.0001 per cent

Population structure and the Demographic Transition Model

Population structure

The term ***population structure*** is used to describe the structure/composition/make up of population in a country or region.

This will include examining the characteristics of age, sex (male or female), fertility (the average number of children born to a woman), mortality (the death rate) and migration (movement of people), race, language, religion, occupation, etc. The two most studied characteristics are age and sex.

These two characteristics are normally shown together in a ***population pyramid***. The pyramids are split in half to show males on the left and females on the right. They have a vertical axis which is normally in 5 year segments, but can be more detailed and have individual years. The pyramids can either use absolute figures in thousands and millions or, more commonly, percentages of the total population.

Population pyramids differ considerably in shape from country to country and in any country over a period of time. They are useful tools in showing and analysing changes and trends in population structure. The changes that take place over time are called demographic transition. A traditional way to study these changes over time has been to use the ***Demographic Transition Model*** **(DTM)**.

The Demographic Transition Model (DTM) is a theoretical model which is used to show these changes that take place in a country over time from high birth rates and death rates to low birth rates and death rates as part of the economic development of a country from a pre-industrial/less developed to an industrialised/more developed economy. It is based on a model put forward by an American demographer called Warren Thompson who recorded the changes, or transitions, in birth and death rates in industrialised societies over the past two hundred years.

The term demographic transition describes the changes in birth and death rates from high levels to low levels over time.

Today most developed countries (***MEDCs***) are beyond stage 3 of the model. The majority of developing countries (***LEDCs***) are in stages 2 or 3. The model was based on the changes seen in Europe so European countries follow the DTM relatively well.

Many developing countries have now moved into stage 3. The major exceptions are the poorest LEDC countries, mainly in Sub-Saharan Africa and some Middle Eastern countries, which are poor or affected by government policy or civil strife, notably Pakistan, Palestinian Territories, Yemen and Afghanistan.

Demographic Transition Model

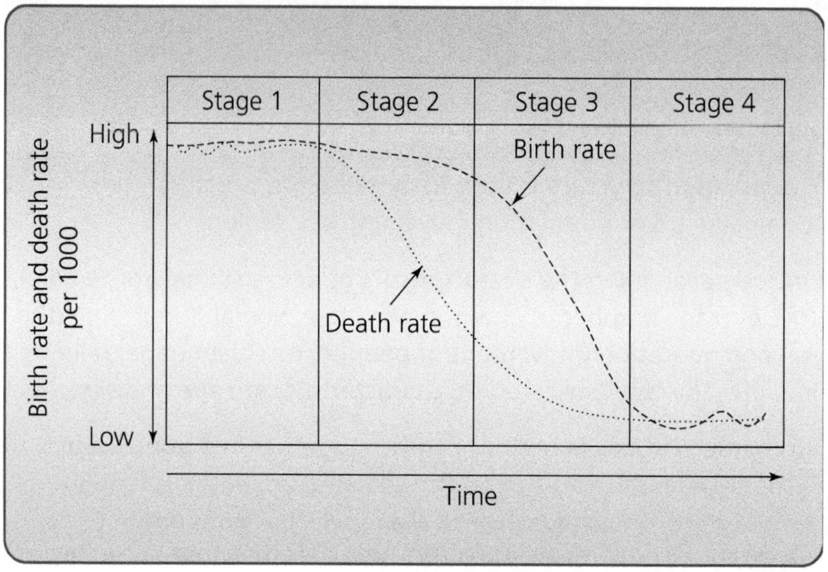

Figure 3

Cambridge 0460 Paper 12 Fig 1 Nov 2011

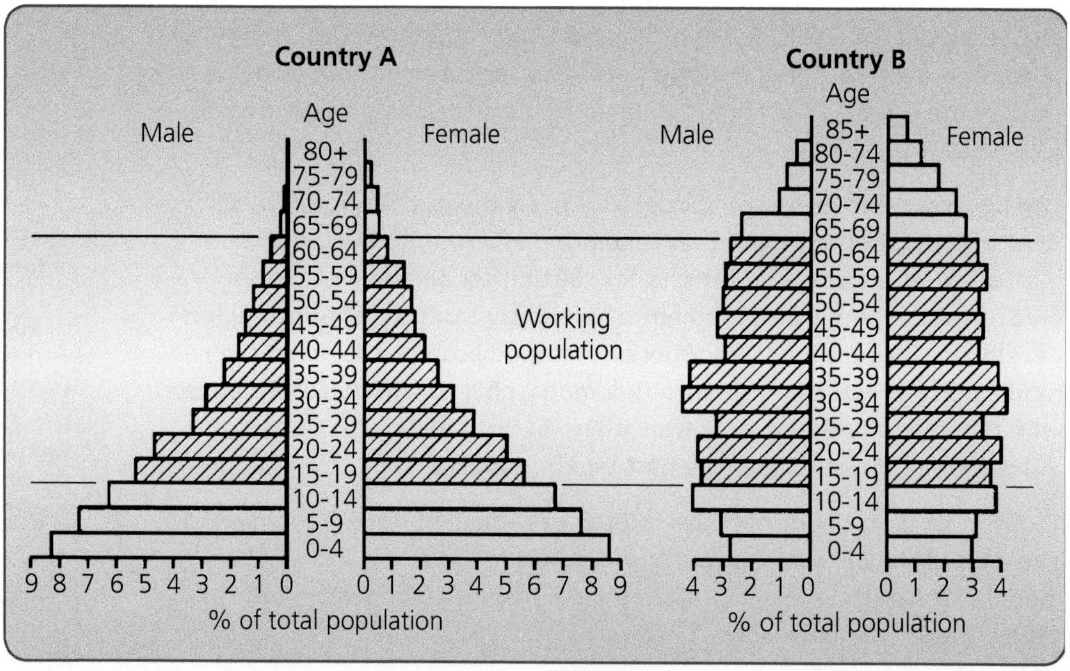

Figure 4

Cambridge 0460 Paper 11 Fig 1 Nov 2011

Two contrasting population pyramids as shown in Figure 4: Country A is in Stage 1 of the DTM and Country B in Stage 4. Country A has a wide base, with a large percentage of young dependents; and tapers quickly, due to higher death rates, to a narrow top.

An example could be Eritrea in north east Africa. Country B has a narrow base and is shaped more like a column than a pyramid. An example could be Japan. Note the much larger percentage of the population who are 65+ in Country B making it taller and reflecting the higher life expectancy of Country B. On both pyramids the ***economically active*** portion of the population between the ages of 15 and 65 is shaded

The model has countries going through a transition which involves going through ***four stages*** (or possibly five). In ***Stage One***, in a pre-industrial society or a very poor LEDC, both the death rates and the birth rates are high – about 35 per 1000 people and they fluctuate.

Birth rates are high in Stage 1 because:

- There is little or no birth control or family planning
- More children will mean that a family will have more help to farm the land, as they cannot afford machinery
- In some societies, a large number of children is seen as a sign of virility
- As so many children die when they are young, parents have several children to try and ensure that some will live and look after them in old age
- Religious beliefs – some religions encourage large families.

Death rates are high in Stage 1 because:

- There is high level of diseases – such as Cholera, Tuberculosis, Malaria and the Bubonic Plague (the Black Death)
- High number of famines producing both starvation and malnutrition
- Poor hygiene – there is a lack of clean water and very poor sewage disposal; many people, especially young children and babies, will die from diarrhoea
- Little or no medication – a lack of doctors, hospitals, medicinal drugs.

In ***Stage Two***, which is typical of a developing (LEDC) country, the birth rates remain high but the death rates drop rapidly (to about 20 per 1000). The drop in the death rates is due to:

- Improvements in farming techniques which increases food supply – so there will be less starvation and malnutrition
- Improvements in transport allowing food to be moved around more quickly and further
- Improvements in basic healthcare – hospitals, doctors, vaccination and immunisation programmes
- Improved water supply and sewage disposal, so there is less deaths from diarrhoea.

All this results in increased life expectancy and as there is no corresponding fall in birth rates and more people are living longer, countries in this stage experience a large increase in population.

In ***Stage Three,*** birth rates fall rapidly (to about 20 per 1000) and death rates continue to fall more slowly (to about 215 per 1000) due to:

- Access to contraception – family size can be planned
- Increases in wages – families are better off and do not need as many children to work
- Increased urbanisation – children are not needed as much for work as they are in farming families
- A reduction in subsistence (where what you grow your family eats – there is little or no extra food to sell for cash) agriculture – not as many children are not needed to work on the farms
- An improvement in the status and education of women
- A reduction in the value of children's work, an increase in parental investment in the education of children and other social changes.

As a result population growth begins to level off in Stage 3.

During ***Stage Four*** there is both low birth rates and low death rates. Birth rates may drop to well below replacement level, as has happened in countries like Germany, Italy, and Japan, leading to a shrinking population. This is a threat to many industries that rely on population growth to provide their workforce; they do not have enough workers to fill the jobs available.

Also, as the large group of people in the country born during stage two get older, it creates an economic burden on the shrinking working population (they will have to pay more taxes) who have to support more retired people.

Death rates may remain consistently low or even increase slightly due to a rise in lifestyle diseases. These are due to people doing less exercise and eating high calorie, fatty foods. This leads to increased obesity and an increase in diabetes and coronary heart diseases.

What was/is life like in the four stages of the DTM?

In Stage 1, death rates and birth rates were/are both high and fluctuated rapidly according to natural events, such as droughts, floods, war and disease, which produced a relatively constant and young population. Children contributed to the economy of the household from an early age by carrying water, collecting firewood, caring for younger children, cleaning, washing, preparing food, and doing some work in the fields. For a poor family raising a child cost little more than feeding the child, also, there was/is no access to education or entertainment expenses.

In addition, as they became adults, the children became a major input into the family business, mainly farming, and they were the main form of insurance in old age.

In India, an adult son was all that prevented a widow from falling into poverty and destitution and while death rates remained high, there was no question as to the need for large families, even if the means to prevent them had existed.

In these societies there was, and is, no government pensions to look after people in their old age when they became too weak to work.

In Stage 2, there is a fall in the death rates and a rapid increase in population. The change to Stage 2 in Europe was started in the Agricultural Revolution of the eighteenth century when better farming techniques meant that more food could be grown which could support a larger population. In the twentieth century, the fall in death rates in developing countries tended to be faster.

Countries in this stage include the following.

Yemen, Afghanistan, Palestine, Bhutan and Laos and much of Sub-Saharan Africa (but do not include South Africa, Zambia, Botswana, Swaziland, Lesotho, Namibia, Kenya and Ghana, all of which have begun to move into stage 3).

The decline in the death rate is due to two factors:

- Improvements in the food supply brought about by higher yields due to better agricultural practices and better transportation of food which helped prevent death due to starvation. These agricultural improvements included crop rotation, selective breeding, and seed drill technology.
- Significant improvements in public health care which helped reduce death rates (mortality), particularly for children. These included medical breakthroughs (such as the development of vaccinations) and, more importantly, improvements in water supply, sewerage, food handling, and improved general personal hygiene. This came from a growing scientific knowledge of the causes of disease and the improved education of mothers.

Even with all these improvements, in 2009, over half a million mothers die in childbirth each year due to a lack of medical facilities in the poorer countries of the world.

One person dies every 30 seconds from Malaria.

The main result of the decline in the death rate in stage two is an increasingly rapid rise in population growth (a 'population explosion') as the gap between deaths and births grows wider. This change in population occurred in NW Europe during the nineteenth century due to the Industrial Revolution. During the second half of the twentieth century less-developed countries (LEDC's) entered stage two, creating the worldwide population explosion that has some people concerned today.

Another characteristic of stage two of the demographic transition is a change in the age structure of the population. In stage one, the majority of deaths are concentrated in the first 5–10 years of life. Therefore, more than anything else, the decline in death rates in stage two sees the increasing survival of children and a growing population. As a result, the age structure of the population becomes increasingly younger and more of these children enter the reproductive cycle of their lives while maintaining the high fertility rates of their parents. The bottom of the 'age pyramid' widens first, accelerating population growth. The age structure of such a population is illustrated by using an example from an LEDC like the countries of Afghanistan and Angola today.

Urban living also raises the cost of dependent children to a family.

In Stage 3, the population moves towards stability through a decline in the birth rate. There are several factors contributing to this eventual decline. In rural areas, continued decline in childhood death means that at some point parents realise they need not require so many children to be born to ensure a comfortable old age. As childhood death continues to fall and incomes increase, parents can become increasingly confident that fewer children will be needed to help in the family business and care for them in old age. Increasing urbanisation changes the traditional values placed upon fertility and the value of children in rural society.

In both rural and urban areas, the cost of children to parents is increased by the introduction of compulsory Education Acts and the increased need to educate children so they can get a better job. Children are now usually stopped by law from working. Partly due to education and access to family planning, people begin to reassess their need for children and their ability to raise them.

Increasing female education has led to more women getting jobs and following careers. Working women have less time to raise children; this is particularly an issue where fathers traditionally make little or no contribution to child-raising, such as southern Europe or Japan. Improvements in contraceptive technology are a major factor. Contraceptives are now more widely available and the knowledge of how to use them.

The resulting changes in the age structure of the population eventually lead to an aging population. The population pyramid becomes less triangular in shape and more like a stretched balloon. Countries that have experienced a fertility decline of over 40 per cent from their pre-transition levels include the following.

Costa Rica, Jamaica, Mexico, Ecuador, Philippines, Indonesia, Malaysia, Sri Lanka, Turkey, Egypt, Morocco, Lebanon, South Africa, India and many Pacific islands.

Countries that have experienced a fertility decline of 25–40 per cent include the following.

Vietnam, India, Bangladesh, Jordan, Qatar, United Arab Emirates, Zimbabwe and Botswana.

Countries that have experienced a fertility decline of 10–25 per cent include the following.

Nepal, Pakistan, Syria, Iraq, Saudi Arabia, Botswana, Kenya, Ghana.

In Stage 4, both birth and death rates are low. Therefore, the total population is high and stable. Some people think that there are only 4 stages and that the population of a country will remain at this level. Countries that are at this stage include the following.

The DTM is only a suggestion about the future population levels of a country. It is not a prediction.

USA, Canada, Argentina, Australia, New Zealand, most of Europe, Trinidad and Tobago, Brazil, Sri Lanka, South Korea, Singapore, Iran and China.

Will there be a Stage Five?

The original DTM has just four stages, however, some people think that a fifth stage is needed to represent countries that have gone through the economic transition from manufacturing based industries into service and information based industries – a process called **deindustrialisation**. Countries such as the United Kingdom (the earliest country to reach stage five), Germany, Italy, Spain, Portugal, Greece and Japan. These countries are now reproducing well below their replacement levels and are not producing enough children to replace their parents' generation.

China, South Korea, Hong Kong, Singapore, Thailand and Cuba are also below replacement levels, but this is not producing a fall in population yet in these countries, because their populations are relatively young due to strong growth in the recent past.

The population of southern Europe is already falling, and Japan and some West European countries will soon begin to fall. However, many countries that are not replacing their population did not reach this stage gradually but rather suddenly due to an economic crisis as a result of the change from Communism in the late 1980s and 1990s. Examples include Russia, Ukraine, and the Baltic States.

The population of these countries is falling due to fertility decline, emigration and, particularly in Russia, increased male mortality.

The death rate can also increase due to 'diseases of wealth', such as obesity or diabetes, leading to a gradual fall in population in addition to aging.

The population of 51 countries, including Germany, Italy, Japan and most of the former Soviet Union, is expected to be lower in 2050 than in 2005.

In 2000–2005, migration in 28 countries either prevented population decline or it doubled the amount of natural increase (births minus deaths) to produce population growth. These countries include Austria, Canada, Croatia, Denmark, Germany, Italy, Portugal, Qatar, Singapore, Spain, Sweden, United Arab Emirates and United Kingdom. A greater number of women in developed countries now have their children later in life. The reasons behind this include:

- The emancipation of women and the freedom to be more than a child bearer
- Spending a longer time in education by going on to higher education courses in universities, therefore having a later marriage and less likely to bear children
- Putting their career development and working life first
- Medically safe to bear children later
- More effective birth control methods
- Increased education on birth control and its methods
- Cultural change
- A desire for material possessions which can be achieved by two wage earners in a family rather than one
- The high costs of looking after children in their early years
- Second marriages.

How useful is the DTM?

As with all models, the DTM is an idealised picture of population change in countries. The model is a generalisation that applies to these countries as a group and, therefore, it may not accurately describe individual cases. The extent to which it applies to less-developed societies today remains to be seen. Many countries such as China, Brazil and Thailand have passed through the DTM very quickly due to rapid social and economic change.

Some countries, particularly African countries, appear to be stalled/stopped in the second stage due to stagnant development and the effect of AIDS.

The problems of an ageing population

The 15–65 age group are called ***economically active***. The age groups below 15 and above 65 are called ***economically inactive***. The ratio between the economically active and inactive groups is called the ***dependency ratio***.

As people live longer they place an increasing burden on the economically active group. In the UK, the number of economically inactive people over the age of 65 compared to economically active people has changed remarkably between 1950 and today. In 1950, there were 15 retired people to every 100 working people. This had increased to 20 in 2000 and will be 40 in 2040.

In Italy, the situation is further advanced and 19 per cent of its GDP is being spent supporting the elderly, by 2030 this could be 33 per cent which is unsustainable in the current economic situation in Italy.

In the twentieth century, life expectancy rose by 30 years and by 2050, 75 per cent of people in MEDC's will live to over the age of 75. The effects of an ageing population include:

- A decline in the total population of a country
- Labour shortages – several countries, such as Germany, overcome this by importing workers – migrant workers
- Increased spending on medical services for the elderly – geriatric healthcare and retirement homes to look after the elderly
- The under use and closure of other services like schools
- More people will require a pension for a longer period of time as life expectancy increases.

Describe and suggest reasons for population migrations. Reference should be made to internal movements such as rural-urban migration as well as to international migrations both voluntary and involuntary.

Migration

Migration is the movement of people to live or to work. Migration can be either ***internal*** (movement within a country) or ***external*** (movement to another country). People who leave a country are called ***emigrants***. People who arrive in a country are called ***immigrants***.

Migration can be ***permanent*** – where the migrant moves away forever, ***temporary*** – where the migrant returns to their home country at some time in the future or ***daily***.

The reasons for migration can be ***forced***, where there is no choice for the migrant or ***voluntary*** where it is the own choice of the migrant. The reasons why people migrate may be one or more of a two sets of factors, called – ***push and pull factors***.

Push factors are those that cause people to move/migrate away from an area.

Pull factors attract people to an area. In many countries, there has been a large migration from rural to urban areas. Both can be a mixture of either natural or human factors.

Push factors include the following.

- Natural disasters and events – such as volcanic eruptions, earthquakes, tsunami, hurricanes, floods, drought and rising sea levels
- Unemployment
- Lack of work opportunities
- Escape from poverty and low incomes
- War
- Racial, political or religious intolerance
- High crime rates
- Housing shortages
- Land shortages
- Famine or lack of food.

Pull factors include the following.

- Employment
- Higher wages
- Availability of food supplies
- Better housing and education opportunities
- Higher standard of living
- Greater racial, political and religious tolerance
- More attractive living environment
- 'Bright lights' syndrome
- Less crime.

Voluntary migrations are often for economic reasons as people look for employment or for improved wages. One of the most common migrations taking place in the world is rural to urban migration – from the countryside to the cities and towns – a process called ***urbanisation***.

The ***push factors***, forcing people away from the rural, countryside areas, can include lack of jobs, poor wages, drought, lack of health care and few, if any, educational opportunities.

The ***pull factors***, attracting people to the urban areas – towns and cities – can include job opportunities, higher wages, health care and educational opportunities. Plus, the so called '***Bright lights***' syndrome – people are attracted by the perceived better lifestyle that cities can provide compared to remote, isolated rural communities.

Rural to urban migrations have an impact on both the *donor* rural area and the *receiving* urban area. Rural areas can become depopulated; fewer farmers can lead to a drop in food production and there are less people to help with harvesting crops and many of the people who migrate are males, often husbands and fathers, who leave their families behind for several months or years at a time.

City areas can find their ability to cope with large numbers of migrants difficult with regard to housing, health care, education and in providing enough jobs.

Many of the migrants will be very poor and will end up in squatter settlements.

In some MEDC's rural areas are losing population, such as Snowdonia – an upland area in North Wales, UK. The reasons include:

- Few jobs as job opportunities are limited to sheep farming, forestry and water supply, all of which require few workers and the slate quarries which used to employ many people have closed.
- Highland including many mountains which are unsuitable for building and have poor road communications due to winding roads through mountains such as the A5 road in North Wales.

Kuwait is an excellent example of a country receiving large numbers of economic migrants. The wages earned in Kuwait by migrants are often sent back to their families where it improves their standard of living and their quality of life. It also has an impact on local communities in the areas they have left, like those in Kerala in Southern India. 21 per cent of the GDP of Kerala comes from money being sent back home by migrant workers. It also has over one million 'Gulf wives' living apart from their husbands. The money from remittances is spent in local shops and in the building industry as people either build new homes or improve the quality of their homes. In the UAE, of the total population of 6.4 million, 5.5 million are expat workers and their families.

Migrants who move to a new country can face several problems and difficulties. These include the following.

- A lack of qualifications/skills/education/no experience
- Many cannot speak the language
- Many will end up doing low paid, unskilled jobs
- Some are unable to obtain employment or there may not be enough jobs
- They may find that there are higher living costs and they may be unable to buy homes and end up living in poor, overcrowded conditions
- They may encounter discrimination; some people may think that their jobs are being lost to the immigrants
- Many migrants may have entered the country illegally and cannot access services for fear of being caught and deported
- They may be exploited by business and factory owners.

It is estimated that in Mexico for every dollar sent home by migrant workers mainly in the US, three dollars more is generated in the form of construction materials, food or contract work. Workers can earn 10 times the wages that they could earn in Mexico. Over 1 million Mexicans migrate to the US every year. USA desperately needs seasonal workers for the large farming and food processing industries in states like California.

In 2003 remittances worldwide reached $100 billion.

In some MEDCs, there is the opposite of rural to urban migration taking place – urban to rural migration. This is called ***counter-urbanisation***. The push factors for this are high cost of housing, traffic congestion, noise and air pollution, high levels of crime and a poor quality living environment with a lack of open space.

The pull factors are the higher quality living environment, lower cost of housing, less crime and the ability to commute longer distances to work with improved road and rail links to urban areas.

The central areas of some cities, such as Detroit in the US, have become depopulated – the ***Do-Nut Effect***, with abandoned housing and services declining as there is a lack of tax revenue coming in from a smaller population.

The rural areas find themselves under pressure to release more land for housing, house and land prices may rise which can mean that local people, especially the young adults, are unable to afford to live in their local area.

Today there are at least 13 million refugees, according to the UN, spread across most of the countries of the world.

Forced migrations are often for political or religious reasons or they may be as a result of civil wars. **Refugees** are people who have been forced to leave their homes because of these reasons. Examples include the recent civil wars in the countries of Rwanda, Democratic Republic of the Congo and Sudan in Africa.

The slave trade which was carried on until the middle of the nineteenth century, when people were forced to move from West and East Africa to the Caribbean and the US involved millions of people. The partition of Pakistan from India saw a huge migration of Hindus and Muslims between the two countries.

When taking information off such graphs use a ruler to locate values on the axes exactly instead of making a visual estimate.

You may be given different types of graphs, maps and diagrams to compare, contrast and analyse the information shown on them. In Figures 1a and 1b the origin of migrants to the US is shown and how the areas of origin have varied over time. You may also be asked how different types of diagram or graph, which show similar information in different ways, may have advantages over each other. For example in the first two graphs the first graph contains more detail and data, covers more years and provides a continuous picture of migration than the second graph. However, the second graph has a better visual effect and shows the locations of the origin of the migrants.

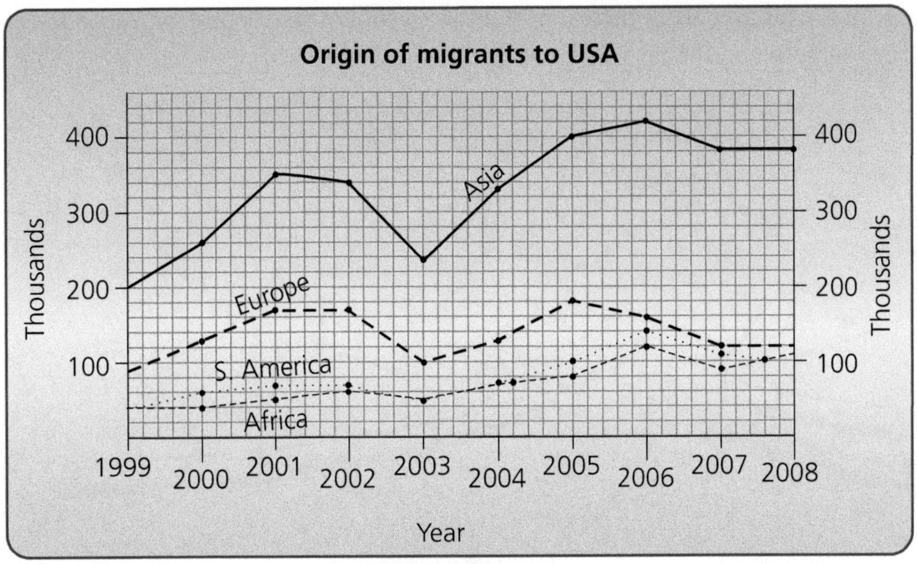

Figure 5 (a)

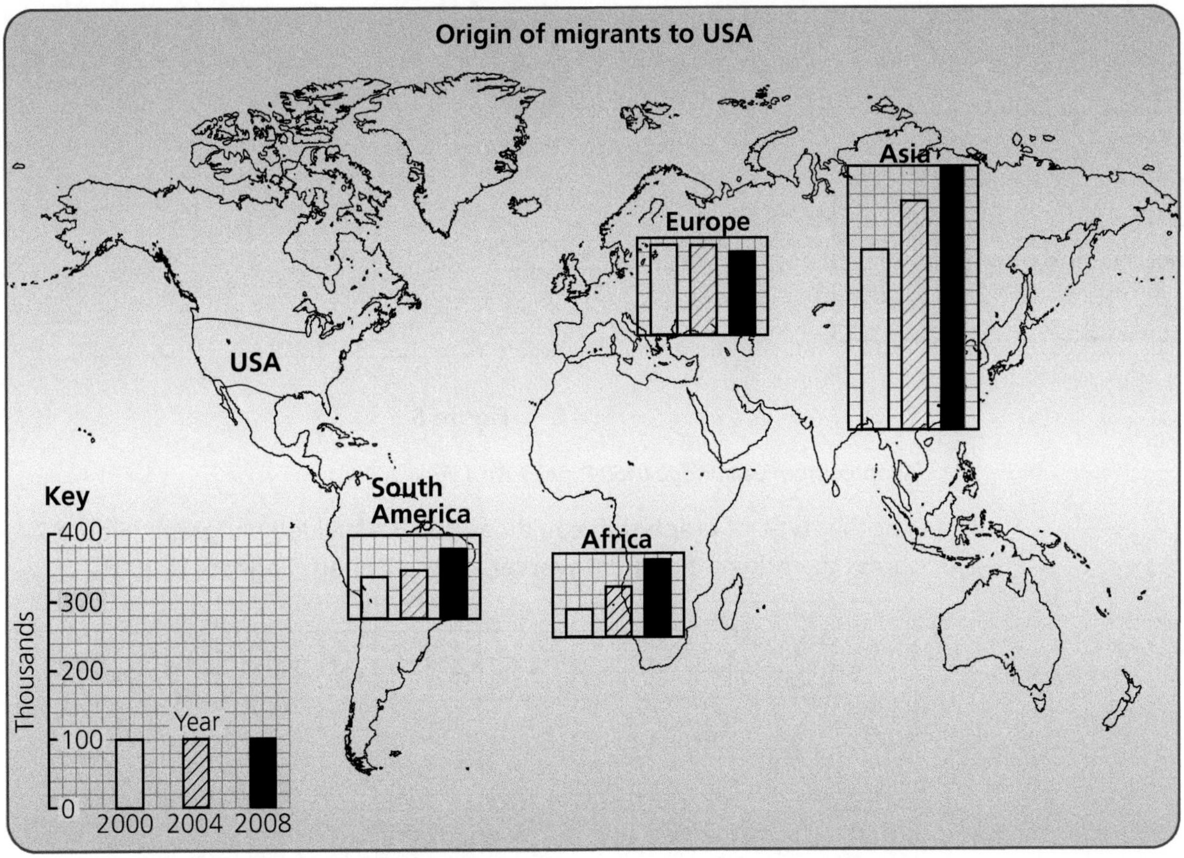

Figure 5 (b)

Cambridge 0460 Paper 23 Figs 8 and 9 Nov 2010

Figure 6 uses arrows of different widths to show the number of migrants from ***selected*** countries to USA in 2000.

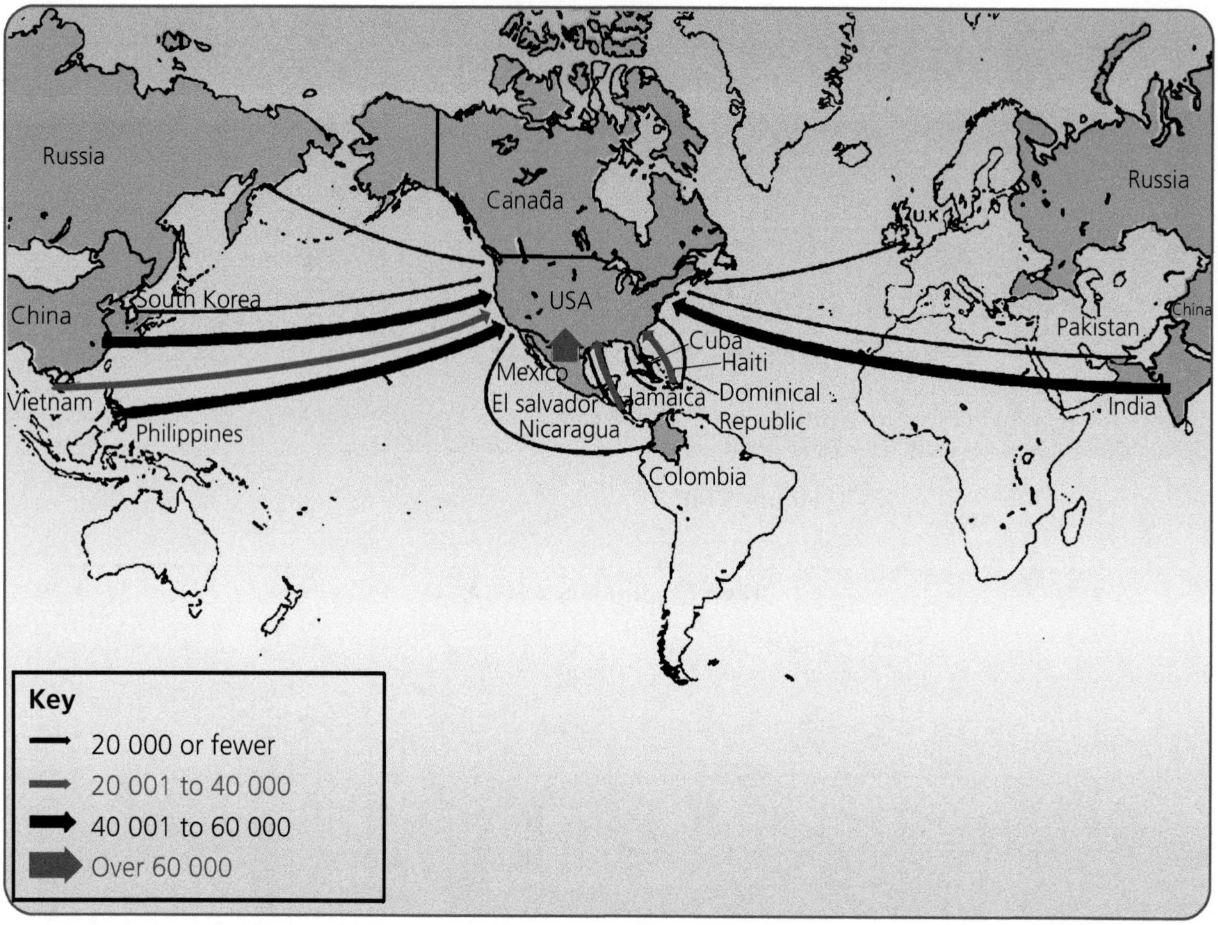

Figure 6

Adapted from *Cambridge 0460 Paper 1 Fig 1 June 2009*

Another type of graph that could be used is a divided bar graph. Figure 7 shows the origin of migrant workers in the United Kingdom in 2003.

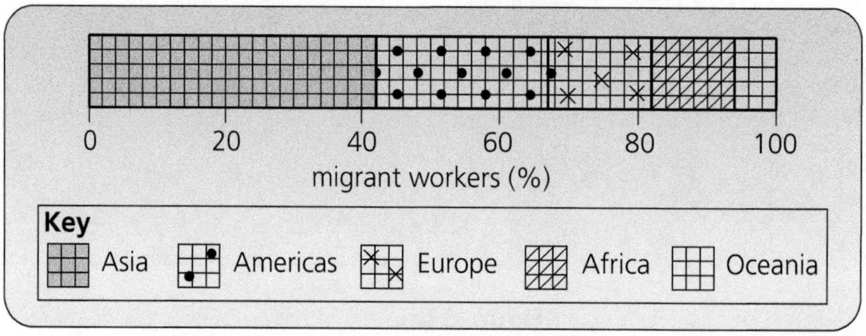

Figure 7

Cambridge 0460 Paper 2 Fig 7 Nov 2008

The impact of HIV/AIDS

Although, for most of the world, death rates are falling there are several countries where it is rising. HIV/AIDS is one of the major reasons for this. It is the major cause of deaths in the continent of Africa. In the 12 countries worst affected in Africa, 1 in 10 people between the ages of 15 and 49 are HIV positive. In some parts of Southern Africa, like Botswana, 40 per cent of adults are infected.

About 70 per cent of the world's HIV cases live in Sub Saharan Africa. Two thirds of children in many Sub-Saharan African countries are projected to have HIV infection by the time they have reached age 50 (or die from HIV before).

The AIDS epidemic is concentrated in 7 countries in Southern Africa, such as Botswana and South Africa (22 per cent). In these 7 countries, the population will drop by 26 million (19 per cent) by 2015 and 77 million (36 per cent) by 2050.

The impact on countries affected by HIV/AIDS

There are 6 main impacts as listed below.

1. ***Labour supply and the economy*** – as more people catch HIV/AIDS in the economically active 15–49 age group there will be less people available to work and the development of the country and its economy may actually go into reverse. In agriculture, this means that less food can be grown and harvested. A country will have to increase its investment in health care which will reduce investment in other aspects of development.
2. ***Family*** – the death of the parents in many families mean that the grandparents and the children are left to look after the family. Where there are no grandparents children are orphaned with nobody to look after them. This has meant that there are now thousands of orphaned children in Southern Africa.
3. ***Education*** – with a lack of government money in poorer LEDCs to spend on education about HIV/AIDS, many people are not aware of how they can avoid catching HIV. Also, a very large number of teachers, in countries like Botswana, have HIV/AIDS and are too ill to teach which will have a serious impact on the future development of these countries.
4. ***Poverty*** – the lack of money in LEDCs means that most people are unable to buy the cost of the drugs that are now available to treat the disease. Many people go into debt to pay for the drugs.
5. ***Infant and Child Mortality*** – AIDS can be passed on to children by their mothers which means that the numbers of infant and child deaths increases.
6. ***Dependency Ratio*** – the ratio between the economically active, 15–65 years old, and economically inactive, under 15 and over 65 years old, population.

The people who get AIDS are normally in the economically active age range who look after and support the economically inactive group. They also pay the taxes which funds government projects.

What strategies are being used to try to reduce the spread of disease in developing countries?

- The education of the general population to make them aware of how HIV/AIDS is spread and the dangers of unprotected sex. For example, national poster campaigns and radio and TV advertisements, through theatre groups and road shows visiting rural areas.
- The issuing of free condoms.
- Effective legislation against prostitution.
- Free syringe exchange for drug addicts.
- The careful screening of blood transfusions.
- Better health treatment to reduce early deaths from diseases to which AIDS victims are less resistant.
- Cheap antiviral drugs developed and distributed to slow the growth of the AIDS virus.

Possible problems of growing population

The problems include the following:

- Not enough resources to supply a larger population
- Lack of work
- Inadequate food supplies
- Poor access to education and health care
- Overcrowded housing/lack of space for development
- Lack of housing leading to the development of shanty towns example, Nairobi in Kenya or the favelas of Sao Paulo and Rio De Janeiro in Brazil
- Increased traffic congestion
- Increased atmospheric pollution
- Inadequate clean water supply and sewage disposal
- Lack of facilities for waste/rubbish disposal
- The overuse of agricultural land and increased overgrazing
- The deforestation and loss of natural vegetation and habitat.

Population control

Population control normally involves the practice of limiting population increase, usually by reducing the birth rate. However, some MEDCs which are experiencing falling populations are trying to encourage the growth of population. France, for example, gives parents money in the form of child benefits and it also gives the parents maternity and paternity leave from work after the birth of the child.

The practice has sometimes been voluntary; as a response to poverty, environmental concerns, or out of religious ideology, but in some times and places it has been the law. It is generally done to improve the quality of life for a society or as a solution to overpopulation. Population control is introduced by some societies to improve people's lives, giving them greater control of their family size.

The population control movement was active throughout the 1960s and 1970s setting up many family planning programs in many countries.

Population control across the many different societies of the world may involve one or more of the following practices:

- Increasing the access to contraception
- Abstinence
- Increasing access to abortion
- Encouraging emigration to other areas in a country
- Decreasing the numbers arriving through immigration
- Practising infanticide – particularly of females
- Advertising campaigns forwarding the advantages of a smaller family
- Offering bonuses to those people who have smaller families
- Educating women about family planning
- Improving health care so that infant and child mortality rates drop, reducing the need to have more children.

The methods chosen can be strongly influenced by the religious and cultural beliefs of the community's members. Failures of the other methods can lead to the use of abortion or infanticide, in which case it is regarded as a necessary drastic last resort. A specific practice may be allowed or mandated by law in one country while prohibited or severely restricted in another and this generates great controversy between and within different societies.

Case Study – China

One of the most famous examples of government population control is China's 'One Child' Policy in which having more than one child is made extremely unattractive. China's 'One Child' policy caused a very significant slowing of China's population growth which had been very high before the policy was introduced.

A number of measures were introduced by the government such as the following:

- Couples were allowed only one child
- Men could not get married until they were 22 and women 20
- Couples had to apply to the authorities to get married and again when they wanted a baby
- Couples were rewarded for doing this by being given a salary/wage bonus – an extra 10 per cent, free education, priority housing, family benefits
- Priority in education/health facilities/employment/housing
- Those who did not conform lost these benefits and were given large fines

One unfortunate result of this policy is that those parents who wanted a boy as a child sometimes abandoned female children or illegally practised 'infanticide' – the killing of the child!

- Women who became pregnant a second time were forced to have an abortion and women who became repeatedly pregnant were sterilised
- A 'workplace snooper' is employed by most factories and businesses who can grant permission for employees to have child
- The government advertises the benefits of small families such as having a greater amount of disposable income available.

The policy came under criticism because it involved forced abortions and forced sterilisation. However, at the present time, while the punishment of an 'unplanned' pregnancy is a fine, both a forced abortion and a forced sterilisation is against the law and can be punished with up to 10 years' imprisonment.

The Chinese government introduced the policy in 1979 to help solve the social and environmental problems it was facing at that time, including the problem of possibly not being able to feed a fast growing population which could have left millions facing starvation and malnutrition.

According to Chinese government officials, the policy helped prevent 400 million births.

However, some people believe that the reduction in fertility could be more due to the modernisation of China than government population policies.

In 1999, the Chinese government started relaxing the policy as the birth rate had fallen from 31 to 19 in the twenty years from 1979 to1999. They allowed families in rural areas to have two children. Also, if two 'one child only' people reach marriageable age, they can have two children.

The policy is controversial both within and outside China because of the issues it raises; because of the manner in which the policy has been implemented; and because of concerns about the negative economic and social consequences in China. For example, boys are more valued than girls which led to female babies being abandoned and that China will face the problems of an ageing population in the future.

Exemption from the One Child Law

Following the catastrophic earthquake in May 2008 in Southern China, which killed at least 70 000 people, many of them children, the government relaxed the law and allowed couples who lost a child in the earthquake to have a new replacement child. In fact, the government sent specialists to the area to reverse sterilisation procedures and help couples with fertility issues.

China is now realising that it has an ageing population which will have a future impact on its fast growing economy. For example, in providing the labour force of the future and in the provision of care for the elderly – something that was carried out by sons and daughters in the past, whereas in the future each married couple may have four elderly parents to look after.

Progress check

1. What factors influence the density and distribution of population?
2. What are the reasons for the rapid increase in the world's population?
3. What are the main components influencing population growth – birth rate, death rate and migration.
4. What is the relationship between population growth and resources?
5. What problems may result from population growth?
6. How are the patterns of population growth in different world areas influenced by differences in birth rate, death rate and migration?
7. What are the consequences of different patterns of population growth?
8. What are the reasons for different types of population structure in the different stages of the Demographic Transition Model?
9. What are the reasons for population migrations?

Examination style questions

1. Italy is a European MEDC and it has an ageing population. It now has twice as many people who are over 60 years old than it has children below 10 years of age. What problems may this cause for the country in the future? **[4]**

Example answer:

One problem is that Italy will have to find the money to look after all the old people by paying them pensions and building retirement homes for them to live in. Also, with so few younger people, they may not have enough people to work in their factories and businesses in the future. In the future, the population of Italy will decrease because when the older people die there will be less people to replace them. Another problem with less number of young people is that some of the schools might be empty and have to close.

2. The number of international migrants increased in the world is increasing rapidly. Using named examples that you have studied, explain why people migrate from one country to another. **[6]**

Example Answer:

Many people migrate to get a job because they cannot get one in their own country and some people will move to get a better job which pays them more money. Some people are escaping to get themselves away from war zones. Some people move because they want to escape from earthquakes and volcanoes and droughts while others move to get an education.

Comment: A good answer for the first part of the question on the problems of an ageing population. In the second part of the question, though, there are no examples. The question does say 'Using named examples that you have studied' and this is a common mistake made by many. Their reasons are also not explained fully.

Overall mark: 6/10

Examination style questions for you to try

1. Explain why:
   (i) The birth rates are high in many LEDC's **[4]**
   (ii) The governments of some LEDC's are attempting to lower their birth rates **[4]**
   (iii) The death rates have started to come down in many countries in recent years. **[4]**
2. Describe both the positive and negative effects that the migration of people may have on the area to which they migrate. **[6]**
3. Using examples describe the policies that can be used by governments to change rates of natural population growth. **[7]**

Chapter

2 Settlement

Learning Summary

In this chapter you will learn about:

- ***The factors influencing the size, development and function of urban and rural settlements and their spheres of influence***
- ***The characteristics of land-use zones of urban areas in LEDCs and MEDCs***
- ***The problems of urban areas in LEDCs and MEDCs, their causes and possible solutions***
- ***The impact on the environment resulting from urbanisation and possible solutions***

Size, development and function of urban and rural settlements

The location, site, size and development and function of a settlement depend on a number of factors. These factors often change with time so some settlements become more important or less important with time. A topographic or similar map can give you a great deal of basic information about a settlement. These may be used in the IGCSE Paper 2 as a practical exercise as well as on the theory Paper 1.

The **site** of a settlement is the actual building site. The growth of the settlement would then depend on the **situation** of the settlement to the surrounding area relative to other surrounding settlements, large physical features such as valleys and hills and what natural resources were available – fertile soils, fuel, minerals, and routes etc.

In the past, the main factors affecting the location of a settlement included the following.

- A ***wet point site*** to be near a reliable source of water – beside a river, stream or spring or oasis
- A ***dry point site*** to avoid flooding
- A ***good defence site*** – this was often a high point, such as a hill top, surrounded by steep slopes or inside a meander
- Having **building materials nearby**
- ***Flat or gently sloping land*** that was easy to build on
- A ***supply of fuel*** – firstly wood and then coal
- ***Fertile land*** for growing food

- A ***sheltered site*** – often in the lower parts of valleys. This often meant being on warmer south facing slopes compared to colder north facing slopes in the Earth's northern hemisphere and the opposite in the southern hemisphere.
- ***Good transport links*** – often where several tributary valleys joined which became a route centre (sometimes called a ***Nodal point***), a ***bridging point*** of a river (particularly the lowest bridging point of a river before it enters the sea) or a port.

Most sites would have more than one of these factors.

Some of these factors have become unimportant for many settlements in the MEDC's particularly. For example, the need for a defence point or a reliable source of water as most people get their water in MEDC's from piped water, food is bought from shops and supermarkets and flood prevention schemes stop or reduce the threat of flooding.

Settlements take on certain **shapes** when they form. The most common are the following.

Nucleated – this looks circular in shape with the buildings mostly concentrated around a route centre.

Linear – where a settlement is spread out along either side of a road and looks like a long line.

Dispersed – where individual buildings are spread out across a landscape.

The maps in Figure 1 show three different settlements in rural areas. **X** is dispersed, **Y** is nucleated and **Z** is linear.

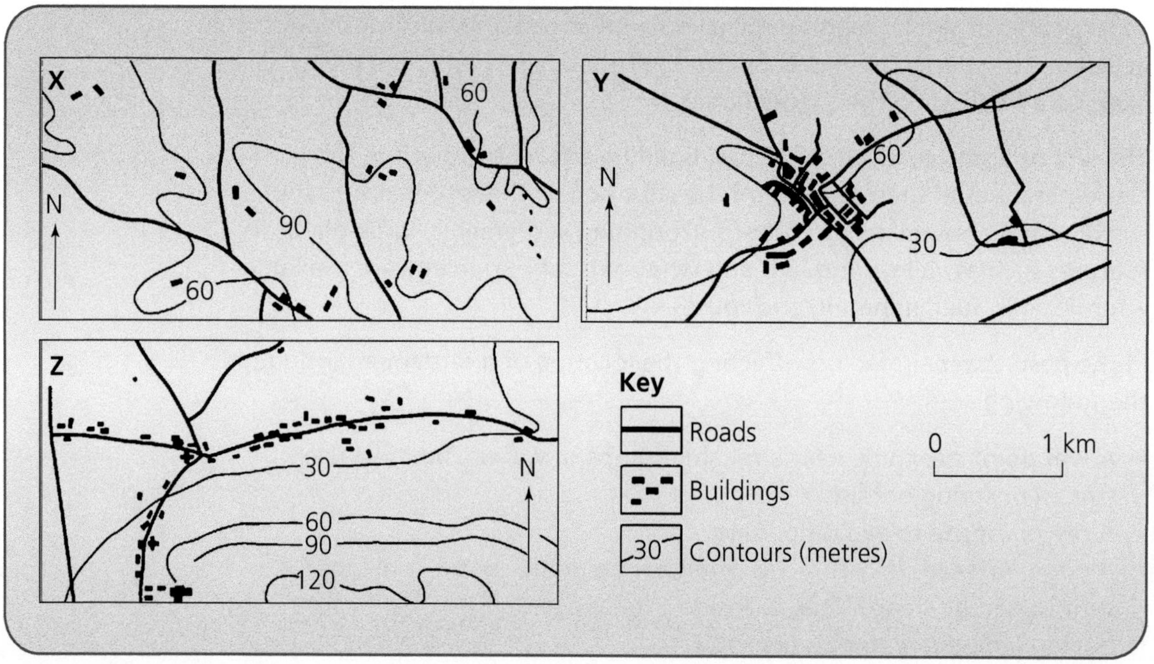

Figure 1

Cambridge 0460 Paper 2 Fig 3 Nov 2002

Figure 2 shows the ***hierarchy of services*** and their relationship to the ***sphere of influence*** and the ***threshold population***.

The **function** of a settlement describes what a settlement did, or does. Again, some settlements may have several functions. These include ***defence, administration*** (containing several government functions some of which may be national, some state or local), ***commercial*** (shops and offices), ***industrial, mining, route centre, market town, education*** (may contain a university), ***tourism, and residential***.

A successful port, such as Liverpool in the northwest of England for example, would be found where there was:

- A ***deep water estuary*** such as the mouth of the Mersey River
- A ***deep water anchorage*** so that it could accommodate large ships
- A ***sheltered anchorage*** so that ships can anchor, load and unload safely
- A ***large, flat area*** beside the port for the building and the expansion of warehouse and industrial activities
- Near important ***sea routes***, such as Liverpool being on the opposite side of Atlantic facing the US, which will encourage trade
- Have a large ***hinterland*** of nearby cities and industrial towns, such as the cotton manufacturing towns surrounding Liverpool in England into which imports in to the port could be distributed and the finished goods can be brought in for export
- Well-developed ***road and rail communications*** from the port to its hinterland.

After their initial siting and building, many settlements have continued to grow and expand in size because they also provide excellent sites for industry and factories to set up, for example:

1. A large river nearby will provide a water supply for a factory; the water can be used for cooling, or as a raw material in processing materials. The river would provide any easy means of disposing waste.
2. Relatively cheap, flat land is likely to be found on the floodplains beside rivers. This can be drained and factories could be built with room to expand.
3. They could have or be near excellent transport routes/rivers/railways/air transport for the easy, fast, efficient and cheap access for either obtaining or sending out raw materials, component parts and finished goods.
4. They have nearby work/labour force available.

Settlement hierarchies

A **settlement hierarchy** is found by putting the settlements in a region or country in to a ***rank order*** using either their population size or the type and range of services that they provide. A typical settlement hierarchy would have, in ascending order the following.

Hamlet, Village, Town, City, Conurbation, Capital city/Primate city or Megalopolis.

The term 'settlement hierarchy' is often used in classifying places according to the number and size of shops and services that they contain. At the top end of the hierarchy, in a city, there is a ***high order settlement*** which will provide with ***high order services*** and ***goods***. At the bottom end of the hierarchy, in small towns and villages, there will be ***low order settlements*** which will provide ***low order services*** and ***goods***. A typical large town or city may provide a ***range of services***, which would include the following.

- Retailing such as specialist shops/department stores
- Leisure such as cinemas/theatres
- Educational institutions such as schools/university
- Medical facilities such as hospital
- Financial and insurance services such as banks
- Estate Agents selling houses in the local area
- Large supermarkets for weekly shopping
- Provide a market for local farmers.

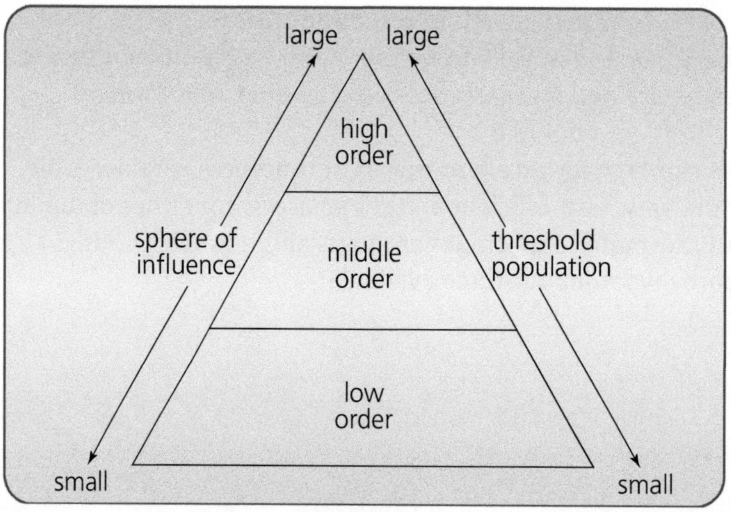

Figure 2

Cambridge 0460 Paper 11 Fig 2 Nov 2010

A city may have major national chain and department stores, shopping malls containing international chain stores like GAP, FCUK, Top Shop, Next, H&M, Bhs, Dean and Deluca, Marks and Spencer, etc. Whereas, near the bottom, a village may have a small village shop which provides ***convenience goods*** – goods that people need to buy perhaps two to three times a week such as water, vegetable, fruit, milk and newspapers. At the other end of the hierarchy, a hamlet may have no shops or services and the people who live there may have to travel to a nearby village or town to obtain the goods and services that they need.

Spheres of influence

A sphere of influence is the area surrounding a settlement that is served by the settlement in terms of its services such as shops, jobs, healthcare, education and government services. The size of a settlement's sphere of influence will depend on a number of factors such as:

- The number and type of services it provides
- The transport facilities available to the settlement
- The level of competition from surrounding settlements.

The different size settlements in a settlement hierarchy will also have a different sized sphere of influence.

Higher order settlements will have several advantages over ***lower order*** settlements because of the high order services they provide, which will mean that:

- People will travel further for higher order services. For example, to buy ***specialist goods***, such as furniture, computers, flat screen TV's, cars, 'white goods' such as washing machines, cookers, fridges and freezers, etc.
- People travel further to buy ***comparison goods*** (goods where you would like to compare quality and price as they are expensive – such as the specialist goods mentioned above) rather than ***convenience goods*** (inexpensive items that people buy two or three times a week – such as milk, bottled water, bread, fruit, vegetables, newspapers and magazines).
- High order settlements offer more shops/wider range/opportunity to shop around/get cheaper prices.
- People travel further for some services to seek better quality.
- People will travel to buy specialist services, such as the financial and legal services provided by banks, insurance, and law firms.
- People who live in settlements with low order services will have further to travel than people who live in high order settlements for services etc.

Important in this process is the ***range*** of a good or service – the maximum distance people are prepared to travel to obtain a good or service. This will have a different size hierarchy depending on the good or service that is needed.

Each service or good will have a ***threshold*** population – the minimum number of people needed to ensure that a service or shop will have enough demand or users to be successful. In the UK, for example, it has been estimated that a village shop needs 350 customers, 2 500 patients for a doctor, 10 000 people for a secondary school or a Boots Chemist, 50 000 for a Marks and Spencer store and 60 000 people for a large national supermarket chain such as Sainsbury, Asda or Tesco.

Land-use zones of urban areas

An increasing number of people move to towns and cities to live – the towns and cities grow as a result – a process called urbanisation. The pull factors attracting people to towns and cities are mainly:

- The prospect of getting a job
- The prospect of getting a better paid job
- Nearer to the place of work
- Better housing, services (such as schools, health care and hospitals), shopping and entertainment.

In the developing world, LEDCs, there is also the following.

- Increased availability of food supplies – they can buy food from shops rather than rely on unproductive farmland
- Increased opportunities for education for their children
- Better provision of health care/doctors/hospitals
- The perceived attractions of a city – called the 'Bright lights' syndrome
- To escape from the persecution of religious or political minorities
- Joining family members who have already moved to the city
- Better standard of living
- Better sanitation
- Better water supplies.

There are also push factors causing them to leave the countryside/rural areas:

- To escape wars and conflicts
- Mechanisation of farms – this means that there are fewer jobs available
- Land fragmentation – if a farm is divided up amongst sons there might be too small an area to support a family and so they will be forced to move.

As towns and cities grew, several urban geographers realised that cities in MEDCs were not growing in a haphazard way and they began to recognise patterns in the land use appearing in the cities and towns. Several Urban Geographers then produced theoretical models of urban land use that could be applied to MEDC cities. Although each urban area, i.e. town or city, is unique and has its own distinctive shape and land use patterns, these models attempt to show that they all share certain common characteristics.

Two of the earliest and simplest models were put forward by two American researchers called Burgess and Hoyt. The **Burgess Concentric model** came first in the 1925 and saw a city showing a pattern of concentric rings around one centre called a ***CBD – Central Business District***. A typical CBD will have distinctive features such as the following.

> **Their models of urban land use were based on US cities and were named after them**

- High cost of land – which can only be afforded by shops and offices
- High rise buildings – to make full use of the expensive land
- Few houses/residences – due to high cost and rents charged for land
- A lack of open space – the land is so expensive and valuable
- A transport focus – most roads and railways will focus on the centre of the city or town and make it the most accessible part of the city or town. It will have transport links with all parts of the town/city.

Outside the CBD was a ring/zone of ***light industry***, followed by three rings/zones of ***low, middle and upper class residential housing***. The low class housing was often terraced, with no gaps between houses as they were cheap and quick to build near the inner city. Workers were then close to the factories in which they worked as they could not afford to pay for the cost of transport to get them to work. The better off/richer you were the further away from the crowded city centre (CBD) and industry you could afford to live. As the urban areas grew so did the concentric rings.

The ***Hoyt Sector model*** came later in 1939 when public transport had been developed in the cities of the US. In his model, land use developed along the main transport routes going out, radiating, from the central CBD. This formed a series of ***wedges, or sectors***. Next to the industrial sector, low class housing developed as the workers could not afford to be far from their place of work and the high class sector was furthest away.

The value of land also changed with the changes in land use. The most expensive sites were always in the CBD. The CBD was always the most accessible part of the city for everybody and so businesses competed with one another for these sites. With competition came higher prices of land. The major land users were banks, shops and offices as they needed access to as many customers as possible and they could afford the land prices – unlike industry and housing.

> **The low class housing had the cheapest land because there was very little competition for these sites.**

By the 1970s, urban land use and both cities and towns had further evolved and changed. Another model, the ***Composite model***, appeared that was a combination of both the concentric and sector models. Mann developed this model after studying medium sized UK cities like Nottingham. In LEDCs, the theoretical models differ in several ways from those in the MEDCs:

- Firstly, most of the better housing is located in or near the city centre compared to being on the edge of the city.
- The quality of housing decreases as you go towards the edge of the city instead of improving.

- Industry tends to locate along the main roads leading in to the city centre rather than being in a distinct zone or sector on the edge of the city.

With time several factors have changed, which has seen several new patterns and trends of development in cities across the world. For example, CBDs have become increasingly crowded and congested. They have become less accessible as cities grow and people have found themselves living much further away from the centre. There have been several important developments which include the following.

Out of town shopping centres began to develop with shopping malls which had easy access, free parking and 'one stop shopping' – you could get all your shopping done in one large shopping centre or mall as well as have a meal, and entertainment in multiplex cinemas. Shops started to leave the congested city centre sites and set up in the new out of town locations. This has produced the ***Do-Nut effect*** – a run-down city or town centre abandoned by shops and businesses – an urban settlement with a hole in the middle. Many cities and towns have now put in place ***regeneration schemes*** to attract businesses back into the centre – a process called ***reurbanisation***. These schemes have involved several new initiatives.

1. ***Creating pedestrianised zones or precincts*** – certain streets in the centres have been closed off to traffic or only allow public transport vehicles, like buses, and sometimes delivery vans for shops to enter. This has improved the environment with less traffic pollution of the air and less noise. Also, there have been less traffic accidents with pedestrians safe to walk around the centres. The increased space provided by the roads has also meant that new sitting areas can be provided, small trees, shrubs and flower beds can be put in the area. Cafes can have outside tables and street theatre has been encouraged in some cities.
2. ***Old office blocks and shops have been pulled down and redeveloped as shopping malls*** where shopping can be done under cover in a controlled environment and shops are closer together, as well as providing eating, drinking and entertainment facilities.
3. ***Gentrification*** – this is where old houses and buildings in or near the city centre, which are often large and well-constructed, are renovated and brought up to modern standards.

Gentrification has several advantages over pulling down old areas and rebuilding.

Advantages

- They can then be used for shops, offices and apartments.
- It is often a cheaper option than pulling down the buildings and constructing new buildings.
- Older houses add character/retain culture/image. They provide a convenient residential/housing location close to people's workplaces/CBD.

There are several social advantages of improved housing rather than building new flats.

Advantages

- People have lived there for many years
- Cannot afford to move to a costly new house
- There is an established community spirit as many of the people will know each other
- Area already has convenient small corner shops/cafes/pubs etc.
- It is a cheaper option for the local government authority who have to pay for any new developments
- It helps to restrict the outward expansion of the town or city
- It minimises the disruption caused by demolition.

Just outside and adjacent to the CBD, many cities and towns had large areas of old, traditional industry. As industry has changed and developed, these inner city sites became unsuitable for modern industry which needed large, flat easily accessible sites. Many became derelict and abandoned. These areas have also been regenerated (called ***urban regeneration***) and their functions have been completely changed. In the UK, during the 1980s, ***Urban Development Corporations (UDCs)*** were setup. Many were river and coastal industrial sites which have been cleaned up to provide excellent residential and business sites.

Such regeneration is often financed by the government.

The ***London Docklands Development Corporation*** (LDDC) is a very famous example and was one of the first two UDCs (the other was in Liverpool – the ***Merseyside Development Corporation – MDC***) in 1981. 10 more were setup in England and one in Wales by 1993.

After they had served their purpose they were all wound up by 2000.

These UDCs were given the power to buy and acquire land, reclaim it and then attract private investment into the areas to set up new businesses, industry, housing and community developments.

This has not stopped new developments. The new Olympic sites in Sydney 2004 and for London in 2012 are both in old industrial areas and have been set up to regenerate these areas for the long term future.

The rural-urban fringe

Apart from the changes in the central parts of cities and towns, there has been a great deal of change over time on the edge of the urban areas where they meet the rural countryside.

In the UK, the rest of Europe and in North America during the 1920s and 1930s, urban areas spread out dramatically – a process known as ***urban sprawl.*** This process is still very obvious in most countries, such as in Kuwait where development has spread south from Kuwait City towards Fahaheel.

In the UK and elsewhere, there have been many attempts to limit and control this development and growth. One of the first attempts was the setting up of ***Green Belts*** in1947.

Most of the larger UK cities have such green belts.

A ***Green Belt*** was an area of land surrounding an urban city area where any new housing or industrial development was to be stopped or severely restricted. The land would be kept as farmland or used for recreation.

The pressure on this rural-urban fringe has not disappeared though and they have proved very attractive sites to many land users, including the following:

- New housing
- Science and Business parks – for footloose businesses especially
- Retail parks and hypermarkets
- New hotels, conference centres
- New road developments
- New sports areas and stadiums
- Landfill (rubbish) sites and sewage works.

The reasons for these developments at these locations include the following.

- The land is much cheaper than in the centre of towns and cities.
- There is much less traffic congestion.
- There is room to expand the development in the future.
- There is a larger area for car parking.
- Less pollution and a much more attractive place for people to live being surrounded by countryside.

The sites in the urban areas which were redeveloped are called Brownfield sites.

These new sites in the countryside rural areas are called ***Greenfield sites.*** Historically, people have always been migrating into cities however, in MEDC's there has been a move in the opposite direction – a process called ***counter urbanisation***. As people have wanted to live in better environments they have moved to the countryside, often to new housing developments attached to existing villages – producing expanded villages called ***suburbanised villages***.

These villages and the land on the fringe/edge of towns and cities have many attractions for people who want to move out of town and city centres as they provide:

- Houses with a modern design, services and amenities/electricity/water
- They are usually brick built
- Have space to park cars
- They will have relatively easy access to local services
- Relatively low cost compared to houses and property in a town or city centre

- Gardens/space/close to open space/play areas
- No air pollution as there are no nearby factories
- Close to their workplaces which are now also built on the urban fringe
- Good public transport access/main road access to the CBD if they still work or want to go into the centre for higher order shops and services.

Many of the people, who live in these settlements however, do not work in them as they travel/commute to work in the cities and towns every day. This has given these villages the name of either ***Commuter or Dormitory settlements***. The services and functions in these settlements are fewer than expected for a settlement of that size; as the people live in them but work elsewhere and obtain much of their shopping and services in the towns or cities. The people in these villages form part of an area called a ***Commuter Hinterland*** around cities. However, these new developments on the edge of towns and cities can generate new problems.

Disadvantages

- Traffic congestion as many people who live in new developments commute to work in CBD.
- Loss of farmland due to new housing developments/road construction.
- Atmospheric pollution from increased traffic.
- Growth of squatter settlements where disease spreads rapidly.

Problems of urban areas in MEDCs and LEDCs

Some of these have been looked at earlier – urban decay and dereliction causing the Do-nut effect and urban regeneration. In addition to these, many city centres in both MEDCs and LEDCs suffer from traffic congestion, overcrowding, housing shortages, unemployment, deprivation and racial conflict along with various forms of pollution – air, water and noise. The cities in LEDCs also suffer from squatter and shanty settlements. Most of the growth in cities in the last 30 years has been in LEDCs. Examples include Sao Paulo and Rio de Janeiro in Brazil, Delhi, Kolkata and Mumbai in India, Nairobi in Kenya, Manila in the Philippines, Bangkok in Thailand and Jakarta in Indonesia.

The people and migrants who live and arrive in these cities face a number of major problems which include the following.

- Inadequate housing and/or not enough houses
- A lack of local authority investment in housing and services
- The poverty of the people – they cannot afford to buy houses/houses are too expensive/rents for houses are too high

- They are often unqualified/uneducated and find it very difficult to get a job
- As a result, many will be unemployed, or working for low wages
- They face overcrowding/lack of space near their workplaces.

Over 100 million people living in the cities of the developing world have no shelter of any kind and over one third of the population of these cities live in squatter settlements/ shanty towns.

Most city authorities would like to remove these squatter settlements but very few authorities have the resources to replace the housing that would be lost. As a result, many of these settlements become permanent homes, though many authorities do help by supporting and helping to set up ***self help schemes*** and ***community housing projects*** in which the residents can improve their houses and the infrastructure of the areas they live in. They also help build up a community spirit.

Rio de Janeiro in Brazil is typical of many LEDC cities in that there is an enormous inequality between the rich and the poor. The richest 1% earns 12 per cent of the city's income, while the poorest 50 per cent earn 13 per cent of the income. It continues to grow at a staggering rate – over 1 million people are added every 10 years. With a population of over 5 million people, Rio has half a million homeless people who live on the streets with no shelter. Its public services like education and health care struggles to cope with such growth. Physically, it is trapped between high steep mountains and the coast and has little room for growth of buildings or to improve transport.

The largest favela, such as Rocinha, have a population of over 100 000 people.

It has over 750 ***favelas*** (favelas are housing areas of 60 or more families in houses that often lack the basic services of running water, sewerage and electricity and the residents have no legal right to the land on which they live). In fact they make up just 6.3 per cent of the land area of the city but house 17 per cent, about 1.1 million, of the population. The favelas tend to be located either on the rural-urban fringe, or on land that building developers would not normally use, such as steep hillsides or marshland beside rivers. In 1988, heavy rain triggered landslides on the steep slopes, carrying away shacks and causing over 200 deaths. Rio has a problem with crime and the favelas can be centres of organised crime, drug trafficking and violence. There is not enough available and affordable housing to meet demand so that people are forced into the favelas.

There are four main types of favela in Rio de Janeiro:

- Dense areas with self-built housing lacking any infrastructure such as roads, electricity, water or sewerage.
- Areas where land or housing has been illegally subdivided into very small plots or houses.
- Invasions of risky areas such as beside railway lines, electricity lines or streets.
- **Corticos** – areas of old and decaying housing that is being illegally rented out to the poor.

There are several possible solutions to the lack of available and affordable housing in LEDC cities like Rio de Janeiro.

- The government buying land and building houses that are cheap to rent – very few people will be in a position to buy.
- Providing interest free or low interest loans for people to either build their own homes or to improve their current homes or neighbourhoods.
- Provide the infrastructure and services like clean drinking water, sewage systems, refuse/rubbish disposal, health care and schools to improve the quality of life of the people in the favelas.
- Supporting small businesses in the favelas to provide employment and incomes, often through microfinance schemes.
- Teaching basic building and construction skills to the people and providing low cost building materials so that they can improve their houses.

An example of a successful scheme is the Favela Bairro project (the ***Favela Neighbourhood Project***) which was set up in Rio in 1994, in two phases, to provide 120 of the medium sized favelas – those with a population of between 500 and 2 500 households.

The first phase started with providing essential services, including paved roads, water and sewage systems, sport and leisure facilities, relocation of families in landslide threatened areas, channel engineering of rivers to reduce the threat of flooding. The second phase has involved reducing the threat of crime and providing education and employment for the residents. It is also helping people to own their homes. The results of these improvements can greatly improve the quality of life of the people who live in squatter settlements and areas of poor housing by:

- Increasing the availability of clean water from communal taps
- Reduce the incidence of disease – helped by the building of new toilets to prevent the contamination of water by sewage
- Building surface drains to reduce the amount of standing water – which is likely to smell and be polluted
- Constructing paved roads which will mean people can travel more easily in cars or on bikes. This could lead to better quality and more regular and widespread public transport
- Security lighting in housing areas which will improve personal safety, so that there is less danger of muggings
- Provide free education for street children
- Provide low cost building materials.

Rubbish bins and skips and the regular collection of rubbish will mean less litter dumped on streets and in rivers, which will further help reduce disease and pollution.

While all this has been going on in the favelas, those people who can afford to have often moved away from the congestion and moved to cleaner, safer environments further along the coast from Rio to new '***edge towns or cities***' such as ***Barra de Tijuca***.

This new town is 20 kms along the coast linked to Rio by a four lane highway which goes through tunnels in the mountains and is raised up along the coast. It now has a population of over 140 000 stretching 5 kms along the coast, with a beach that stretches for 20 kms. Three quarters of the housing is in 10–30 storey apartment blocks.

Impact of urbanisation on the environment

Rio de Janeiro also illustrates well, unfortunately, the many environmental problems faced by cities in LEDC's.

- It has very poor air quality as a result of the traffic congestion which produces a photochemical smog from the exhaust fumes.
- It has poor water quality – raw sewage flows into the sea off Rio and this pollution, as well as that from industry in Rio, has seen a 90% drop in fish catches off the coast in the last 20 years.

Transport solutions – in an attempt to reduce transport problems and traffic congestion in cities and towns, a number of solutions have been used. These solutions aim to do the following.

- Reduce congestion
- Save time for those travelling to the centre saving on the transportation costs
- Reduce accidents
- Reduce personal stress levels
- Create a more pleasant urban environment by reducing atmospheric pollution from exhaust fumes and noise pollution
- Save space – less car parks will be needed.

The solutions include the following.

- Providing more frequent, modern public transport systems so that people do not have to come to work in their car. This will include buses and ***mass transit systems*** like trams, light railways and underground railway systems such as the Dubai Metro system in the UAE.
- ***Park and ride schemes*** where people can leave their cars in car parks on the edge of cities and towns and be taken to their place of work or to shop, etc. by frequent bus, rail or underground system.
- ***Congestion charging*** – used in London, England where people who wish to drive in to the centre of cities are charged extra to do so. A silicon chip is attached to their car and their bank accounts are automatically charged when they enter a congestion charge zone.
- ***Providing discounted travel tickets*** for commuters who can use them for all forms of public transport in city or town centres by bus, train, metro or water. Examples include the Oyster Card in London and the Nol Silver cards in Dubai.
- ***Increase parking charges*** or ***restrict parking*** in city centres and fine or tow away offenders.

- ***Provide less polluting forms of public transport*** in cities – electric and gas fuelled vehicles and trains.

Progress check

1. What factors influence the size, development and function of settlements?
2. What factors influence the size of a settlement's spheres of influence?
3. What are the characteristic features of land-use zones in the urban areas of more economically developed countries (MEDCs)?
4. What are the characteristic features of land-use zones in the urban areas of less economically developed countries (LEDCs)?
5. What are the causes of the problems of urban areas in LEDCs and MEDCs and what are the possible solutions?
6. What are the impacts on the environment resulting from urbanisation and what are the possible solutions to?

Examination style questions

1. Describe three differences between the services provided in a village and those provided in a city. **[3]**

Example Answer:

A city will provide many more services than a village. A village may only have one small shop compared to the hundreds you might get in a city and the services that are provided by a city will be much higher order services. There will also be more specialist services in a city like banks and law firms. People will be prepared to travel much further for these high order specialist services in a city, compared to the low order goods, like bread and milk that you get in a small village shop.

2. Explain why many cities have a large sphere of influence. **[4]**

Example Answer:

Cities have such large spheres of influence because they offer so many different types of services and they will have such a wide variety of shops. If you want to buy expensive things for your house like T.V's, computers, fridge freezers and washing machines which cost a lot of money you will be prepared to travel a long way to city to compare different shops and different prices to get the best deal. They also have the best entertainment with large cinemas and theatres to go to and lots of good things to do like watching football matches and visiting museums. It's easy to get to them as well as there are good, fast roads and lots of buses and trains going to them.

3. Explain why many new shopping and entertainment centres are being built in suburban areas rather than in the centre of cities. **[5]**

Example Answer:

It is much easier to build new shopping and entertainment centres in a suburban area rather than in the centre of a city because they will be much easier for people to drive to because they will be nearer the motorways on the edge of the city and people will not have to get through the crowded streets of the city centre. Shops will like it better because their supply lorries will be able to get to them more easily. The land in the suburbs will be cheaper than the land in the city centre and so big shopping malls can be built. There will also be more space to build a large shopping mall. Parking will be easier because there will be more land for car parks and it might be free. People will be able to do one stop shopping and not have to go and park again near another shop or walk for ages to get to it. The shopping mall will be nice and warm in winter and cool in the summer as it will be climate controlled and you will not get wet from the rain. It will also be away from the noise and air pollution of the city centre.

Comments: A very good answer in all parts of the question. Many good points made which may have picked up all the available marks and they make a good point about being close to the residential population in the suburbs in the last part of the question.

Overall mark: 12/12

Examination style questions for you to try

1. (i) What is meant by the terms nucleated, linear and dispersed settlements? **[3]**

(ii) What is counter urbanisation? **[2]**

(iii) What is gentrification? **[1]**

2. (i) Explain why many people only travel short distances to use their local shops and services, but travel longer distances to use a large out of town shopping centre. **[5]**

(ii) In many of the world's urban areas there are housing shortages. For a named urban area which you have studied where there is a housing shortage. Describe and explain why there is a shortage and what attempts which have been made to solve the problem. **[7]**

(iii) Describe the characteristic features of a Central Business District (CBD) for a named urban area which you have studied. **[7]**

Theme 2:

The natural environment

Chapter

3 Plate tectonics

Learning Summary

In this chapter you will learn about:

- ***The distribution of earthquakes, volcanoes and fold mountains***
- ***Plate movements and their effects***
- ***The causes and effects of earthquakes and volcanic eruptions***

The layers of the Earth

The Earth, when seen in cross section, has four main layers.

- At the centre, is the ***inner core*** which is about 1 400 kms across. Here the rocks are solid and extremely dense – they are about five times denser than the rocks at the surface. They are made of iron (about 80 per cent) and nickel and are extremely hot, about 5 500°C.
- On the edge of the inner core is the ***outer core*** which is made up of dense, semi molten rock with a temperature of 5 000–5 500°C. It is about 2 100 kms thick.
- Outside the core is the ***mantle***. This is also semi molten, but is less dense and makes up a layer which is about 2 900 kms thick.
- At the surface is the **crust**. It varies in thickness and there are two types – ***Oceanic crust*** and ***Continental crust***. The main differences between them are summarised below.

Oceanic crust	Continental crust
Relatively thin – 5 to 10 kms thick	Relatively thick – 25 to 90 kms thick
Younger	Older
Heavier/Denser	Lighter/Less dense
Continually being formed and destroyed	Cannot be destroyed

If oceanic and continental crusts collide the oceanic crust, being denser, will go ***under*** the continental crust. This process is called ***subduction***. Relative to the other layers, the crust is actually quite thin.

If the Earth was the size of an apple, the crust would be the thickness of the apple skin!

Plate tectonics is the study and explanation of the global distribution of tectonic plates, fold mountains, earthquakes and volcanoes.

The Earth's crust is split into many huge pieces called ***tectonic plates***. These pieces of crust float and move on top of the much denser mantle below them. The movement of the plates is due to movements of huge ***convection currents*** in the mantle below. The movement of the plates produces several distinct landforms, as well as earthquakes.

The map below shows the location of the largest plates and their edges, called ***plate margins***. These plate margins are the location of Fold Mountains and many of the world's volcanoes and earthquakes.

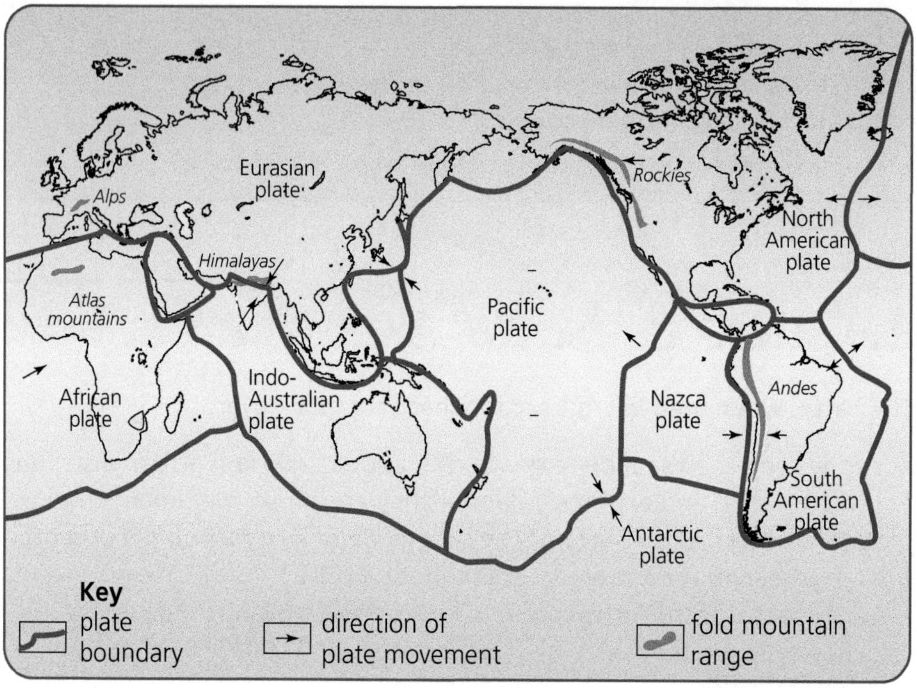

Figure 1 Major plates, plate boundaries and major fold mountains

Cambridge 0460 Paper 1 Fig 6 June 2008

Fold Mountains are formed from the Earth's crust/rocks/strata which have been uplifted by massive movements of the crust. Examples include the Himalayas in Asia, the Rocky Mountains in North America, the Andes in South America, the Alps in Europe and the High Atlas mountains in North Africa.

Fold Mountains are formed when two plates, either two continental plates or an oceanic and a continental plate, move towards each other and collide. The material to make the Fold Mountains come from layers of deposited sediment eroded from the land – forming sedimentary rock – which accumulates in depressions in the Earth's surface called ***geosynclines***.

These sedimentary rocks get compressed by a combination of the weight of rocks lying on top of them and two plates colliding. They then become uplifted, bent and crumpled into a series of folds and form Fold Mountains as a result.

Fold Mountains are usually found along the edges of continents where the thickest deposits of sedimentary rock accumulates, such as the Himalayas, where the Indian and Eurasian plates are in collision.

Types of plate boundary/margin

Where two plates meet, it is called a ***plate boundary or plate margin***. There are four types of plate boundary/margin.

Constructive boundaries/margins

This is where two plates move away from each other. Any gap that appears between these plates, fills with molten magma and the lava that comes out forms/constructs new crust. One of the biggest and longest constructive margins is the ***Mid Atlantic Ridge*** which stretches down the middle of the North and South Atlantic Oceans where the North and South American plates are moving away from the Eurasian and African plates. There are many undersea volcanoes along the Ridge and minor earthquakes occur along it as the plates move. Both volcanic activity and earthquakes on these margins tends to be relatively gentle in comparison to the other margins.

Mid Atlantic Ridge opens up by 3 cms every year.

Destructive boundaries/margins

These are found where plates made of heavier oceanic crust move towards plates made of lighter continental crust. Where they meet, the heavier oceanic crust is forced down under the lighter continental crust and forms a ***subduction zone***. As the oceanic crust sinks deeper, it melts and forms ***magma***. This may rise to the surface and emerge as lava. It forms very explosive volcanoes, as in the Andes Mountains in South America, where the Nazca plate is moving under the South American plate.

Where this process takes place in an ocean, the volcanoes may form a line of volcanic islands – called ***Island Arcs*** as in the islands of the West Indies in the Caribbean and in the Aleutian Islands, south west of Alaska. Destructive margins often suffer from very powerful earthquakes, such as Chile earthquake of 1960 which was the largest ever recorded at 9.5 on the Richter scale and the Japanese earthquake of March 2011 which was 8.9 and the fifth largest ever recorded.

Collision boundaries/margins

This is where two continental plates converge/move towards each other. These lighter plates are not dense enough to sink into the mantle. As the plates collide, they fold up and form fold mountains, such as the Himalayas. These collisions can also produce powerful earthquakes, but they do not produce volcanic eruptions.

Conservative boundaries/margins

These occur where plates slide past each other. Sometimes they become locked together and pressure builds up until they tear apart, along a fault line. These movements can produce very powerful earthquakes, such as in Haiti in January 2010, but they do not produce volcanic eruptions and land is not created or destroyed. The San Andreas Fault in California is another famous example.

Earthquakes

An earthquake is the result of a sudden release of energy that causes the Earth's crust to shake, sometimes violently. Every day there are at least 8 000 earthquakes on Earth. In a typical year, about 49 000 earthquakes are actually strong enough to be felt and noticed by people and an average of 18 of these can cause serious damage to buildings and possibly injure and kill people.

The majority of earthquakes take place within 300 kms of the Earth's surface.

Most of the world's earthquakes (90 per cent of them and 81 per cent of the largest) take place in the 40 000 km long, horse shoe-shaped zone known as the ***Pacific Ring of Fire***, which for the most part is found along the edge of the Pacific Ocean. As plates move, the rocks on their edges may become locked together until, at the weakest point along a plate margin – a ***fault*** line, they tear apart, or rupture, and this releases the strain.

Earthquakes can also be produced by the movement of magma inside volcanoes. These earthquakes can serve as an early warning of volcanic eruptions, such as during the Mount St Helens eruption of 1980 in the north west of the US. Some human activities can also trigger earthquakes, such as underground nuclear explosions and the creation of large reservoirs behind dams, the weight of which compresses and depresses the crust below them.

An earthquake's point of initial tearing or rupture inside the Earth's crust is called its ***focus***. Earthquakes with a deep focus are found in the subduction zones beneath destructive plate boundaries. Those with a shallow focus are found along conservative and constructive plate boundaries. Shallow earthquakes like these can sometimes be very violent, as in Haiti in 2010, because their energy is not absorbed by the relatively thin crust above them and appears on the surface very quickly.

The term ***epicentre*** refers to the point on the Earth's surface directly above the focus where the energy bursts onto the surface and spreads out in a series of shock waves. Earthquakes cause two major effects on the Earth's surface, – ***shaking*** of the crust and the ***slipping*** of the crust. Surface movement by slipping, in the largest earthquakes, can be more than 10 metres. A slip that occurs underwater can create a huge wave called a ***tsunami***.

Earthquakes are recorded with a ***Seismometer*** or ***Seismograph***, with the results displayed on a ***Seismogram***. The word comes from a Greek word meaning 'shake'. Records of the ***seismic waves*** produced by earthquakes allow ***seismologists*** to map the interior of the Earth, and locate and measure the size of earthquakes.

There are two common **scales** used to measure the size of an earthquake:

- The ***size*** of an earthquake is reported by the ***Richter scale***. On this scale, an earthquake with a magnitude of three or lower is almost imperceptible, while one with a magnitude of seven or higher can cause serious damage over large areas, as in Haiti.
- The ***intensity of shaking*** is measured on the ***Mercalli Scale***. After a major earthquake, it is common for there to be ***aftershocks***. An aftershock is an earthquake that occurs after a previous earthquake. An aftershock is in the same region of the main shock but is always of a smaller magnitude. Aftershocks are formed as the Earth's crust, around a fault, adjusts to the effects of the main shock.

There are several reasons why earthquakes cause damage.

- ***Ground movement*** can cut lines that cross faults; example tunnels, highways, railroads, power lines and water and gas pipes.
- ***Shaking*** is the greatest threat. Modern buildings can handle the shaking through earthquake engineering, but older buildings can get damaged.
- ***Liquefaction*** occurs when shaking turns what looked like solid ground into mud. This happens in areas covered in sediments, such as in sands and gravels, found on floodplains and beside the coast.
- ***Aftershocks*** can cause the final collapse of the structures damaged by the main earthquake.
- ***Subsidence***, where the land drops during an earthquake, can damage tunnels, roads, railways, power and gas lines and harbours. In flat, coastal areas a drop in the land can allow the sea to permanently invade and destroy forests and farm land.

The actual amount of damage caused by earthquakes will depend on a combination of factors listed below.

- The ***strength*** of the initial earthquake and the aftershocks that may follow it. The Haiti earthquake in January 2010 was 7.0 on the Richter scale which was powerful enough to destroy buildings. It was also followed by strong aftershocks which further weakened already damaged buildings.
- The ***depth*** of the earthquake – many earthquakes take place deep in the crust below 150 kms so, much of their energy is absorbed by the crust above them. The Haiti earthquake was less than 10 kms in depth and so appeared at its epicentre on the surface with much more energy.

- ***Distance*** from the epicentre – as the shock waves spread away from the epicentre they become weaker.
- The ***Geology*** of the rocks in the area – loose sedimentary rocks may liquefy and cause buildings and structures to sink into the ground; while more solid harder rocks will provide the safest foundations for buildings.
- ***Building construction materials and designs*** – steel framed buildings are better able to absorb movement than concrete framed buildings.
- The ***space between buildings*** – as buildings sway they may hit each other, if they are built too close to each other and become damaged.
- ***Number of storeys*** – in a tall high rise building, shock waves becomes amplified as they move up the building which can cause them to sway and collapse.
- The ***density of population*** living in an area – a densely populated urban area is likely to suffer many more casualties and damage than a low density rural area.
- The ***time of the day*** when the earthquake occurs – at night in residential areas most people will be inside their homes and asleep. During the working hours, people in cities and towns will be working or going to school and be inside buildings.
- People may be exposed to ***secondary hazards*** – these can include tsunamis on the coast, landslides and rock falls in mountainous areas, fires in urban areas – many caused by broken gas pipes and electricity lines. After earthquakes, water supplies may become contaminated as they mix with sewage, hunger may be a problem where food and water cannot reach affected communities.

In winter, people without shelter and winter clothing may suffer from hypothermia.

Living in an earthquake or active volcanic zone

There are several things that can be done to help people live more safely in earthquake prone areas and active volcanic zones.

- ***Improved technology and use of historical data*** can improve prediction and forecasting rates of earthquakes and volcanoes to provide warnings.
- ***Mapping of high risk areas*** where buildings are at risk from Liquefaction, mudslides, landslips, lahars, lava flows and Pyroclastic flows can ensure that such areas are not used for building.
- ***Improved building designs and materials*** can mean that buildings do not collapse during earthquakes. Buildings with deep foundations made of special rubber can absorb shock waves better. Steel framed buildings, with steel cross braces can move more than rigid concrete buildings and stay intact. Automatic shutters that close on windows can stop glass falling on people below the buildings. Tall buildings, like the Taipei 101 in Taiwan (the world's second tallest), can have counter weights built inside them to halt the swaying of buildings. Triangular shaped buildings, like the Transamerica building in San Francisco, have less weight in their upper storeys and are more stable as a result. Flexible pipes can be used for water and gas, as well as systems that shut off water and gas flows automatically when an earthquake occurs.

Shatter-proof glass can be used in windows.

- ***Ensuring that adequate emergency drills and procedures are in place***, both at home and for people at work and in schools and hospitals. The stockpiling of emergency supplies of medicines, drinking water, tinned food, tents and blankets can mean that there can be a rapid response to any earthquake or volcanic eruption.

The impact on humans

The impacts will vary according to a combination of factors at any particular place, but earthquakes and volcanic eruptions may have several results, including the following.

- ***Loss of life*** from collapsing buildings, bridges and elevated roads, fire, and disease. Children and other dependents can be orphaned or left without any family support. Survivors may face serious psychological and emotional problems for many years afterwards.
- The ***cutting of basic necessities*** such as power, water, sewage due to damage to power lines, water and sewage pipes.
- The ***collapse of buildings*** or the destabilisation of the base of buildings which may lead to collapse in future earthquakes and general damage to houses and buildings. People may be homeless for weeks, months or years.
- ***Road, railway and bridge damage*** can make access difficult or impossible to earthquake affected areas.
- The ***spread of disease*** due polluted water and lack of medicine when water and sewage pipes are broken and water becomes polluted with sewage.
- ***Loss of jobs and businesses*** when factories, offices and places of work are destroyed.
- ***Higher insurance premiums*** for those people in earthquake affected areas where insurance companies are not prepared to take the potential risk.
- Most people agree though that ***human loss of life*** is the most significant human impact of earthquakes and volcanic eruptions.

LEDCs, like Haiti, Afghanistan and Pakistan do not have the resources to adequately deal with such disasters, compared to MEDC's like the US, Japan and Italy.

Case study of an earthquake

Sichuan province, China May 2008

This was a very powerful earthquake – 7.9 on Richter scale. It occurred in the mid-afternoon when children were at school and adults were at work. Many buildings collapsed as they may have been poorly constructed and were not earthquake proof. It affected a wide area containing large settlements as the region was densely populated. There were many gas leaks and fires as gas pipelines where ruptured by the movement. Roads were blocked and badly damaged which further delayed emergency services.

The rupturing of sewage and freshwater pipes meant that there was contamination of water leading to a lack of drinking water. The area was poorly prepared for an earthquake. There was lack of education concerning earthquakes and there were poor emergency services which could not cope with the disaster. Over 69 000 people were killed in this earthquake and over 4.8 million were left homeless. There were many long-term effects which resulted from this earthquake:

- Damage to workplaces due to which people were unable to earn a living.
- The negative impact on the economy and industrial production.
- Damage to infrastructure – roads, railways, power lines, water, gas and sewage pipelines.
- The economic cost of rebuilding the infrastructure and housing.
- Damage to schools and the disruption of education.
- The psychological trauma of experiencing an earthquake and the loss of family and friends.
- The earthquake led to homelessness on a large scale.

There are several ways to protect people in Sichuan from future earthquakes. These include the following.

- Build houses and schools which are more stable and designed to sway but not collapse.
- Make sure that planning regulations are followed.
- Build deep foundations of the buildings.
- Use flexible water and gas pipes.
- Make sure there is an automatic gas switch off when an earthquake occurs.
- Have frequent earthquake drills and make sure there are education of safety procedures and that people and the government stockpile supplies of drinking water, food, clothing/blankets and tents, etc.
- Build structures on solid ground.
- Better preparation of emergency services.
- Restrict building heights and improve their design.

The reasons why so many people live in areas such as Sichuan, even though they are at risk from earthquakes include the following.

- They have lived there all their lives and have a sentimental attachment to the area.
- They are close to family/friends.
- There are good services/schools/hospitals in the area.
- There is a lot of work to be done in the area as it has fertile farmland. This means that they can make a good living.
- They cannot afford to move.
- There is pressure of living space in an area that is very mountainous.
- They are confident about their safety and are willing to take the risk as an earthquake has not occurred for many years.

Volcanoes

Volcanoes normally form in ***two*** possible types of location.

1. Where two plates move ***away*** from each other – i.e. the plates diverge, at constructive margins and a gap/line of weakness is created in the Earth's crust. Molten magma emerges through the gap and the lava solidifies to form volcanoes, etc.
2. Where two plates move ***towards*** each other – i.e. the plates converge at destructive margins, where a heavier, denser, oceanic plate moves down under a less heavy continental plate (the process of subduction). Friction and intense heating takes place which results in the destruction of the oceanic plate, which melts and turns into magma. The build-up of magma creates enormous pressures on the crust above it and the magma rises through lines of weakness and appears on the surface of the plate as lava. The lava solidifies to create a volcano.

The opening in the Earth's crust where the lava appears is called a vent.

Some volcanoes though are found in thinner, weaker areas of the Earth's crust, called ***hot spots***, well away from the plate margins, where magma can force its way to the surface, such as in the Hawaiian Islands.

Apart from lava the magma may come out in two other ways.

- It may explode out and fall as ***volcanic bombs***.
- It may appear as very fine ***ash***.

All these are potential hazards to the people who live near volcanoes. Ash, for example, can cover and kill crops or cover buildings to such a depth that they collapse. However, they may also face other hazards.

Lahars refer to a mixture of melted snow and ice from the top of the volcano, often combined with rain water, which mixes with ash and runs off the volcano, flooding valleys and flatter areas with mud.

Pyroclastic flows are clouds of red hot, poisonous gases mixed with ash that flow down the sides of volcanoes at speeds upto 200 kms per hour.

Over time all this material may build up to form a volcano.

There are three main types of volcanoes based on their shape and what they are made of.

1. **Shield volcanoes** – these are made from lava only and form on constructive plate boundaries or at hot spots like Mauna Loa in Hawaii, where lava appears at the surface as two plates pull apart. They form large volcanoes, sometimes hundreds of kilometres across, because the lava that forms these are alkaline and very runny traveling a long way on the surface before cooling and going solid.

> Indonesia has over 200 of the world's active volcanoes.

2. **Dome volcanoes** – these are also made from lava only but their lava is acidic and thicker and cools quickly. It does not flow very far and so these volcanoes become very steep sided and high, such as Mount St Helens in USA.
3. **Composite volcanoes** – these are made from both lava and ash, often in alternating layers as both lava and ash come out of the vent during an eruption. They form on destructive plate boundaries where oceanic crust has melted as it is subducted. The lava forces its way up through the crust and emerges as a violent explosion – such as Mount Etna in Sicily, Italy.

Volcanoes can be **active, dormant** or **extinct**.

- An **active** volcano is one that has recently erupted and is likely to erupt again. There are about 1 700 active volcanoes in the world today.
- A **dormant** volcano is one that has erupted in the last 2 000 years and may possibly erupt again – these can be dangerous as they are difficult to predict – the one on the Caribbean island of Montserrat last erupted 500 years ago but has made up for this with its massive eruptions in the last few years.
- An **extinct** volcano has long since finished erupting and has cooled down – the UK's volcanoes last erupted over 50 million years ago.

Predicting volcanic eruptions

There are a number of ways to help predict and then prepare people for volcanic eruptions. These include the following.

- ***Seismometers*** recording the increasing number of earthquakes that are caused by huge amounts of magma pushing up under a volcano.
- ***Tilt meters*** which measure the changes in the volcano's shape as they start to bulge with the upward movement of magma.
- ***Thermometers*** measuring increases in temperature.
- ***Gas sensors*** monitoring the release of gases from the volcano.
- ***Satellites*** can help monitor changes in the shape of a volcano and increases in temperature.

Once lava has erupted it may be possible to ***halt or divert lava flows*** by building concrete dams or spraying water on their fronts to solidify the lava and help tame and divert it.

Many people live in areas where there are natural hazards such as volcanic eruptions. People live in these volcanic areas for a number of reasons.

- ***Volcanic soils are often very fertile*** and yield of crops are high; in the case of Mount Etna in Italy the fertile volcanic soils support extensive agriculture with vineyards and orchards spread across the lower slopes of the mountain and the broad Plain of Catania to the south.
- ***People can obtain hot water for heating*** and also ***generate electricity*** from the volcano using the hot steam to produce geothermal power.

- Volcanoes provide ***raw materials*** such as sulphur, zinc, gold and diamonds which can be mined and sold.
- ***Volcanoes can attract tourists*** and they can get jobs as tour guides. For example, the people who live in towns near Mount Etna, such as Messina and Catania, can earn money from renting accommodation to tourists.
- ***Governments,*** as in Italy, can set up volcanic and earthquake ***prediction equipment*** and then local people may feel more secure in living in high risk areas.
- ***Many people have lived near volcanoes and earthquake zones all their lives***. They are close to their family and friends, they work in the area and also, many just cannot afford to move away to another area.

Case studies of volcanoes

Krakatoa, Indonesia

Some eruptions are violent and spectacular others are very gentle. The Indonesian island of Krakatoa eruption was the most violent in recent history and took place in 1883. The noise could be heard 4 700 kms (3 000 miles) away and it completely blew away the top of the volcano and produced a massive tsunami.

With a ***Volcanic Explosivity Index*** of 6 it was equivalent to 200 megatons of TNT and four times the yield of the largest nuclear weapon ever built.

The eruption ejected approximately 21 cubic kilometres of rock and ash. Near Krakatoa, 165 villages and towns were destroyed and 132 seriously damaged, at least 36 417 people died, and many thousands were injured by the eruption – mostly from the tsunamis that followed the explosion.

The eruption destroyed two-thirds of the island of Krakatoa. Eruptions at the volcano since 1927 have built a new island in the same location, named Anak Krakatau (Indonesian for 'Child of Krakatoa'). This island currently is about 4 kilometres across and 300 metres high, growing 5 metres each year.

Mount St Helens, Washington, USA

Mount St Helens is most famous for its catastrophic eruption on May 18 1980 after lying dormant for 123 years. It was the deadliest and most economically destructive volcanic event in the history of the United States.

Sixty two people were killed; 250 homes, 47 bridges, 24 km of railways, and 298 km of roads were destroyed.

The eruption caused a massive debris avalanche, reducing the height of the mountain's summit from 2 950 m to 2 550 m and replacing it with a 1.6 km wide horse shoe-shaped crater. Over 2.5 kms^3 of mountainside slid away in flows that reached 250 kms per hour. Lahars carried magma, ash, trees into the adjoining Spirit Lake and generated waves approximately 200 metres high. The debris deposited by the lahars was over 45 metres deep. Pyroclastic flows with temperatures of over 300°C travelled off the volcano at speeds of over 400 kms per hour. An area over 500 kms^2 was scorched by these flows.

The following map shows some of the effects of the eruption of Mount St Helens, USA, in May 1980.

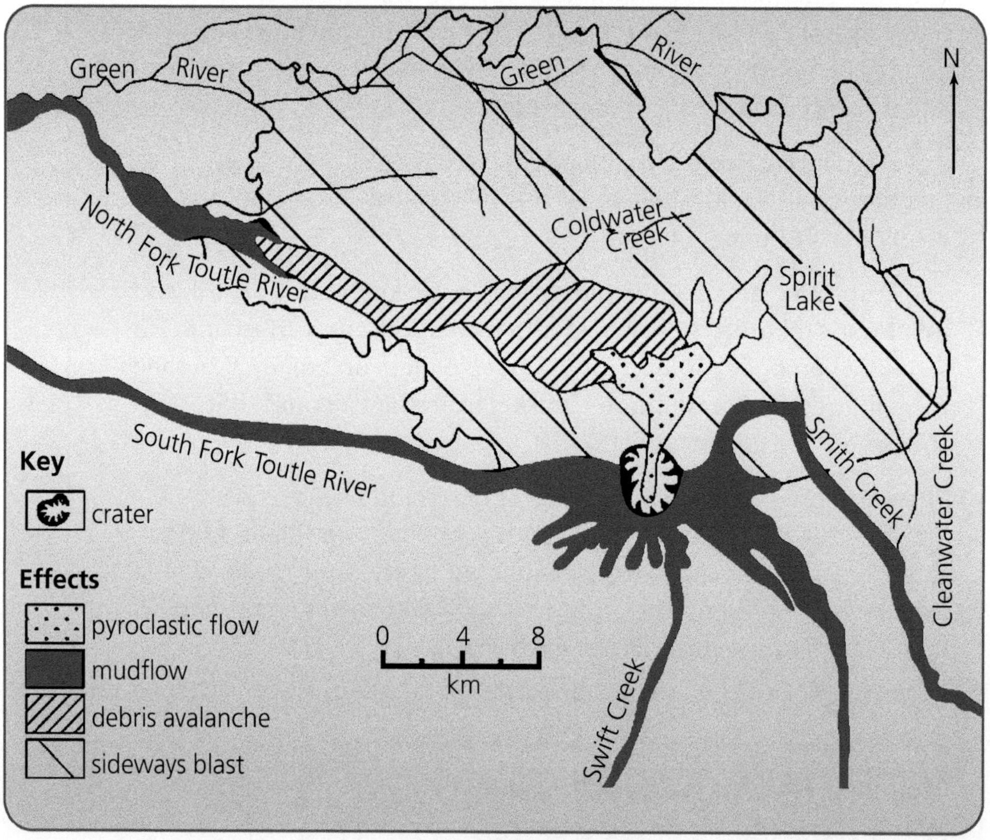

Figure 2

Cambridge 0460 Paper 21 Fig 7 Nov 2010

The map shows four main effects of the eruption. You may be asked to use maps like this to identify the location and size of certain features and effects, using the scale line and compass directions provided on the maps.

Mauna Loa, Hawaii

In contrast to Krakatoa, Mauna Loa in Hawaii – a shield volcano, is the largest volcano on Earth, has been gently pouring out lava for at least 700 000 years and may have emerged above sea level about 400 000 years ago. It has poured out about 75 000 km³ (18 000 cubic miles) of lava in that time!

Tsunamis

Earthquakes and volcanic eruptions, when they take place under an ocean, can move large areas of the ocean floor over distances measuring from a few kilometres to a 1000 km. These movements can generate tsunamis. The word **tsunami** is Japanese for 'harbour wave': Tsu – harbour, nami – wave. Japan's coastal harbour communities have long suffered from these phenomena and hence the name.

A tsunami is a series of large waves which have extremely long wavelengths (upto 50 kms) and long wave periods (4 minutes travelling at speeds of up to 800 kph i.e., 500 mph).

Asian tsunami 2004

The Asian tsunami of the 26 December, 2004 highlighted the devastation that can be caused. It was generated by the third largest earthquake in the last 100 years measuring 9.2 on the Richter scale.

The earthquake triggered a series of devastating tsunami along the coasts of most landmasses bordering the Indian Ocean. It killed more than 250 000 people in eleven countries, and flooded coastal communities with waves of upto 30 meters high. It was one of the deadliest natural disasters in recorded history. Indonesia, Sri Lanka, India, and Thailand were hit the hardest by the tsunami.

The Asian tsunami actually changed the speed of the earth's rotation by 3 milliseconds.

Japanese tsunami 2011

The 2011 earthquake off the Pacific coast of Japan was a magnitude 9.0. It was the most powerful known earthquake ever to have hit Japan, and one of the five most powerful earthquakes recorded and triggered powerful tsunami waves that reached heights of upto 40.5 metres and which, in the Sendai area, travelled upto 10 km inland.

This earthquake occurred where the Pacific oceanic plate moves ***under*** the plate beneath northern Honshu. This happened along a 500 km length of the plate margin, parallel to the coast of Japan.

The tsunami flooded a total area of approximately 561 km² in Japan within one hour of the earthquake.

Japan's ***Earthquake Early Warning system*** sent out warnings to millions of people in Japan and this early warning saved thousands of lives (compare the number of deaths in this event with the Asian Tsunami in 2004). The warning for the general public was delivered about 31 seconds after the earthquake occurred. There have been 15 844 deaths confirmed, 5 893 injured, but 3 394 people are still missing. Over 125 000 buildings were either damaged or destroyed. Around 4.4 million households were left without electricity and 1.5 million without water. The tsunami also caused a number of nuclear accidents at the three reactors in the Fukushima nuclear power station, and 200 000 residents nearby had to be evacuated. The estimated economic cost was $235 billion, making it the most expensive natural disaster in world history.

Progress check

1. Describe the general distribution of Fold Mountains, volcanoes and earthquakes.
2. Explain how their distribution is related to movements at plate boundaries.
3. Give a basic explanation of plate tectonics describing the global pattern of plates, their structure, and be aware of plate movements and their effects.
4. What are the different types of plate boundary and what are the differences between them?
5. What are the main features of volcanoes (and their eruptions) and earthquakes?
6. What are the disadvantages of living in an earthquake zone?
7. What are the advantages and disadvantages of living in a volcanic area?
8. How can the risks of living in areas of earthquakes and volcanoes be reduced?

Examination style questions

1. Suggest different ways to protect people from earthquakes. **[4]**

Example Answer:

There are many different ways to protect people from earthquakes. Firstly, their houses can be built stronger so that they do not collapse during the shaking of an earthquake.

A steel frame can be used which can move and bend rather than collapse like a concrete building. They can also be built on deeper foundations. People should make sure that they stick to building rules and regulations and they do not allow people to build with the wrong materials and they build on solid ground. They should make sure that everybody knows what to do when an earthquake hits and that they have emergency supplies ready of water and medicines.

2. Explain why many people continue to live in areas where they are at risk from earthquakes. **[4]**

Example Answer:

Many people have lived for generations in earthquake areas so they are surrounded by their friends and family and they have built their homes and developed their farms in that area. Many people are just not rich enough to be able to move away and set up a new farm or buy a new house – they may not get much money for their land or sell their house because it is in a dangerous area. When they balance the advantages and disadvantages of moving they may decide to stay and take the risk, especially if an earthquake has not happened for many years and they feel safe because of that.

3. Explain the causes of an earthquake which has occurred in a named area that you have studied. **[6]**

Example Answer:

California is in an earthquake zone and has had lots of earthquakes. Many of them are along the San Andreas Fault line which is a line of weakness between two plates called the North American and Pacific plates. These plates are sliding past each other along this fault line along what is called a Conservative margin. Sometimes the two plates get stuck and pressure builds up until they suddenly slip a few metres. This big movement sends out shock waves which can destroy buildings and it has done this in both Los Angeles and San Francisco.

Comment: An excellent answer. In the first two parts of the question, there is a good list of ways to protect people and very good reasons as to why people still live in earthquake zones.

In the third part of the question, the example is not only naming a fault line but two cities affected by earthquakes. Their explanation of a conservative plate margin is well thought out and explained.

Overall mark: 14/14

Examination style questions for you to try

1. (i) What are Fold Mountains? **[2]**

(ii) Use labelled diagrams to explain how Fold Mountains can be formed beside some plate boundaries. **[3]**

(iii) Explain why some volcanoes are different in size and shape from each other. **[4]**

2. (i) With the aid of a labelled diagram, describe four of the main features of a composite volcano. **[4]**

(ii) Why do mudflows occur during volcanic eruptions and what problems do they cause? **[2]**

(iii) Explain why earthquakes of the same strength may cause different numbers of deaths. **[4]**

3. Explain why many volcanic areas are popular places to live but can create problems for the people living in those areas. **[5]**

Chapter

4 Weathering

(Landforms and landscape processes)

Learning Summary

In this chapter you will learn about:

- ***Weathering which involves the breakdown of rock in situ and, as such, should be distinguished from erosion***
- ***What is meant by different types of weathering***
- ***The main factors influencing the type and rate of weathering***
- ***The influence of climate on the rate of weathering***

Weathering and erosion

There is often a lot of confusion over the terms ***weathering*** and ***erosion***, many people think that they are the same process.They are, in fact, very different.

Weathering is the ***breakdown*** of a rock where it lies, sometimes called ***'in situ'***. ***Erosion*** is the ***removal*** of the weathered rock by water, ice or wind. There are 3 types of weathering as explained below.

Physical/mechanical weathering

It includes ***Freeze-thaw weathering*** and ***Exfoliation*** (sometimes called onion skin weathering).

Freeze-thaw weathering – is most common in polar and temperate climates where freezing temperatures cause water to freeze in rocks. When water freezes, it expands its volume by 9 per cent. It takes place when water gets into small spaces and cracks the rock. If it then freezes and expands it can put enormous pressures of up to 2 000 kg/cm² on the rock and split the rock apart. Where bare rock is exposed on a cliff or slope fragments of rock may be forced away from the face. These fragments of rock may then fall to the bottom of the cliff or slope where they form a large pile of rocks called ***scree***.

Exfoliation (or onion skin weathering) – is most common in hot tropical climates where the surface temperatures of rocks exposed to the sun can reach over 90°C during the day and then drop below 0°C during the night! Bare rock surfaces will expand and contract each day as temperatures rise and fall.

These daily stresses can cause the surface layer of the rock to separate and peel away from the rock.

Chemical weathering

It includes the processes of solution, carbonation and oxidation.

Solution – rainwater contains a cocktail of dilute acids. The most common is carbonic acid, formed by carbon dioxide gas, CO_2, combining with the rain water. Rainwater becomes more acidic as it passes through the soil – because soil air contains 25 per cent CO_2, compared to the 0.04 per cent in the atmosphere. Certain minerals are put into solution by these acids – the carbonate rocks like limestone and chalk are very susceptible to this process.

Carbonation – Carbonation occurs in rocks with a high content of calcium carbonate such as limestone and chalk. Carbon acid reacts with the calcium carbonate to form calcium bicarbonate. Calcium bicarbonate is soluble so therefore the rock is dissolved and carried away. This type of weathering can produce landforms in limestone areas such as underground caverns, caves, limestone pavements and sinkholes.

Oxidation – occurs when minerals combine with oxygen destroying the structure of the original mineral. Iron minerals are especially susceptible to this process, often the oxygen comes from that dissolved in water producing a rusty colour.

Biological weathering

Burrowing clams on the English coast have lowered chalk by 2.3 cms a year, while 100 periwinkles can scrape away 86 cm³ a year!

It can include both physical and chemical processes. The physical processes can include animals such as limpets, marine worms and fish grazing on and burrowing into rocks.

However, one of the most common ways in which biological weathering takes place is when trees extend their roots through cracks in rocks as they search for water. As they grow, the tree roots can open up cracks in rocks and break up the rock as a result.

Factors influencing the type and rate of weathering

As can be seen from the descriptions of the different types of weathering, two factors the climate and geology (rock type and structure) can have a major influence on rates of weathering.

Climate

The amount of Freeze-thaw weathering that will take place will depend on the number of times that temperature moves above and below freezing in a year.

In contrast to this, the amount of chemical weathering will increase as the amount of heat and moisture increases. The rate of chemical weathering increases by 2–3 times for every 10°C rise in temperature – up to a maximum of 60°C. As a result, in warmer humid tropical areas chemical weathering is more rapid than in the cooler, temperate regions of the world.

Geology

The physical and chemical characteristics of the rocks that are being exposed to weathering will help determine the degree to which a rock is weathered.

The ***rock type***, including its mineral composition and grain size, will affect the degree to which a rock will react to physical and chemical weathering. Rocks that contain calcium carbonate will be very susceptible to solution – carbonation. In sedimentary rocks, the type of natural cement that binds together the grains of rock will be important. Those rocks with iron oxide cements will be affected by oxidation, while those with silica cements will be very resistant to erosion.

Rocks with ***different grain sizes*** will weather at different rates. Those that are coarse grained will weather more quickly than fine grained rocks as they absorb water more easily.

The ***rock structure*** will determine the presence of lines of weakness, such as fault lines, bedding planes, joints and cracks etc. Such lines of weakness will increase the surface area of the rock which can be exposed to water, air and freezing; while plants will find it easier to develop their roots in rocks where lines of weakness exist.

Progress check

1. What is meant by the terms weathering and erosion?
2. Name and describe two processes of physical weathering.
3. Name and describe two processes of chemical weathering.
4. Describe and explain how biological weathering can take place.
5. Describe and explain the formation of scree.
6. Why is weathering more rapid in humid tropical regions than in temperate regions?
7. How can the rock type and structure affect the type and degree of weathering that takes place?
8. How can climate affect the type and degree of weathering that takes place?

Examination style questions

1. Explain how chemical weathering can cause the weathering of limestone. **[4]**

   Example Answer:

   Carbon dioxide in air will react with rain drops to form a weak carbonic acid. When this falls onto a rock like lime stone it reacts with the calcium carbonate that limestone contains to form calcium bicarbonate which is soluble in water and will be carried away and this will increase the size of the cracks in the rock.

2. Explain how biological weathering may help to break down rocks. **[4]**

   Example Answer:

   If a seed falls into a crack in a rock it may germinate and its roots may grow in the crack. As the roots grow the cracks may be widened and the rocks may be broken up. Also some animals may burrow into some types of rock which will weaken the rock.

Comment: A very good answer, gives a good explanation of both chemical weathering detailing the change from calcium carbonate to soluble calcium bicarbonate. Also mentions two types of possible biological weathering by both plants and animals.

Overall mark: 8/8

Examination style questions for you to try

1. Describe the climatic conditions of temperature and precipitation where:
   (i) Strong chemical weathering may take place.
   (ii) Strong physical weathering may take place. **[2]**
2. Describe one weathering process and the possible results of this weathering in an area where strong physical weathering can take place. **[5]**
3. Explain how one named process of chemical weathering may operate. **[4]**
4. Describe how two rock features/characteristics can influence the rate of weathering. **[4]**

Chapter

5 River processes

(Landforms and landscape processes)

Learning Summary

In this chapter you will learn about:

- ***The processes at work in a river – eroding, transporting and depositing***
- ***The erosional processes of hydraulic action, abrasion (corrasion), solution (corrosion) and attrition***
- ***The processes by which a river transports its load – traction, saltation, suspension and solution***
- ***The reasons why and where in a river's course deposition takes place***
- ***The ways in which the effectiveness of the river processes concerned will vary***
- ***The landforms associated with these river processes***
- ***The interaction between rivers and human activities with reference to natural hazards and landscape processes***

River erosion, transportation and deposition

Processes of erosion

There are ***four*** processes of river erosion.

- ***Hydraulic action***: This is where the weight and force of the water flowing in the river removes particles of rocks from the river channel's bed and sides.
- ***Abrasion (sometimes called corrasion)***: This is where the river's ***bed load*** (boulders, pebbles, gravel, sand and silt) as it rolls, bounces and collides with the channel bed and sides, removes particles of rock from the channel bed and sides.
- ***Solution (sometimes called corrosion)***: Some minerals (mainly the ***carbonate*** minerals found in rocks like limestone and chalk) are put into solution by the weak acids found in river water. These weak acids include ***carbonic acid*** which is formed as carbon dioxide gas in the atmosphere joins with rainwater. This has a great impact on limestone in particular.
- ***Attrition***: This process does not actually erode the river channel bed and sides but it is the process that breaks up the river's bed load. It takes place when the rocks on the bed of the river are rolled along and they collide with each other and become smaller and rounder as a result. This means that the average size of rock particle (sediment) becomes smaller as it moves down towards the river mouth.

Processes of transportation

There are ***four*** processes of river transportation which carry the load of the river.

1. ***Traction***: This is where the larger, heavier material that makes up the river's ***bedload*** (boulders, pebbles and gravel) is rolled along the river bed.
2. ***Saltation***: This is where the lighter material that makes up the river's bedload (gravel, sand and silt) is bounced along the river bed.
3. ***Suspension***: This is where the smaller, lighter material that makes up the river's ***suspended load*** (clay size) is ***carried/suspended*** by the river.
4. ***Solution***: This is where dissolved material that makes up the river's ***solute load*** is moved by the river in solution.

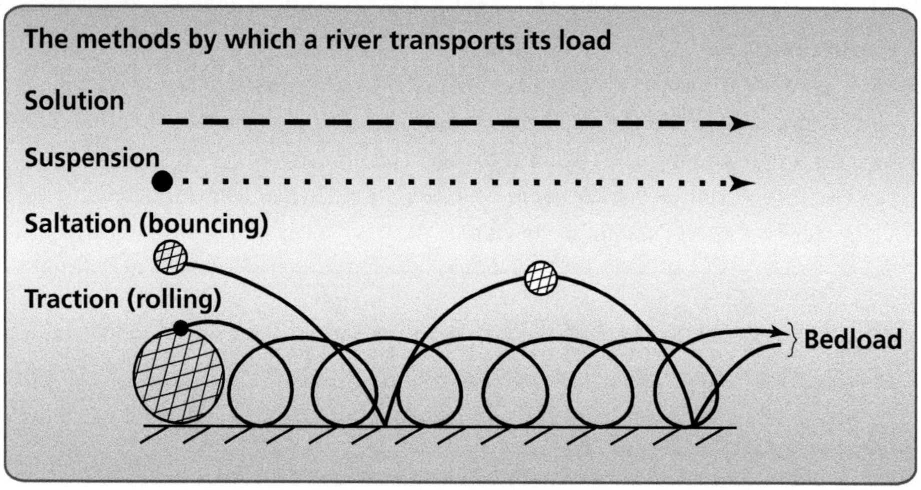

Figure 1 Types of river transportation

Larger bolders and stones are ***rolled*** (called ***traction***) along the river bed. Lighter, smaller rocks are ***bounced*** (called ***saltation***) along the bed. Very small particles will be called ***carried*** in ***suspension***. Some minerals will be carried in ***solution***, especially in areas of limestones and chalk which are ***calcareous*** rocks. The load that is transported along the river bed, either by traction or saltation is called the ***bedload***.

Processes of deposition

Where the river loses energy, it will start to drop/deposit its bedload and suspended load. This may take place in the river channel, on the inside of a river meander, on its floodplain, or on its delta. The heavier material will be deposited first and as the river continues to slow down and become shallower, the smaller material will get deposited.

The river's velocity/speed will slow down when:

- the ***gradient*** of the river channel decreases/becomes less
- the river channel bed becomes rougher and shallower
- the river meets a large body of water such as the sea or a lake.

The landforms associated with the processes

All the landforms are found within a ***river basin***, sometimes called a ***drainage basin*** or ***river catchment***. All the precipitation that falls within a river basin will make its way towards the river channel, either on the surface or underground, and eventually to the river mouth. The dividing line between river basins is called the ***watershed***. Smaller river channels leading to the main river channel are called ***tributaries***. Where two river channels meet, it is called a ***confluence***. The amount of water flowing down a river can be measured at any point at a measuring or gauging station. This is called the rivers' ***discharge*** and it is measured in how many cubic metres of water is passing the gauging station every second. This figure is often abbreviated to the term **cumecs**. All these features are shown in Figure 2.

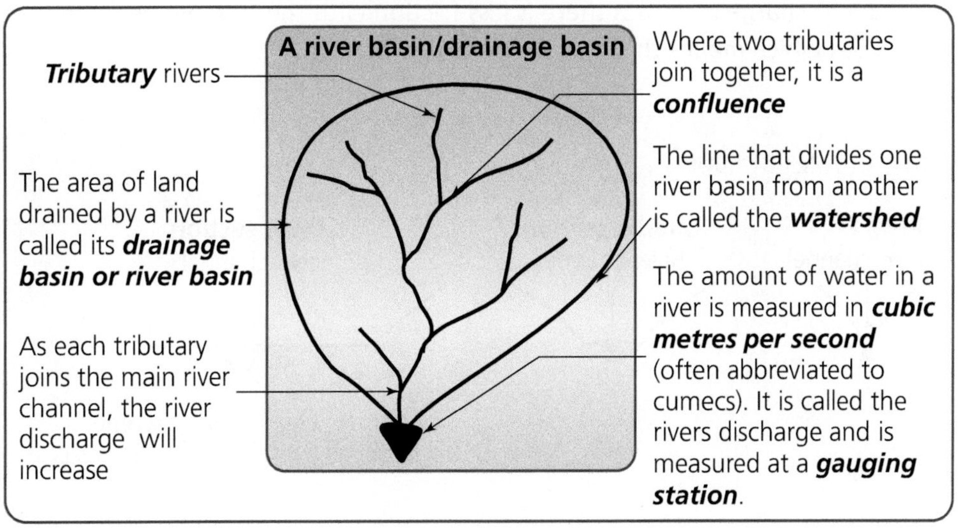
A river basin/drainage basin
Tributary rivers
The area of land drained by a river is called its drainage basin or river basin
As each tributary joins the main river channel, the river discharge will increase
Where two tributaries join together, it is a confluence
The line that divides one river basin from another is called the watershed
The amount of water in a river is measured in cubic metres per second (often abbreviated to cumecs). It is called the rivers discharge and is measured at a gauging station.

Figure 2 Features of a typical river basin

Forms of river valleys

Rivers have a ***long profile*** and a ***cross profile***. The ***long profile*** is drawn from the ***source*** to the ***mouth*** of a river and shows the changes in the steepness/angle of the river from the source to the mouth. In a typical river, the angle will be steeper in the upper section of a river than in the lower section.

The ***cross profile*** is drawn across the river valley and will also change. In the upper section, it will be steep-sided and narrow, in the lower section it will normally be gentle-sided and wide. Each section will have certain other characteristics, these are summarised below and in Figure 3 that follows.

- ***Upper section*** – a narrow V shaped valley, a narrow river channel; the river channel will often completely fill the valley floor; the river channel will be full of large, angular boulders and stones which makes the water turbulent; it will be flowing slowly as it has a very rough channel; it will have a smaller discharge lower down its course. Vertical erosion dominates this section.
- ***Lower section*** – a very wide valley and larger channel; often a floodplain will be found beside the river channel; the river channel will contain much smaller, rounder rocks, often sand-sized or smaller. It will normally be flowing faster as the channel will be smoother. Lateral erosion dominates and deposition takes place.
- As the river moves between the two sections there is a ***middle section*** where there is a combination of features as the river changes its characteristics.
- The ***discharge*** of the river will increase from the source to the mouth as smaller tributary channels add more water to the main channel.
- The ***velocity*** will also increase from the source to the mouth because as the discharge increases there is less friction with the channel bed and sides which means that the river will flow faster.

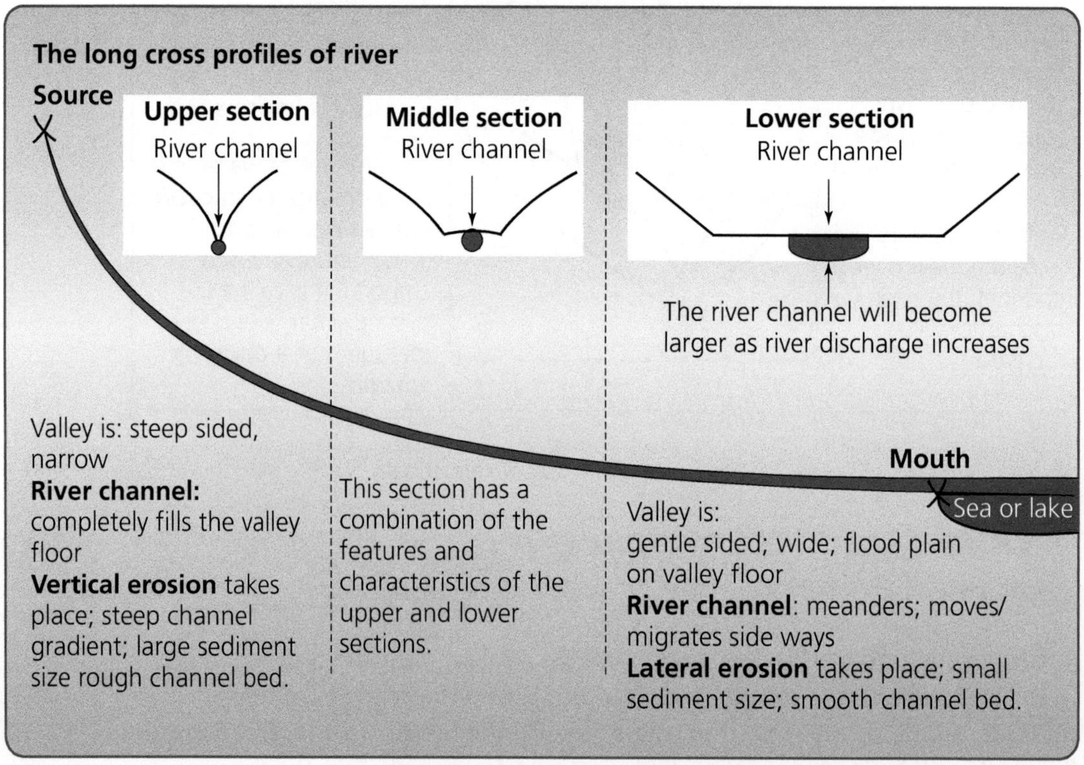
The long cross profiles of river
Source
Upper section
River channel
Middle section
River channel
Lower section
River channel
The river channel will become larger as river discharge increases
Valley is: steep sided, narrow
River channel: completely fills the valley floor
Vertical erosion takes place; steep channel gradient; large sediment size rough channel bed.
This section has a combination of the features and characteristics of the upper and lower sections.
Mouth
Sea or lake
Valley is: gentle sided; wide; flood plain on valley floor
River channel: meanders; moves/migrates side ways
Lateral erosion takes place; small sediment size; smooth channel bed.

Figure 3 River long and cross profiles

Potholes

Potholes are found in the bed of a river which is flowing over solid rock. They usually start to form when in the following cases.

- A weakness or crack or fault line is exposed in the rock in the river bed.
- Differential erosion takes place – as the processes of ***abrasion*** and ***hydraulic action*** erodes the weakness/crack or fault.
- This produces a small hole in the bed of the river – a pothole.
- The potholes enlarge until they begin to merge/join up with one another. The end result of this process is that the river bed is lowered – vertical erosion.

Diagrams, such as Figure 4, can be used to illustrate your answer.

The formation of potholes

1.

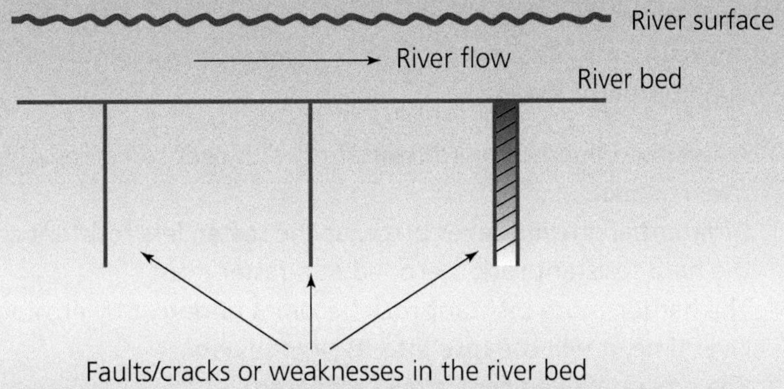

2.

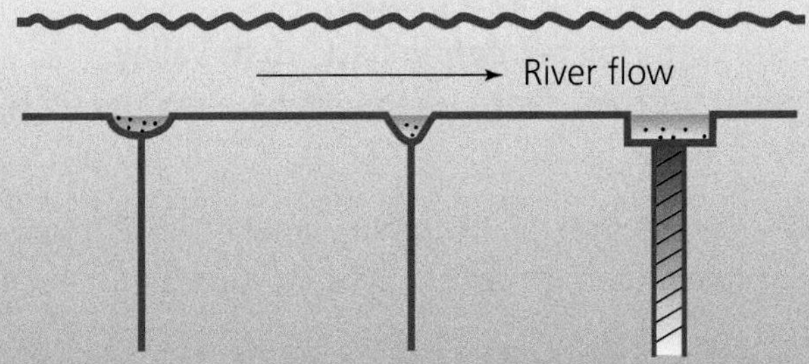

As they are weaker than the rocks on either side of them, the faults/ cracks or weaknesses are eroded by ***hydraulic action*** and ***abrasion*** at a faster rate called ***differential erosion***.

3.

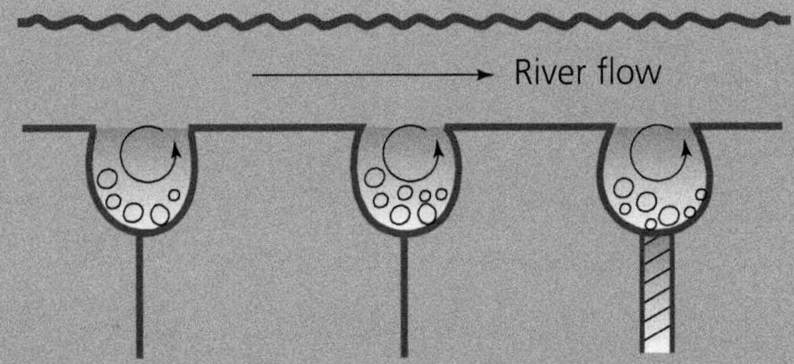

The potholes are enlarged as the flow of the river spins rocks around the hole. ***Abrasion*** by the rocks enlarges the potholes. They may join up and so vertical erosion takes place.

Figure 4 The formation of potholes in a river bed

Waterfalls

Waterfalls are vertical breaks in the smooth long profile of a river channel. They vary enormously in size. There are ***three*** common ways for a waterfall to form in a river channel.

- By ***differential erosion*** – where a band or layer of more resistant rock runs across the river channel. The softer, less resistant rock is eroded at a faster rate causing a drop in the river bed – a waterfall.
- By a drop in sea level, leaving the mouth of the river suspended above the lower sea level – this type of waterfall is sometimes called a knick point.
- By an earth movement – often triggered by an earthquake, causing a drop in the river bed along a fault line.

You may be asked to describe a waterfall formed by differential erosion. With the use of a diagram or a set of diagrams, as in Figure 5, you can explain how this happens.

- A layer/bed/band of more resistant rock is exposed across the bed of a river channel.
- ***Differential erosion*** takes place; as the softer, less resistant rock, below the hard resistant rock is eroded at a faster rate.
- The harder, more resistant rock becomes ***undercut*** by erosion.
- Over time, it will ***collapse*** into its ***plunge pool***.
- The process will be continually ***repeated***.
- Resulting in the waterfall ***retreating*** back up its valley.
- Leaving behind a ***narrow***, ***steep sided valley*** below the waterfall, called a ***gorge***.

This often results in the waterfall becoming smaller until it just leaves a steeper section of river which produces a set of ***rapids***.

The formation of waterfalls

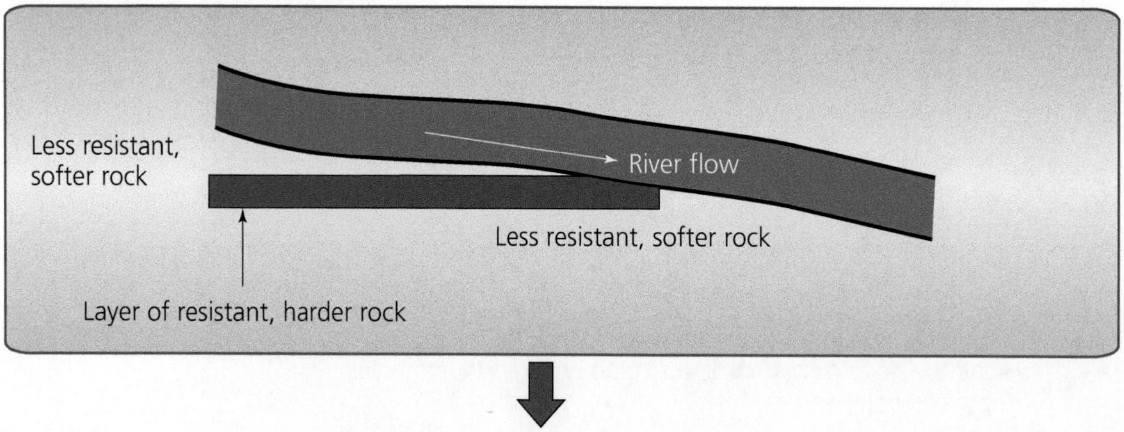

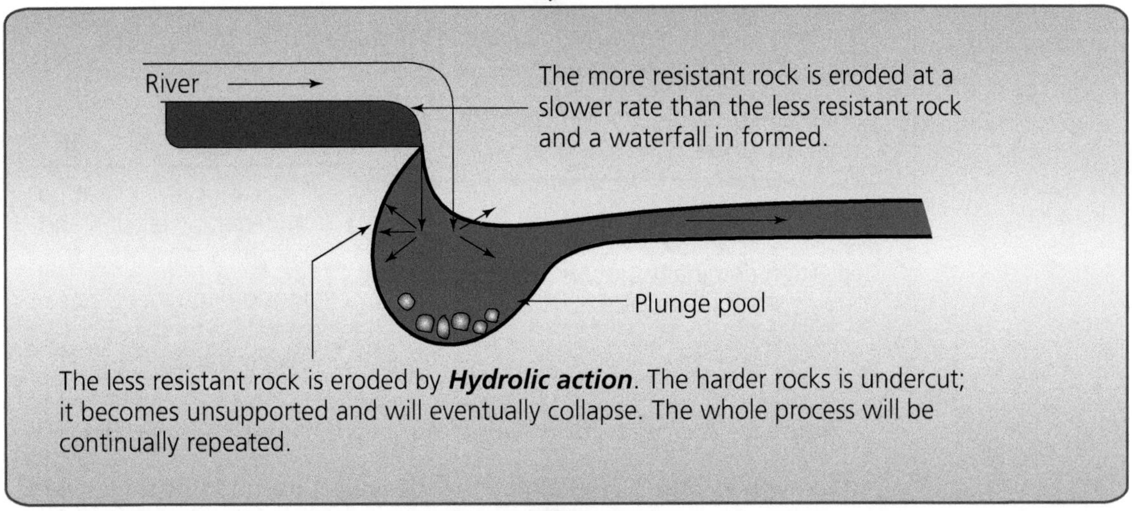

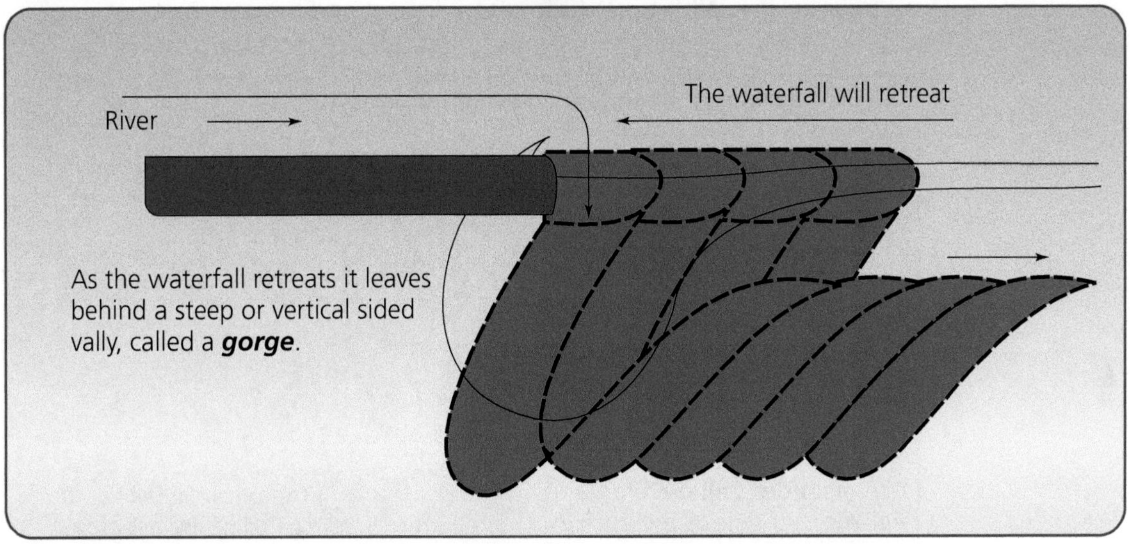

Figure 5 The formation of a waterfall through differential erosion

Meanders and oxbow lakes

Make sure that you correctly identify which side of a meander is A and which is B – a typical task.

In their natural state, unaffected and unaltered by people, rivers rarely flow straight – normally for a distance less than ***ten*** times their channel width. When rivers bend, they are said to ***meander*** and this term is used to describe any bend in a river. Meanders have a very distinctive shape and this is illustrated in the diagram taking a cross section, A to B, from Figure 7.

As shown in Figure 6, the ***outside*** bank of the meander where the full force of the river is felt is called a ***river cliff*** or ***bluff*** – this side is deep, fast flowing, is often ***undercut*** by the river and has a large sediment size.

The ***inside*** bank is called the ***slip off slope*** or ***river cliff*** – this side is shallow, slow flowing and has a small sediment size.

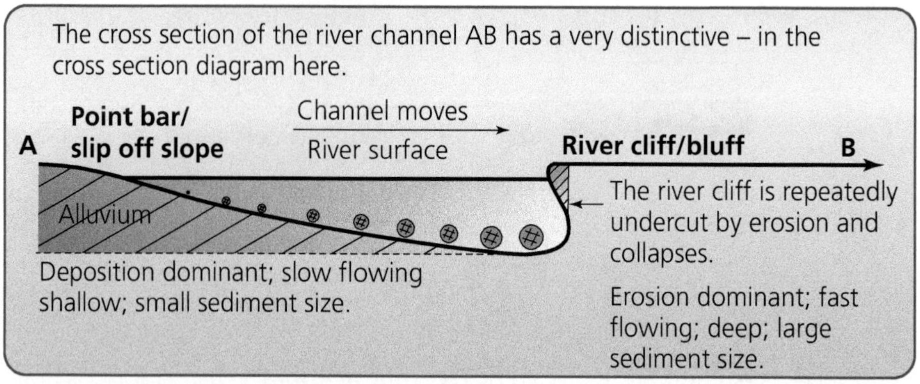

Figure 6 A cross section A–B taken through a typical meander

As can be seen in Figure 7, as a meander develops, its 'neck' becomes very narrow. With time this may be broken through – often during high flow conditions, as in a flood event. This leaves an isolated section of river called an ***oxbow lake***. With time these often dry out and become ox-bow scars.

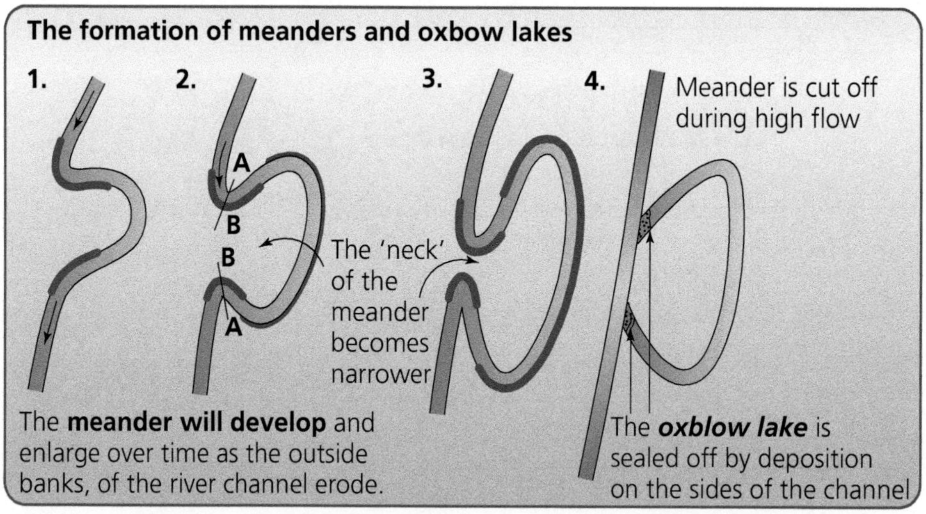

Figure 7 Meanders and the formation of Oxbow lakes

You may need to identify features and processes taking place along the course of a river. Figure 8 shows a river meandering through its floodplain and, below the diagram, a typical cross section A-B through a meander.

The steep slopes represent the river cliffs. P, Q and R show three locations along the river, only one of which is the cross section A-B, in this case it is Q. X marks the location where at some future date the river is likely to cut off the meander to form an oxbow lake.

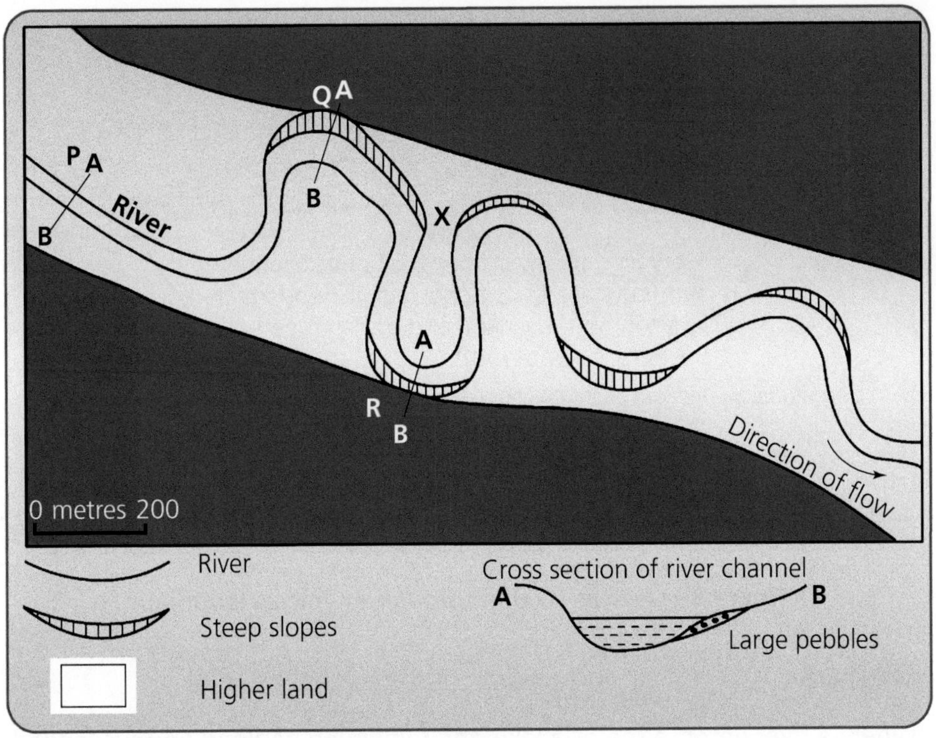

Figure 8 A meandering river

Cambridge 0460 Paper 1 Fig 5 June 2003

Levées and flood plains

The middle and lower sections of a river are characterised by having wide, flat areas beside them made out of material that has been deposited by the river during flood events, as illustrated in Figure 9. These features are called ***floodplains***.

A river will flood when water in the river channel reaches the top of the river banks and flows over them. When a river reaches this level, it has reached what is called ***bankfull discharge***.

As the river water flows away from the river channel, it carries with it the bedload and suspended load that it has been transporting down the river. As it flows across the flat floodplain it quickly loses velocity/speed and its energy and so deposits/drops the material it is carrying. The name given to all this deposited material dropped by a river is ***alluvium***.

The larger, heavier material, like pebbles and gravel, is dropped first which means that the parts of the floodplain nearest the river channel are higher than the rest of the floodplain. These higher areas parallel to the river channel are called ***levées***.

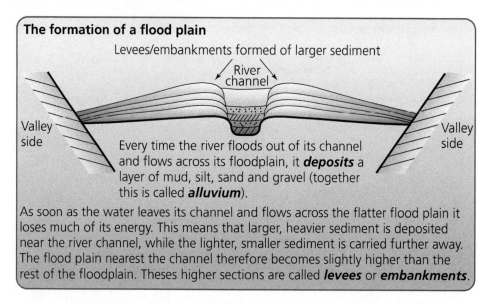

The formation of a flood plain

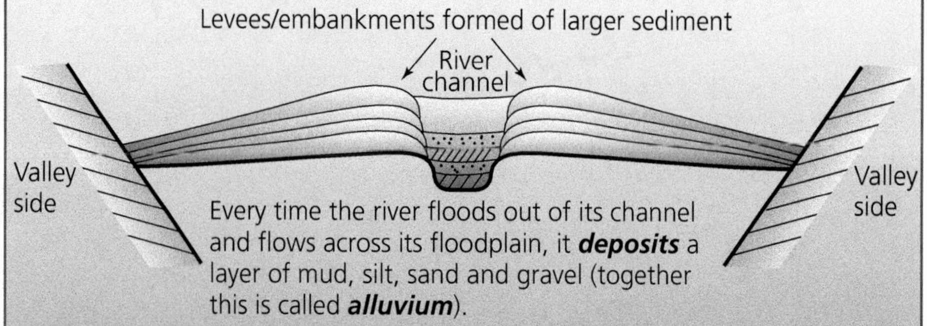
Levees/embankments formed of larger sediment
River channel
Valley side
Valley side
Every time the river floods out of its channel and flows across its floodplain, it ***deposits*** a layer of mud, silt, sand and gravel (together this is called ***alluvium***).

As soon as the water leaves its channel and flows across the flatter flood plain it loses much of its energy. This means that larger, heavier sediment is deposited near the river channel, while the lighter, smaller sediment is carried further away. The flood plain nearest the channel therefore becomes slightly higher than the rest of the floodplain. Theses higher sections are called ***levees*** or ***embankments***.

Figure 9 A cross section through a typical Floodplain

Deltas

Where a river enters a sea or a lake, the remaining bedload and suspended load that it has been transporting will be deposited at its mouth.

If there are strong tidal currents, as found on many coastlines, the material carried as bedload and suspended load by the river will be transported away and it often ends up on the beaches along the coast. However, if there are no tidal currents, the material will build up to form a **delta**.

The deposition of the very small, fine sediment is helped by the fact that the salt particles in the sea cause the fine clay particles to 'stick' together (a process called ***flocculation***) and as they become heavier they drop to the sea bed.

A typical delta is made up of three sets of deposits and this is illustrated in Figure 10.

- The heavier bedload material is dropped first to produce ***fore-set beds***.
- The lighter, suspended material is carried further away from the coast and forms ***bottom-set beds***.
- On top of the fore-set beds as they build up, water will flood across them and deposit more layers of alluvium, these are called ***top-set beds***.

On top of the delta the river channel may split up into several smaller river channels, called ***distributaries***. Its bed fills with alluvium/sediments and partly blocks the channel so that the water starts to flow around the blockage. These then spread across the delta. The growth of vegetation on the delta will help trap more sediment and raise the delta above sea level.

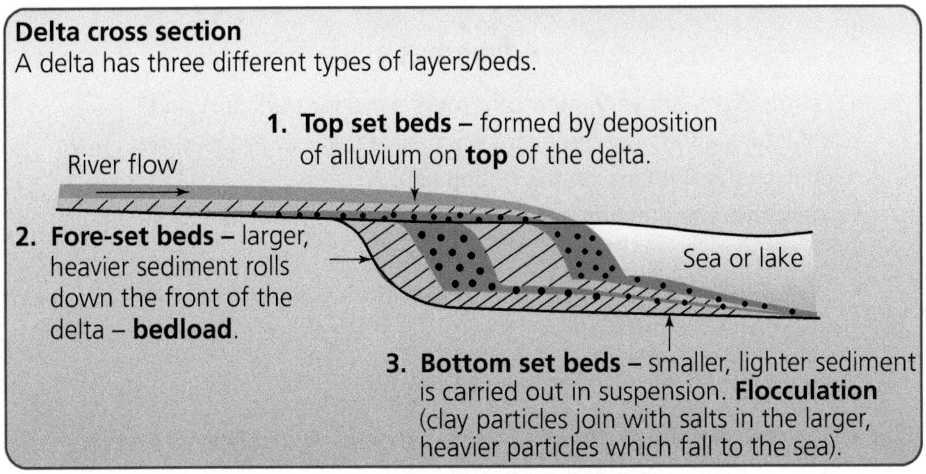
Delta cross section
A delta has three different types of layers/beds.
1. Top set beds – formed by deposition of alluvium on top of the delta.
River flow
2. Fore-set beds – larger, heavier sediment rolls down the front of the delta – bedload.
Sea or lake
3. Bottom set beds – smaller, lighter sediment is carried out in suspension. Flocculation (clay particles join with salts in the larger, heavier particles which fall to the sea).

Figure 10 A cross section through a delta

Deltas may form a variety of shapes, the two most common are as following.

- ***Arcuate*** deltas, for example the Nile delta, which flows into the Mediterranean Sea. They have a triangular fan shape.
- ***Digital*** deltas which have a shape that looks like the fingers on a hand. In some parts of the world they are called ***bird's foot*** deltas, for example, the Mississippi delta near New Orleans, USA which flows into the Gulf of Mexico.

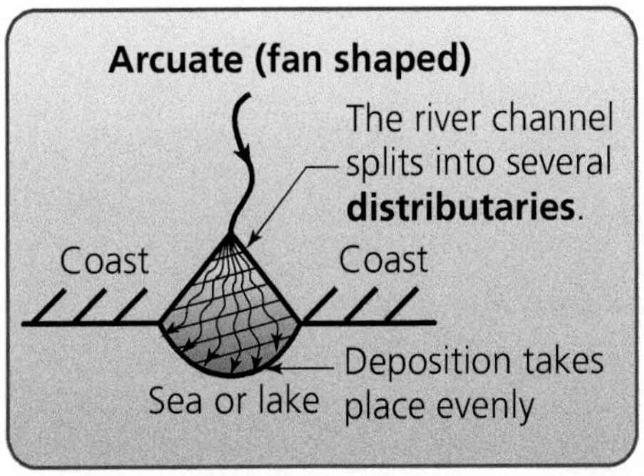
Arcuate (fan shaped)
The river channel splits into several distributaries.
Coast
Coast
Deposition takes place evenly
Sea or lake

Figure 11a The two common types of delta – Arcuate

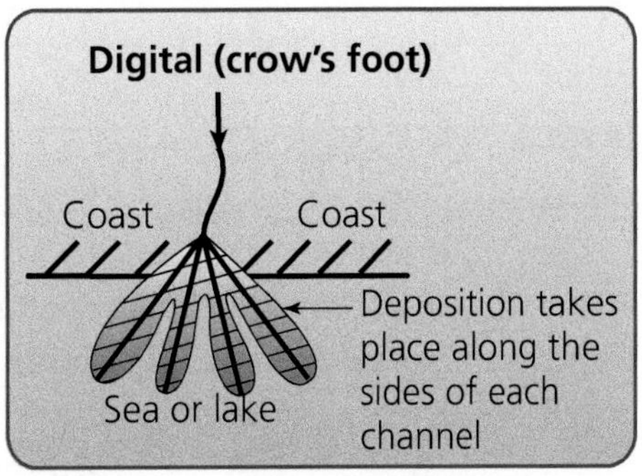
Digital (crow's foot)
Coast
Coast
Deposition takes place along the sides of each channel
Sea or lake

Figure 11b The two common types delta – digital

People experience several advantages and disadvantages when choosing to live on floodplains and deltas.

Advantages

- The ***alluvium*** that has been deposited on them during floods provides extremely fertile soils which mean that they are often very important for agriculture – such as the River Nile in Egypt.
- The water from the river can be used for irrigation, allowing land that lacks water to be used for agriculture.

Advantages

- Larger rivers are very important route ways for transport and communications (by the rivers themselves and by roads and railways built on the flat land on the floodplain).
- Many rivers are an important source of food with the fish they contain.
- They are important sources of fresh water.
- They provide large areas of flat land that can be used for building houses and industry.

Disadvantages

- They are liable to flood which destroys crops and buildings. Floods can also kill people and animals.
- They can be sources of water related diseases because they provide a breeding ground for certain animals that spread disease, such as the mosquito which can spread malaria and dengue fever, and the Bilharzia snail. Polluted water can also spread diseases such as cholera and diarrhoea.
- The alluvium that makes up a floodplain and delta is not very stable for building so foundations need to be carefully constructed.
- It is often very difficult and expensive to cross or bridge a large river.
- Floodplains and deltas are often very densely populated and so there is great competition for space.

The building of dams on rivers

The building of dams normally produces both advantages and disadvantages to both people and the natural environment.

Advantages

- The generation of cheap, renewable, clean electricity – hydroelectric power. The Three Gorges Dam on the Yangtze River in China is now the world's biggest power station.
- This cheap electricity may attract industrial development.
- They provide water for many uses – for people's domestic use, industry and for farming including the irrigation of farm land.
- They regulate river flow and can be used to prevent flooding below them.
- They create employment during the construction phase of the dam.
- They can become important fisheries if stocked with fish.
- They can make transport easier in rivers and can improve communications.

Advantages

- They can provide tourism and leisure facilities, such as sailing, fishing, water skiing, swimming.

Disadvantages

- The lakes and reservoirs they form behind them can flood large areas of fertile farmland.
- They can drown settlements and people's homes which can destroy communities and cause thousands of people to be forced to leave their land and homes. The Three Gorges Dam has forced 1.1 million people to move.
- They cause the loss of a natural river and its valley.
- They can drown important ecosystems and can have an impact on rare plant and animal species.
- They may mean that there is a loss of a large recreational area.
- A large concrete dam can have a big visual impact in a beautiful mountain area.
- They can be very expensive to build.
- Clear water erosion – as they trap the rivers' load behind them so that the water coming out of the dam no longer spends it energy carrying the load. As a result, it is more powerful and has more energy for erosion. This erodes the banks faster which mean that they need protection from erosion.

River flooding

Rivers flood when the water in their channel reaches the top of their banks (this is called ***bankfull discharge***) and then flow across their floodplain. This usually happens **either** when there has been a short period of heavy, torrential rain which the land cannot absorb quickly enough (the water cannot ***infiltrate*** fast enough) – these are often called ***flash floods*** when too much water arrives too quickly for the river to transport away, or when there has been a long period of steady rain and the soil and rocks below the ground are full, ***saturated***, with water so that any more rain that falls cannot infiltrate the soil and so it is forced to stay on the surface of the ground and then flows quickly towards and fills the river channel.

Sometimes, both these situations occur at the same time and these floods can be extremely, serious and dangerous. Predicting floods can save lives and property. ***Flood hydrographs*** are one of the methods used to help in flood prediction.

Flood hydrographs

A flood hydrograph plots ***river discharge*** (in cubic metres per second – CUMECS) and ***rainfall*** (measured in millimetres) over time.

There are several important parts of a typical hydrograph, illustrated in Figure 12 – as the rainfall reaches its peak it is called the ***rainfall peak***, as the river discharge rises on the graph it is called the ***rising limb***. When the discharge reaches its peak it is called the ***flood peak***. As the discharge then drops, it is called the ***falling limb***. The gap of time between the rainfall peak and the flood peak is called the lag time. This lag time is a very important time period as people and animals, businesses can prepare for the flood. It can be for several hours or several weeks on large rivers.

Every river has its own unique flood hydrograph and its unique lag time. Unfortunately, some rivers have very short lag times and high flood peaks which make them very dangerous for people living beside the river. Prediction of floods is, therefore, increasingly important as more people live on floodplains and deltas than ever before.

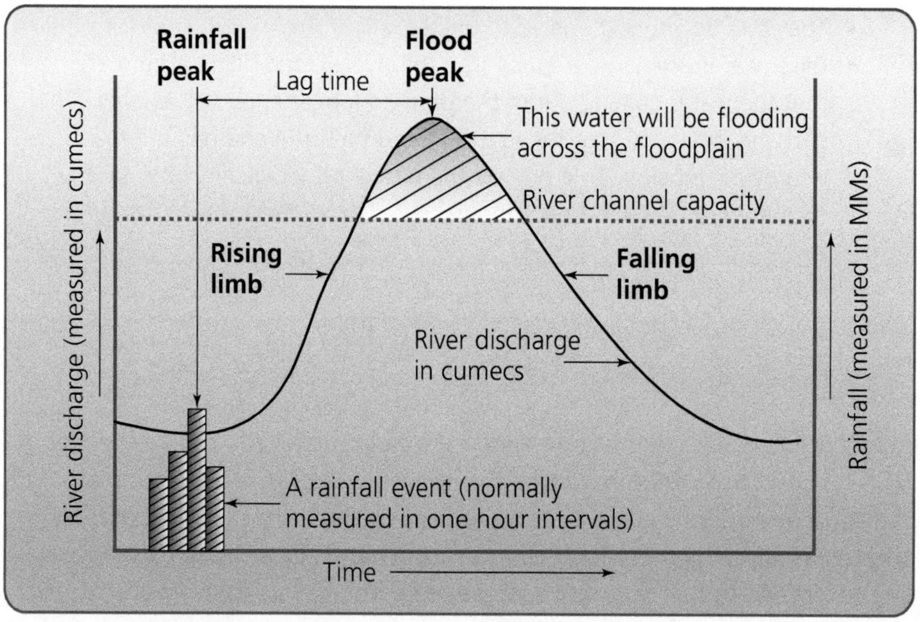

Figure 12 The features of a typical Flood Hydrograph

Flood prevention

There are two main methods of flood prevention. The first set of methods involve intercepting rainwater before it reaches and fills a river channel. The second set involves increasing the size/capacity of a river channel so that it can carry more flood water – this is called ***channel engineering***.

Forests and vegetation naturally intercept rainfall, but on large areas of the Earth ***deforestation*** and farming have removed the trees and vegetation so flooding now occurs where it never existed before or it is much worse than before.

To solve this problem there are several methods which involve keeping water on the valley sides, allowing it to infiltrate into the soil and not allowing it to flow quickly over the surface of the land into the river channel. By preventing this surface run off/overland flow it also prevents the loss of soil – from farmers' fields. The methods include the following.

- Planting trees – called ***afforestation***.
- Leaving ***permanent crops***, such as grass on the valley sides.
- ***Tiered or layer cropping***, where several layers of trees and crops are grown on the valley side by farmers to intercept the rain. For example, a typical field could have:
  (a) palm trees which provide coconut flesh, coconut oil, fibre from their husks for matting and rope, leaves for roofs and wood for fuel and building
  (b) below these, small fruit trees, or tea or coffee trees
  (c) at ground level, vegetables and cereals can be grown or cash crops like pineapples.
- ***Contour ploughing*** – ploughing across a valley side rather than up and down the valley side. Each small bank of soil stops rainwater flowing down the valley side and the rainwater infiltrates into the ground and is available to the growing crops and is not lost as it flows away to the river channel.
- ***Terracing*** – where large level steps are built into the side of a valley which provide areas of flat land for crops to be grown.
- ***Tied ridging*** – creating a grid of raised soil embankments, taking the shape of squares, from which rainfall cannot flow away down the valley side, again the water is kept in the soil on the valley sides and the crops can make use of it.
- Leaving ***crop stubble*** in the fields which both stabilises and protects the soil and stops water flowing to the river channel.
- ***Creating natural wetlands*** – A natural floodplain stores a large amount of floodwater which reduces the threat of flooding further down the river. As many floodplains have now been drained and protected from flooding, the water that they would have stored is now moved further down the river putting flood defences under much greater pressure downstream and many are now not big enough to hold this extra water. In some rivers, like the Mississippi, floodplains that were drained and protected from flooding are now being allowed to flood after heavy rains to store floodwater.

All these methods also prevent soil erosion where valuable, fertile top soil is carried into the river channel.

Much of this soil in the river channel is not transported away by the river and it just builds up on the channel bed. The result of this is that the river channel becomes smaller – its ***channel capacity*** is reduced. This means that less water is needed to cause the river to flood. As a result, floods happen more often and are bigger than they were in the past.

The second set of methods (channel engineering) increases channel capacity so that the river can hold more floodwater. The methods include the following.

- ***Dredging*** – where the bed load is dug out by diggers and there is greater channel capacity as a result. This sometimes means that the soft channel sides may be eroded and collapse into the river channel so the ***channel sides are strengthened*** either by concrete or stone.
- ***Wing dykes*** – these are walls built out from the side of the river made out of concrete and stone on one side of a river channel. The aim is to force the river into a smaller area which means it flows faster and carries away the bed load and alluvium and, therefore, does the job of dredging without the use of machines.

Wing dykes are used on the Mississippi river.

- ***Two stage channels*** – this is where the top of one side of the channel is cut away to increase the amount of room in the channel for flood water.
- ***Building embankments or levees*** – these are high banks of soil, clay, sand and gravel built beside the river channel to increase the volume of the channel. Sometimes, these are built further away from the river channel to make the capacity even bigger.
- ***Straightening the river channel*** – this involves cutting out meanders so that floodwater can flow away much more quickly.
- ***Holding dams*** – these dams are built in the upper sections of rivers and hold back floodwater, from melting snow or heavy rainfall from Monsoons, which they can then release after the flood threat is over. The Mississippi river in the US has over 200 of these.
- ***Check dams*** – these trap the river's bed load as it is being transported down the river in a flood so that it does not fill up the river channel further down the river and reduce its capacity to carry water. They can be emptied by diggers when they fill up.
- ***Overflow channels*** or ***spillways*** which allow water to flow away from the main river channel.

In addition to these methods, and often as a last resort, buildings and homes can be ***flood proofed*** by sealing doors and other openings or raising them up above flood level.

Water resources

The amount of water available to people around the world varies enormously. There are several reasons, both natural and human, why some areas have a shortage of water whereas others can have a surplus. The reasons for this include the following.

- The amount of precipitation received
- The amount of evaporation/evapotranspiration taking place
- Temperatures – the higher the temperature, the greater the amount of evaporation/evapotranspiration taking place
- The type of land use, for example, natural forests compared to farming – farming may consume large amounts of water for irrigation
- The level of economic development – richer MEDC's may consume larger amounts of water

- Population density – more densely populated areas may use more water
- The presence or absence of water bearing rocks or aquifer may mean that more or less water is available to the people
- How close people live to rivers will affect how easy it is to obtain water
- Political decisions – where a river flows through several countries they may not agree on how much water each country may take – the Nile in north east Africa, for example.

The variations are greatest when comparing the rich (MEDC's/developed) countries and the poor (LEDC's/developing/less developed) countries use of water.

- A larger amount could be used for agriculture and irrigation in LEDCs, ***developing*** countries because people are more dependent on the land.
- A larger amount could be used for industry in MEDC's, ***developed*** countries as there is more industry and more factories in developed countries.
- A larger amount could be used for electricity generation (as Hydro Electric Power – HEP) in MEDC's as richer countries consume more electricity, or more may be used for cooling in thermal power stations.

Progress check

1. What is meant by the terms: River basin (sometimes called a drainage basin or river catchment), Watershed, Tributaries, Confluence, River Discharge.
2. Name and describe the four processes of erosion in a river channel.
3. Name and describe the four processes of transportation in a river channel.
4. Describe and explain the formation of potholes, waterfalls, meanders, oxbow lakes, deltas, levées and flood plains.
5. Describe the characteristic features of the long and cross profiles of a river.
6. Why and where in a river's course deposition takes place.
7. What are the advantages and disadvantages of living on floodplains and deltas?
8. What are the advantages and disadvantages of dams?
9. Why do rivers flood?
10. What are flood hazards?
11. What are the features of a flood hydrograph?
12. What are the ways in which floods can be prevented or their impact reduced?
13. Why do some areas have a shortage of water whereas others can have a surplus and why there are global differences in water use?

Examination style questions

1. Using an example which you have studied, explain how and why a delta is formed at a particular location. **[5]**

Example Answer:

The River Nile in Egypt has formed a very large delta where it reaches the Mediterranean Sea. As the river reaches its mouth, it starts to slow down and it no longer has the energy to carry its load. The river will then deposit the sediment (alluvium) it is carrying at the mouth of the river. As there are no major sea currents to carry away the sediment it has built up to form a delta. The salt in the sea water has helped by causing the small clay particles to join together and become larger and heavier so that they have sunk to the sea bed. The growth of vegetation on the Nile delta has helped trap more sediment and raise the delta above sea level. Over time the sediment has accumulated and increased the size of the delta. Lots of people now live on the delta using the fertile alluvium to grow crops.

Comment: A very good answer, an example has been used to describe well how the delta has formed. Could have used the word 'flocculation' in describing the action of sea water and the last sentence on people living on the delta is irrelevant to this particular question as it was not asked.

Overall mark: 5/5

Examination style questions for you to try

1. (i) What is the name given to the line dividing two river basins? **[1]**
   (ii) What is a confluence in a river? **[1]**
   (iii) Explain how the processes of hydraulic action and abrasion may erode the bed and banks of a river channel. **[4]**
   (iv) Name and explain two processes by which a river transports its load. **[4]**
2. (i) Describe three likely impacts of flooding in an area. **[3]**
   (ii) What methods can be used to reduce the impact of flooding? **[5]**
3. Describe the advantages and difficulties for people of living on a river floodplain. You should refer to a floodplain which you have studied. **[7]**

Chapter

6 Marine processes
(Landforms and landscape processes)

Learning Summary

In this chapter you will learn about:

- ***How wave processes erode a coastline and the re-sorting and depositing materials removed through erosion***
- ***The erosional processes of wave action***
- ***How coastal landforms are created***
- ***The types of waves (constructive and destructive) and the components of waves, swash and backwash***
- ***How material is transported along a coastline by onshore and offshore movements***
- ***The action of wind in shaping coastal sand dunes***
- ***The landforms such as beaches, spits and bars; coastal sand dunes and salt marshes associated with these processes***
- ***The conditions required for the development of coral reefs***
- ***Fringing and barrier reefs and atolls***

Coastal erosion, transportation and deposition

Processes of erosion

There are four processes of coastal erosion.

- ***Hydraulic action:*** This is where the weight (this can be up to 20 tonnes per square metre) and force of a wave crashing against a cliff removes particles of rocks from the cliff. It also includes the process where air is trapped by a wave in a crack in the cliff and the enormous hydraulic pressure this creates opens up the crack further weakening the cliff.
- ***Abrasion (sometimes called corrasion):*** This is where the boulders, pebbles, shingle and sand is picked up by a wave and thrown against the cliff. This constant collision removes particles of rock from the cliff and wave cut platform.
- ***Solution (sometimes called corrosion):*** Some minerals (mainly the ***carbonate*** minerals found in rocks like Limestone and Chalk) are put into solution by the weak acids found in sea water.
- ***Attrition:*** This process does not actually erode the cliff but it is the process that breaks up the boulders, pebbles, shingle and sand on the beach. It takes place when the rocks on the beach are rolled up and down the beach by **swash** and **backwash**. As this happens they collide with each other and become smaller and rounder as a result.

Processes of transportation

There are two main processes of transportation.

1. ***Longshore drift*** (see Figure 1) – where sand and shingle is moved by wave action. For this process to take place on a beach, the waves must break across the beach at an ***oblique*** angle. When the wave breaks its ***swash*** transports sand and shingle up and across the beach. When the swash runs out of energy it returns back down the beach, carrying the sand and shingle with it, as ***backwash***. As this process is continually ***repeated***, it means that the sand and shingle will be moved along the coastline.
   Where there is a break in the coastline, it results in the formation of ***spits, bars and tombolos***. To prevent the process, ***groynes*** can be built to trap the sand and shingle. ***Groynes*** are made out of concrete, stone or wood and are built perpendicular (at right angles) to the coast.

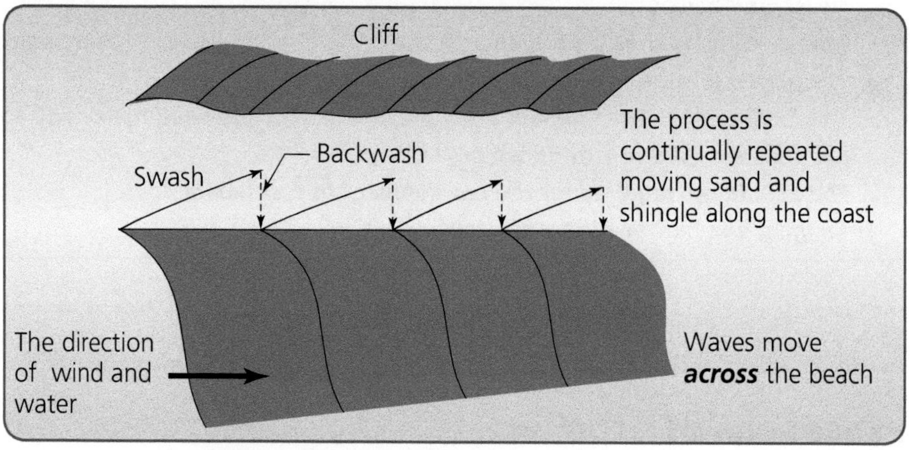

Figure 1 The process of Longshore drift

2. ***Wind action*** – smaller grains of sand can be moved by the wind and can form ***sand dunes*** (see Figure 2) at the back of a beach. For this to happen there needs to be the following.

- A ***large, sand beach*** to supply the sand.
- A ***strong, onshore wind*** to firstly dry out the sand and then transport it inland.
- An ***obstruction*** to trap the sand, such as seaweed at the top of the beach – the ***strand line***.
- The sand will ***accumulate*** (build up) into a small dune, about one metre high, called an ***embryo dune***.
- ***Pioneer species*** of plants, such as ***Marram Grass***, will colonise the small dune. The roots and stems of these plants will trap more sand and speed up the process of deposition so that the sand builds up into bigger ***mobile*** or ***yellow dunes***.
- As this process continues the sand dune will increase in size and height to become ***fixed*** or ***grey*** dunes.

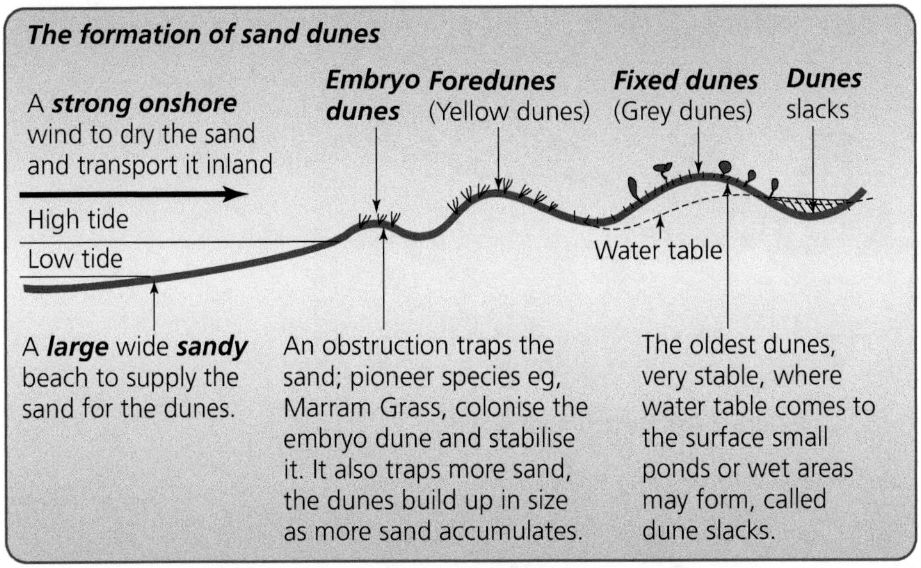
The formation of sand dunes
A strong onshore wind to dry the sand and transport it inland
Embryo dunes
Foredunes (Yellow dunes)
Fixed dunes (Grey dunes)
Dunes slacks
High tide
Low tide
Water table
A large wide sandy beach to supply the sand for the dunes.
An obstruction traps the sand; pioneer species eg, Marram Grass, colonise the embryo dune and stabilise it. It also traps more sand, the dunes build up in size as more sand accumulates.
The oldest dunes, very stable, where water table comes to the surface small ponds or wet areas may form, called dune slacks.

Figure 2 The formation of sand dunes

Constructive and destructive wave action

Waves can be ***constructive*** or ***destructive***. This means that they can either ***build up/construct*** a beach or ***drop/destruct*** a beach.

A **constructive wave** has its swash ***stronger*** than its backwash – which will result in sand and shingle being moved **onshore** therefore building up the beach as it ***brings in*** more sand and shingle than it takes away. Constructive waves are usually small, flat waves with a long wave length – upto 100 metres and they have a low frequency – there will be about 6–8 every minute.

These waves steepen slowly when they reach a beach and gently spill forward.

A destructive wave, in contrast, has its swash ***weaker*** than its backwash – which will mean that sand and shingle will be moved ***offshore*** – it will ***take away*** more sand and shingle than it brings in. They are usually large, steep waves with a short wave length – 20 metres and they have a high frequency – there will be about 10–14 every minute.

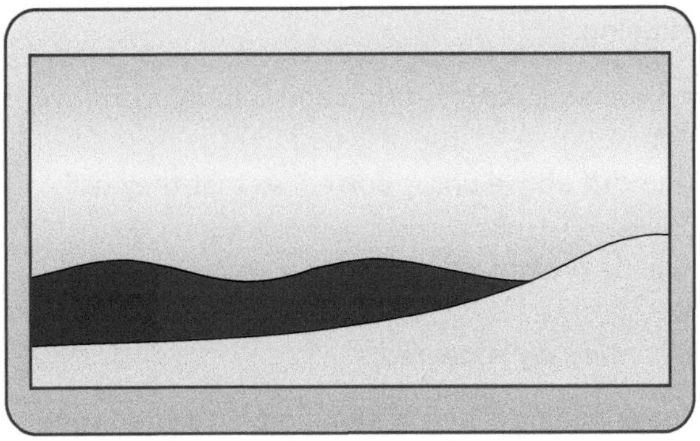

Figure 3 (a) Constructive waves

Cambridge 0460 Paper 13 Fig 5 Nov 2011

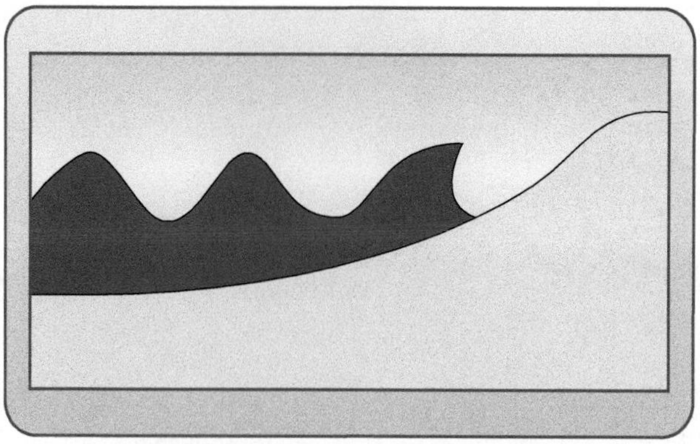

Figure 3 (b) Destructive waves

Cambridge 0460 Paper 13 Fig 5 Nov 2011

Processes of deposition

When a wave loses its energy it will drop/deposit sand and shingle. This results in a number of features of deposition being formed along a coastline. These include beaches, spits, bars, tombolos and salt marshes.

The process of **longshore drift** is very important in forming and shaping many of these features – such as the beaches, spits, bars and tombolos. In addition to the waves and longshore drift, **tidal currents** may transport very large amounts of fine, clay sized, sediment along the coast where much of it may end up in protected low energy estuaries where the sediment often builds up over time to form extensive salt marshes.

Features of coastal erosion

Cliffs and wave-cut platforms

Cliffs are formed when waves erode a coastline (see Figure 4). Cliffs go through a repeated cycle of being:

- ***Undercut*** by hydraulic action, abrasion/corrasion and solution/corrosion.
- This will form a ***cliff notch***.
- This leaves the rocks in the cliff above ***unsupported***, so that they will eventually ***collapse***.
- The collapsed material will be ***broken up by attrition and removed*** by wave action.
- The process will then be ***continually repeated***.

As the cliff retreats, it will leave behind a gently sloping platform of rock called a ***wave cut platform***. Many of these are covered by the collapsed rocks from the cliffs which will form beaches.

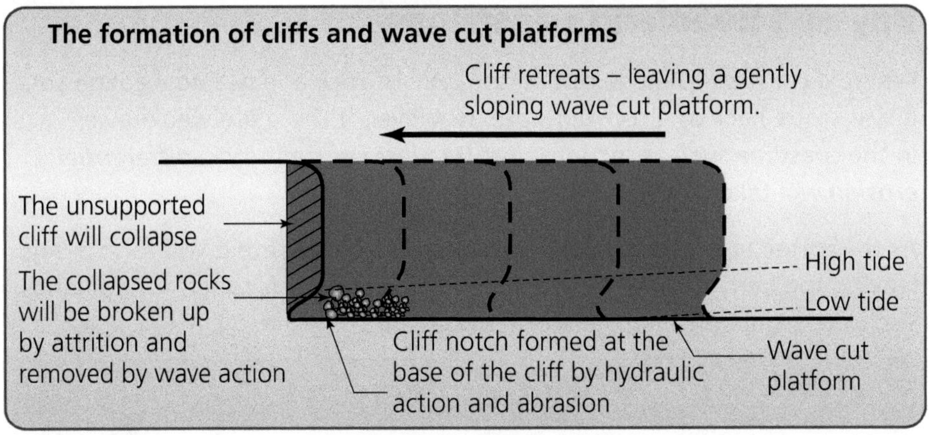

Figure 4 The formation of a cliff and wave cut platform

Caves, arches, stacks, and stumps

These features form in narrow, rocky headlands. The sequence starts when a vertical crack, or fault, in the headland is eroded, by hydraulic action, abrasion/corrasion and solution/corrosion, to form a ***cave***. Sometimes, the crack or fault at the back of the cave may be eroded through to the surface of the headland so that, when a large wave enters the cave, water is pushed out of the top of the cave to form a ***blowhole***. As the cave enlarges, it may erode all the way through a headland to form a natural ***arch***. Over time, the roof of the arch may become weakened and will collapse. This leaves an isolated rock, called a ***stack***. Over time this will become eroded to form a smaller ***stump***. Where a cave forms in a cliff and enlarges, its roof will collapse, leaving a narrow, steep sided inlet in the cliff, called a **Geo**.

A blowhole is sometimes called a gloup.

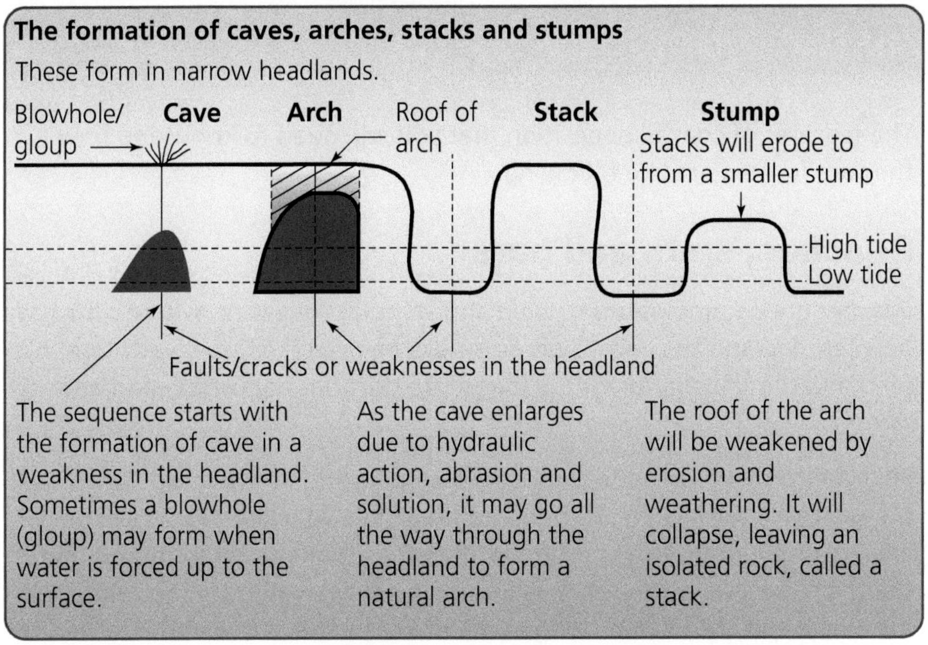

Figure 5 The formation of caves, arches, stacks and stumps

Bay and headland coastlines

Where a coastline is made out of one type of rock and has no weaknesses, it will erode back at a constant rate. However, if there are weaknesses in the coastline such as sections of softer, less resistant rock, ***differential erosion*** will take place.

As the softer, less resistant rock is eroded at a faster rate it will form a ***bay***, leaving the harder, more resistant rocks projecting out to sea as headlands. Such a coastline is called a ***discordant coastline***.

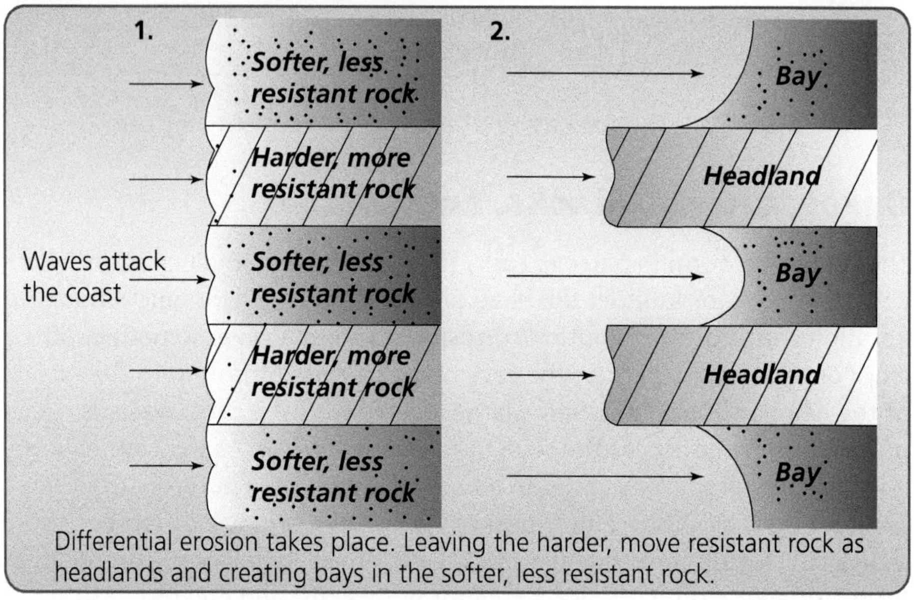

Figure 6 The formation of bay and headland coastlines

Features of coastal deposition

The features of coastal deposition that you will need to know and how they are formed are the following.

Beaches, spits and bars

They are important as they protect many coastlines from erosion by waves.

Beaches are accumulations of sand and shingle. They form where cliffs have been eroded and the collapsed rocks have been broken up by attrition into sand and shingle, and/or where longshore drift has deposited sand and shingle.

Spits are formed when longshore drift is operating, moving sand and shingle along a coastline. If there is a break in a coastline, such as in an estuary or river mouth, longshore drift will continue to deposit sand and shingle. In this case, the beach will start to grow away from the coast, forming a ***spit***. This will be long and narrow and have one end attached to the coast and one end in open water.

If a spit continues to grow, it may stretch completely across a river mouth or estuary until it reaches the other side. It then becomes a ***bar***. The water trapped behind the bar becomes a ***lagoon***. Over time, this will often become filled with alluvium brought down by a river and may disappear.

Should a spit develop and grow until it reaches an island offshore, it will form a feature called a ***Tombolo***.

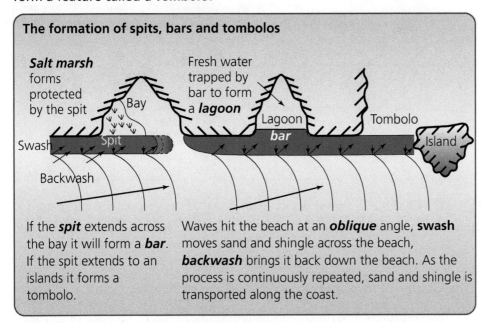

The formation of spits, bars and tombolos

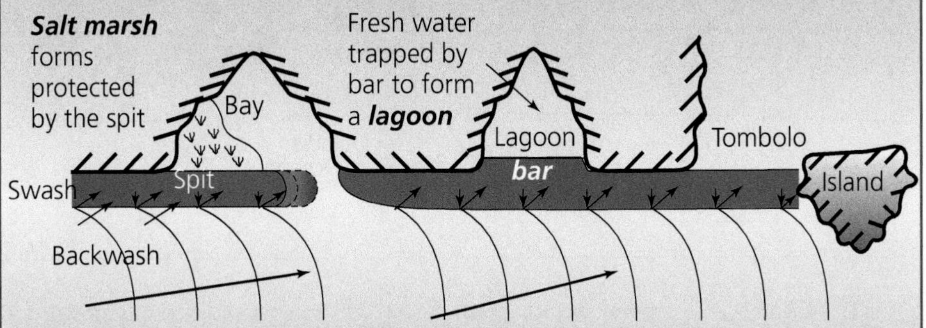

If the ***spit*** extends across the bay it will form a ***bar***. If the spit extends to an islands it forms a tombolo.

Waves hit the beach at an ***oblique*** angle, **swash** moves sand and shingle across the beach, ***backwash*** brings it back down the beach. As the process is continuously repeated, sand and shingle is transported along the coast.

Figure 7 The formation of spits, bars and tombolos

Coastal sand dunes and salt marshes

Salt marshes form in sheltered bays and estuaries or behind a spit or tombolo. In such sheltered places, there is little or no wave action or longshore drift and so very fine sand, silt and clay will be deposited.

Pioneer species of salt tolerant plants will colonise the deposited material which will trap more sediment and bind it together. Each high tide will bring in more sediment which will continue to build up the feature to form a ***salt marsh***.

The formation of Coastal sand dunes has been explained earlier.

Coral reefs

Coral reefs cover 600 000 kms² of the world's oceans bed. They are massive deposits of calcium carbonate (CaCO3) – the mineral used for the skeleton of the coral polyp. Although corals are found throughout the world's oceans, coral ***reefs*** are only found in, or near the tropics.

The following map shows the distribution of coral reefs in the world.

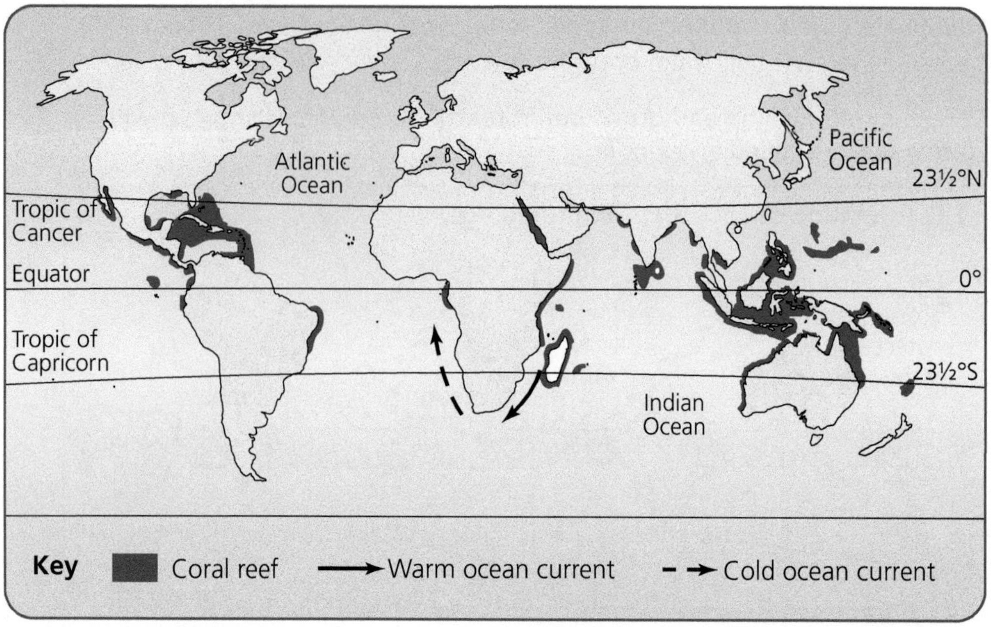

Figure 8

The location of coral reefs is controlled by seven limiting factors.

1. ***Temperature*** – The mean annual temperature has to be over 18°C. The optimal temperature for them is between 23–25°C.
2. ***Depth of water*** – Coral reefs can only grow in depths of water which are less than 25 metres.
3. ***Light*** – The shallow water allows light for tiny photosynthesising algae – called zooxanthellae. In return for the corals providing the algae with a place to live, these tiny algae provide the corals with up to 98 per cent of their food. This is an example of a symbiotic relationship – an ecological relationship which benefits both sides.
4. ***Salinity*** – Corals can only live in sea water, but they can not tolerate sea water of high salinity.
5. ***Sediment*** – Sediment clogs up the feeding structures and cleaning systems of corals. Cloudy water also reduces light penetration in the water reducing the light needed for photosynthesis.
6. ***Wave action*** – Coral reefs prefer areas of high energy wave action. This ensures freshly oxygenated water. It helps to clean out any trapped sediment. It brings in microscopic plankton – a food source for the corals. In areas that are too exposed though corals may too easily be destroyed.
7. ***Exposure to air*** – Corals die if they are exposed to air for too long. They can only survive and grow therefore at the level of the lowest tides.

Most reefs will be damaged at some time by natural and human events – called ***arresting factors*** – because these factors slow/arrest the development and growth of the corals.

There are three types of coral reef as mentioned below.

- **Barrier reefs** – the best example is the Great Barrier Reef running for 2 000 kms off the coast of the state of Queensland in eastern Australia. Barrier reefs are usually the largest reefs and are separated from the land by a deeper water lagoon.
- **Fringing reefs** – these are attached to the land and are found around many Caribbean and South Pacific islands.
- **Atolls** – these are ring shaped and usually rise out of very deep water, well away from the land. They enclose a lagoon and there may be small reefs within the lagoon. Most atolls are found in the Indian and Pacific oceans, such as the 1 100 islands of the Maldives, lying off south west India.

Progress check

1. Name and describe the four processes of erosion on a coast.
2. Name and describe the process of longshore drift.
3. Describe the characteristic features of the types of waves (constructive and destructive) and the components of waves – swash and backwash.
4. Describe and explain the formation of cliffs and wave-cut platforms.
5. Describe and explain the formation of beaches, spits and bars; coastal sand dunes and salt marshes.
6. Describe the conditions required for the development of coral reefs.
7. Describe fringing and barrier reefs and atolls.

Examination style questions

1. Describe how a spit and a bar may be formed on a coastline. **[3]**

Example Answer:

Spits and bars are formed when the process of longshore drift is operating along a coastline. This process moves sand and shingle along a coastline. It takes place when the waves hit the beach at an oblique angle and break across the beach rather than straight up and down. When the waves break, their swash transports sand and shingle up and across the beach. When the swash runs out of energy it returns back down the beach, carrying the sand and shingle with it, this is called backwash. As this process is continually repeated it moves sand and shingle along the coastline. If there is a break in a coastline, such as a river mouth, longshore drift will cause sand and shingle to build up so that the beach will start to grow away from the coast, forming a spit.

If the spit continues to grow it may eventually reach right across a river mouth until it reaches the other side, when it becomes a bar. The water trapped behind the bar is known as a lagoon.

Comment: A very good answer, there is a detailed description of the process of longshore drift, using all the key terms such as oblique, swash and backwash and has not forgotten to point out that this process needs to be continually repeated. It also mentions the need for there to be a break in the coastline such as an estuary or river mouth.

Overall mark: 6/6

Examination style questions for you to try

1. (i) What is a headland? **[1]**

(ii) Name two other natural features which are formed by coastal erosion. **[2]**

(iii) Name and describe three processes of coastal erosion. **[6]**

(iv) Explain how bays and headlands may be formed along a coast. **[4]**

2. Describe the conditions that are required for the development of a coral reef. **[5]**

3. For a named area which you have studied, explain how and why coastal sand dunes have formed in that area. You may use a labelled diagram to help in your answer. **[7]**

Chapter 7 Weather, climate and natural vegetation

Learning Summary

In this chapter you will learn about:

- ***The methods of collecting and measuring meteorological data***
- ***Drawing, describing and explaining the use and siting of instruments at a weather station***
- ***The main types of cloud and how to estimate the extent of cloud cover***
- ***The characteristics, siting and use made of a Stevenson screen***
- ***Making calculations using information from these instruments***
- ***Using and interpreting graphs and other diagrams showing weather data***
- ***The characteristics of the climate and natural vegetation of the two ecosystems***
- ***The relationship between climate and natural vegetation in these two ecosystems***

Weather stations and the instruments used to measure the weather

Measuring the weather takes place all the time globally. The terms 'weather' and 'climate' are often confused with each other. ***Weather*** is defined as being the state of the atmosphere at any particular moment in time. There are thousands of weather stations worldwide, each with several instruments, measuring the different weather variables at any particular moment in time. The more important ones take both remote digital and manual readings every hour of the day and observe these variables constantly.

The measurements that are taken are recorded. This recorded data is then used to describe the ***climate*** (a description of the averages and extremes of weather variables of an area over an extended period of time) of any location. A period of at least 30 years of weather readings is needed to be able to give accurate averages of all the weather variables, but also to give the extremes of these variables.

Weather stations have a number of characteristic features and instruments. A typical weather station will contain several standard instruments. Some of them will be kept inside a raised white box called a Stevenson screen.

A ***Stevenson screen*** is a container in which weather/meteorological instruments can be placed.

This is done to protect them against precipitation and direct heat radiation from outside sources, while still allowing air to circulate freely around them. It allows the shade temperatures to be taken, these being the temperatures shown on weather reports and forecasts. It forms an important part of a standard weather station.

The Stevenson screen will contain several instruments that may include thermometers (ordinary, maximum/minimum), a wet and dry bulb thermometer (hygrometer), and, sometimes, a barometer. Its purpose is to provide a standardised environment in which to measure temperature, humidity and atmospheric pressure. It was designed by Thomas Stevenson (1818–1887), a British civil engineer and father of the author Robert Louis Stevenson. The traditional Stevenson screen is a box shape, constructed of wood, and it has several characteristic, standardised features including the following.

- ***Double louvered sides*** which allows air to circulate freely around the instruments but not blow directly on them.
- A ***standard height for the instruments*** in the screen which is about 1.25m above the ground.
- A ***double roof*** to provide a layer of air between the two roofs which helps insulate the screen from the heat of the sun.
- ***Painted white*** to reflect the sun's radiation.
- The siting of the screen is very important, it needs to be ***in an open space*** to minimise the effects of buildings and trees.
- In the Northern Hemisphere, ***the door of the screen should always face north*** to prevent direct sunlight on the thermometers when it is opened. The ***opposite*** applies in the Southern Hemisphere.

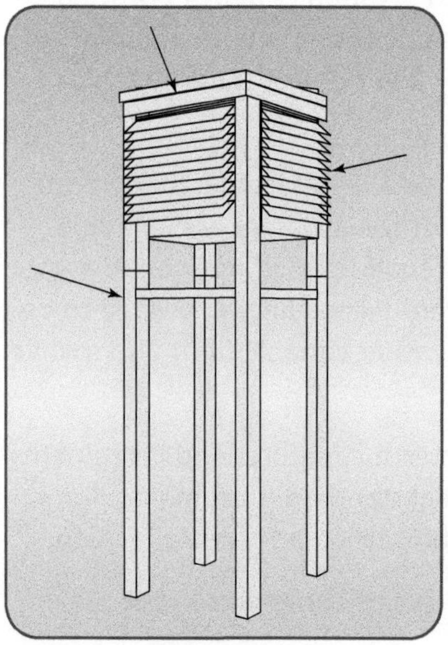

Figure 1

You may be asked to label or annotate the characteristic features of Stevenson Screen on a diagram like this one shown here.

The use of a standard screen allows temperatures to be compared accurately with those measured in earlier years and at different places around the Earth. There are 1 221 Stevenson screens used by the U.S. Historical Climatology Network in the US alone.

Maximum and Minimum thermometers (Six's thermometer)

Temperature is measured using a Thermometer, containing either coloured alcohol or mercury, which expands and contracts in a glass tube as temperatures rise and fall.

This thermometer was invented by James Six in 1782, and named after him.

A Maximum and Minimum thermometer is used to measure the hottest and coldest temperatures recorded during a period of time. This is usually one day – a 24 hour period.

The following diagram shows the typical features of a maximum and minimum thermometer. The ***maximum*** reading recorded at the bottom of the marker on the right is 30 degrees and the ***minimum*** reading recorded at the bottom of the marker on the left is 10 degrees. The ***current*** air temperature being recorded on the instrument is 25 degrees on both sides.

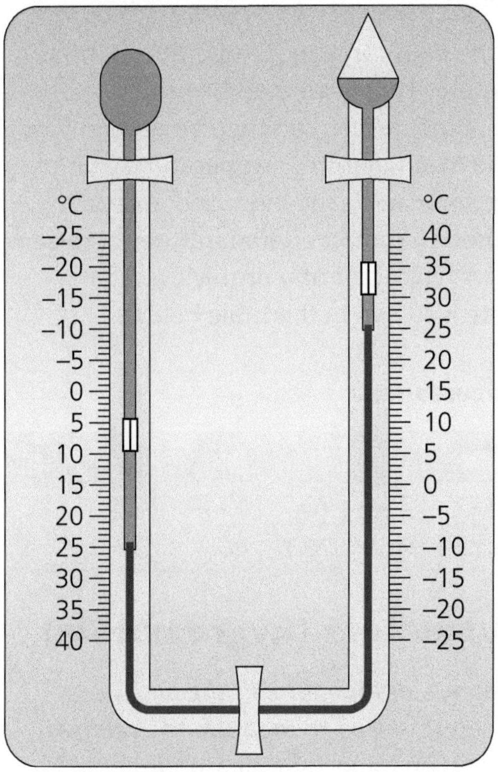

Figure 2

Cambridge 0460 Paper 21 Fig 4 June 2010

Their characteristic features are as following.

- They are made up of a ***U-shaped glass capillary tube*** with two separate temperature readings, one for the maximum temperature and one for the minimum temperature.

- There are ***bulbs at the top of each arm*** of the U-shaped tube. The one at the top of the Minimum tube contains ***alcohol***; the other, at the Maximum end, contains a vacuum.
- In the bend of the U is a ***section of mercury*** which is pushed around the tube by the expansion and contraction of alcohol in the Minimum bulb. It is the alcohol which measures the temperature; the mercury indicates the temperature reading on both the Minimum and Maximum scales.
- As the mercury moves it pushes ***two small steel markers*** which are inside the tube. They record the furthest point reached by the mercury in each side of the tube. When temperature changes, the mercury is moved by the expansion or contraction of the alcohol. The markers remain in the tube at the furthest position they have been pushed to by the mercury.
- They can be ***reset by using a small magnet*** which is used to pull the steel marker back down to the mercury.
- They record the extremes of temperature experienced by the thermometer since it was last reset.

The instrument is used to measure the daily range of temperature; this is called the **Diurnal** range of temperature. These can then be used to work out the daily, or mean temperature. These results can then be used in several ways, usually to work out the mean monthly temperatures, which can then be put on a line graph and compared, and averaged, over a number of years. They can also be used to compare temperatures between weather stations all over the world. A typical set of monthly average temperatures for a hot desert climate is shown in the table below.

Fahaheel in Kuwait average temperatures

	Jan	Feb	Mar	Apr	May	Jun	Jul	Aug	Sep	Oct	Nov	Dec	Annual Mean
°C	14.1	15.7	19.9	23.8	30.1	35.0	36.4	36.3	33.1	28.1	21.5	15.8	25.8
°F	57.4	60.3	67.8	74.8	86.2	95.0	97.5	97.3	91.6	82.6	70.7	60.4	78.4

Wet and Dry bulb thermometers (Hygrometers)

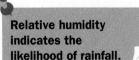

Relative humidity indicates the likelihood of rainfall.

Humidity is the amount of water vapour, or moisture, in the air. A Wet and Dry bulb thermometer (Hygrometer) is used to measure the ***relative humidity*** of the air. Relative humidity is an important measurement as it can be used in forecasting weather.

High humidity makes people feel hotter outside in the summer because it reduces the effectiveness of sweating to cool the body. This is done by reducing the rate of evaporation of perspiration, sweat, from the skin. Low humidity can cause people to dehydrate quickly and also increase the need for the irrigation of some crops.

The following diagram shows the typical features of a wet and dry bulb thermometer. The dry bulb reading 20 degrees and the wet bulb 12 degrees, difference between the two readings being 8 degrees. The table can be used to calculate the Relative Humidity – 37 per cent.

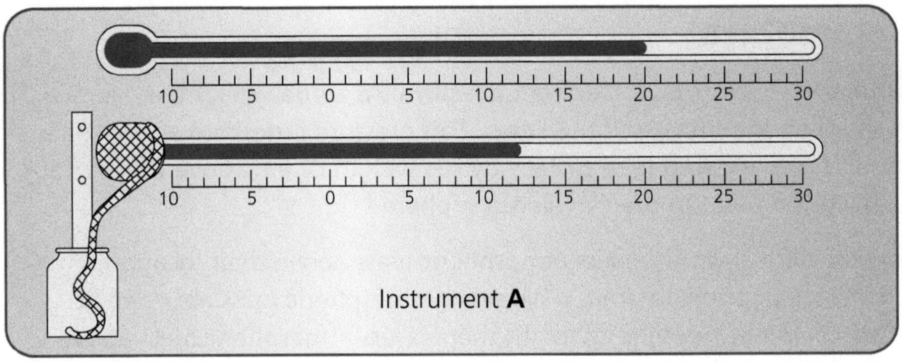

Cambridge 0460 Paper 21 Fig 4 June 2010

dry bulb reading (°C)	wet bulb depression (°C)								
	1	2	3	4	5	6	7	8	9
	%	%	%	%	%	%	%	%	%
24	92	84	77	69	62	56	49	43	37
22	92	83	76	48	61	54	47	40	34
20	91	83	74	66	59	51	44	37	30
18	91	82	73	65	56	49	41	34	27

Cambridge 0460 Paper 2 Table 3 June 2008

Figure 3

The instrument is made up of two thermometers, one of which is a ***Dry bulb thermometer***, which measures the temperature of the air, and the other is a ***Wet bulb thermometer***. This bulb is kept wet by being covered by an absorbent muslin wick which is kept wet by its end being kept in a container of distilled water. It measures the temperature of the air if there was 100 per cent humidity – called ***absolute humidity***.

If the humidity of the air is 100 per cent the readings on both thermometers will be the same – it will normally be raining or there will be mist or fog surrounding the instrument. If it is less than 100 per cent the Wet bulb reading will be lower than the Dry bulb reading.

By recording the temperatures of both thermometers, it is possible to work out the relative humidity of the air surrounding the instrument. This is done by:

- recording the temperatures of both the Wet and Dry bulb thermometers
- recording the difference between the two readings
- looking up the results in a relative humidity table.

Modern digital electronic devices have more or less replaced this instrument. They use the temperature of condensation, changes in electrical resistance, and changes in electrical capacitance to measure humidity changes.

Barometers

Barometers measure atmospheric pressure. As air has weight, it exerts a pressure on the surface of the Earth. This pressure is defined as the force per unit area exerted on a surface by the weight of air, above that surface, at any given point in the Earth's atmosphere.

Low pressure areas have less atmospheric mass above their location, whereas high pressure areas have more atmospheric mass above their location. As one goes up in height there is less atmospheric mass above you, which means that the atmospheric pressure decreases as you go up in height.

At sea level, the atmospheric pressure is about 1.03 kg per cm^2. For approximately every 300 metres you ascend, the atmospheric pressure decreases by about 4 per cent.

By far the most common type used and seen is the Aneroid Barometer.

Worldwide atmospheric pressure is commonly measured in ***millibars*** (mb). The average world pressure is 1013.25 millibars. Above this, we are said to be in an area of ***high pressure***, below it we are in ***low pressure***. Two types of barometer have been used for measuring atmospheric pressure – ***Mercury or Fortin Barometer*** and an ***Aneroid Barometer***.

A ***Mercury barometer*** is created by placing the open end of a metre long glass capillary tube, containing a partial vacuum, in a reservoir of mercury. Mercury is forced up the tube by atmospheric pressure. The mercury will reach a height of about 760 millimeters, or 29.9 inches. As atmospheric pressure changes so will the height of the mercury in the tube – it rises when atmospheric pressure increases and vice versa.

An ***Aneroid barometer*** consists of a small, flexible container which contains a partial vacuum. Small changes in external atmospheric pressure cause the container to either expand or contract. This expansion and contraction moves small mechanical levers and springs so that the tiny movements of the container are amplified and displayed by a needle on the front of barometer. The movements of the needle can then be observed on a scale in either millibars or inches which corresponds to the height of mercury in the Fortin or Mercury barometer.

Most Aneroid barometers include an extra needle index pointer that can be moved by hand externally which is used to mark the current measurement so any changes can be seen.

The following diagram shows the front face of a typical aneroid barometer, giving a current reading of 1018mb after rising from the last recorded pressure of 1006mb – seen by the position of the index pointer.

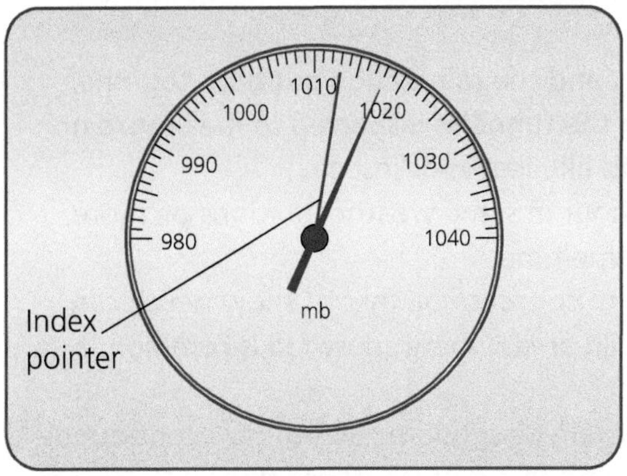

Figure 4

Cambridge 0460 Paper 41 Fig 8 Nov 2011

One form of Aneroid barometer that is seen in some weather stations is a ***Barograph***. This instrument records the changes in atmospheric pressure by means of an ink pen on a small lever attached to the aneroid barometer. It traces a line on graph paper attached to a revolving metal cylinder. The cylinder revolves once in a week. This allows changes in pressure to be seen and recorded during the week. The graph paper is replaced every week.

Rain gauges

Traditional rain gauges are made out of non-corroding copper or plastic. They have a number of characteristic features and their location is very important to ensure that they give accurate readings.

- They have to be ***located away from buildings and trees*** which might affect their collection of rainfall.
- The top of the rain gauge needs to be over ***30 cms high*** to avoid surface water running into them and the spray from rain splash entering them as rain drops hit the ground.
- The ***base of the rain gauge is sunk into the ground*** so that it is not easily blown or knocked over.
- They are normally ***located on either grass or gravel*** which absorbs the impact of falling rain drops and stops rain splash.
- They have a ***collecting funnel*** which has a standardised diameter linked to the size of the measuring cylinder used to measure the rain that is collected.
- The funnel has a ***very narrow opening*** to reduce any possible loss of the water that is collected in the collecting cylinder by the process of evaporation.

- To measure the collected water, it is poured from the ***collecting cylinder*** into the ***measuring cylinder***.
- The measuring cylinder is ***placed on a flat surface*** and the reading is taken from the ***bottom of the meniscus*** formed by the water in the measuring cylinder.
- The water is then poured away and the rain gauge put back together again. The narrow opening on the funnel is inspected to make sure no obstructions have fallen in to it, like leaves or insects.
- Readings may be taken every hour in some weather stations or, more often, once every day at the same time.
- The funnel often has tall sides to collect small falls of snow which can then melt into the instrument. In areas where snow fall is common, a snow gauge is used.
- Increasingly, remote automatic rain gauges are used to give continuous readings. These are usually ***tipping rain gauges***. These transmit the information instantly to weather stations where it is logged automatically.
- The amount of rainfall is then recorded. It can then be graphed or mapped. Annual rainfall is normally mapped using isolines (lines joining places with the same value – a contour line is an isoline which joins places with the same height above sea level, for example) called ***Isohyets***. A typical set of monthly average precipitation readings for a hot desert climate is shown in the table below.

A continuous read out is more accurate than an hourly or daily reading.

Fahaheel in Kuwait average precipitation (rainfall)

	Jan	Feb	Mar	Apr	May	Jun	Jul	Aug	Sep	Oct	Nov	Dec	Annual Mean
mm	18.5	13.0	3.8	7.9	1.4	0.0	0.0	0.0	0.0	2.6	17.9	6.5	71.7
Inches	0.7	0.5	0.1	0.3	0.1	0.0	0.0	0.0	0.0	0.1	0.7	0.3	2.8

Anemometers

These ***measure the speed of the wind***. This can be done by digital anemometers, but in weather stations it is usually measured by ***Cup anemometers***. They must be placed in the open away from buildings or trees that can alter the wind speed. They will normally be placed on a tall mast on top of a building. They normally consist of three, sometimes four, hemispherical cups attached to horizontal arms, which are mounted on a vertical shaft. The air flows past the cups, rotates them and this can be calibrated on a speedometer. The readings can be in metres per second, kms or miles per hour, or more commonly in meteorology, in knots.

The knot is a unit of speed equal to one nautical mile per hour, which is equal to exactly 1.852 km/hour or, approximately, 1.151 mph.

Wind speed is shown by arrows on a weather map, pointing in the direction that the wind is coming from, with 'feathers' attached to the end of the arrow. Each feather is 10 knots of wind speed, half a feather is 5 knots.

In the following figure, A shows a typical Wind Vane, and B a typical Cup Anemometer.

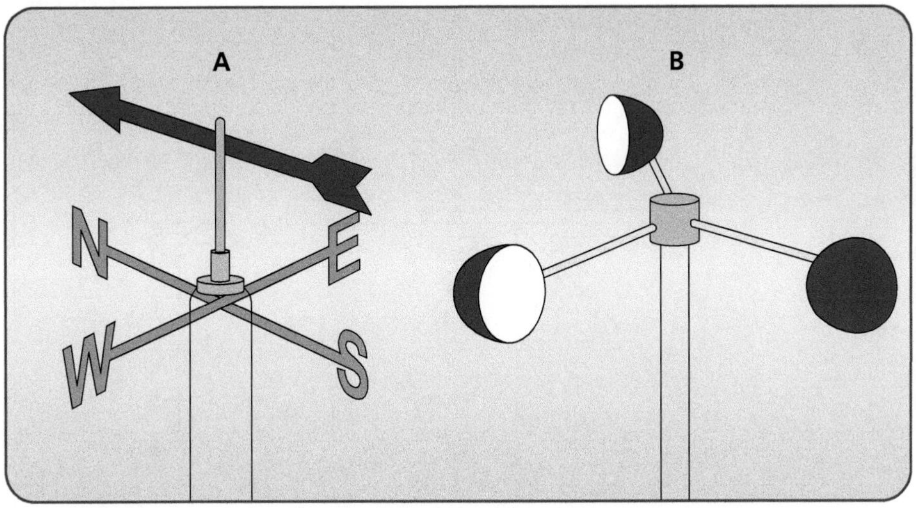

Figure 5

Cambridge 0460 Paper 2 Fig 1 Nov 2005

Wind vanes

These instruments are used to ***indicate wind direction***. Like the anemometers, they need to be in an open space unaffected by buildings and trees, so that they are normally placed on tall masts on top of buildings.

They consist of a horizontal, freely rotating arm placed on top of a fixed vertical pivot. Attached to the shaft of the fixed pivot there are usually four fixed pointers showing the four points of the compass. This means that wind direction can be read visually.

Alternatively, the direction is transferred electronically to an instrument which can give a more accurate reading either in the points of the compass or as a degree bearing. This information can then be transferred to a circular graph to produce a ***Wind Rose***, such as the following example (Figure 6). Each of the eight axes represents one of the eight points of the compass — North, North East, East, South East etc.

Each axis is marked off in segments representing individual days; in this case each axis has five days. Everytime the wind is recorded from one of the eight directions a segment will be filled in when there is no wind to be recorded this has to be written down and recorded beside the figure.

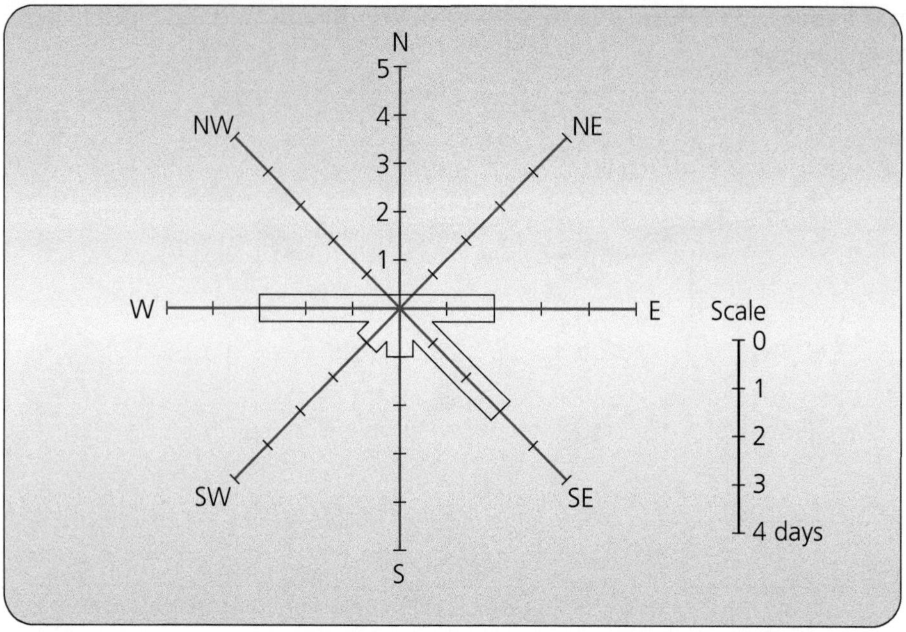

Figure 6 Wind direction at school location (number of days)

Cambridge 0460 Paper 42 Fig 8 June 2010

Cloud cover

The amount of cloud covering the sky can be observed and estimated. It is measured in ***Oktas***. One Okta is one eighth cloud cover. If half the sky is covered in cloud, there would be four Oktas cloud cover; if all the sky is covered in cloud there will be eight Oktas. Sometimes, due to fog, smoke, dust storms or pollution, the sky cannot be seen and so the sky is said to be obscured.

Cloud type

There are several different types of cloud that can be observed in the sky. They are commonly put in to one of three groups according to the level that they are found in the sky – High level, Mid-level and Low level. Their shape and whether they form individual clouds or a complete layer then allows them to be identified and named. They have names which often have their source in the Latin language and which describe their height and shape. It is sometimes helpful to know their meanings. The most common cloud names are:

- Alto – high
- Cirrus – lock of hair
- Cumulus – heap
- Nimbus – precipitation bearing (Latin for 'raincloud')
- Stratus – layer (Latin for 'spread out')

And the most common cloud types are:

- Altocumulus – altus and cumulus – high heap
- Altostratus – altus and stratus – high layer
- Cirrus – lock of hair
- Cumulonimbus – cumulus and nimbus – rain-bearing heap
- Cumulus – heap or pile
- Nimbostratus – nimbus and stratus – rain-bearing layer
- Stratocumulus – stratus and cumulus – layer and heap
- Stratus – layer

The most common are described in more detail below.

High Level

Cirrus clouds form above 6 000 m. At this height water is almost always frozen so these clouds are composed of ice crystals. They tend to be white and wispy in shape, and are often transparent. Isolated cirrus clouds often indicate a stable atmosphere and do not bring precipitation. However, if there are large amounts of cirrus clouds it can indicate that there is an approaching storm.

Mid-level

Altostratus clouds form when a large air mass is lifted, cooled and the water vapour condensed. They can bring rain or snow.

Low Level

Nimbostratus clouds often bring constant precipitation and low visibility. They are a formless layer of cloud that is almost uniformly dark grey.

Stratocumulus clouds look like large lumpy, layered clouds and they can produce rain or drizzle.

Stratus clouds form a continuous horizontal layer and have a level base, and often produce drizzle. They are flat, featureless clouds of low altitude varying in colour from dark grey to nearly white. A 'cloudy day' usually features a sky that is filled with stratus clouds.

Cumulus clouds are very common and are sometimes called fair weather clouds. These are often 'puffy' or 'cotton wool-like' in appearance with clearly defined edges. They are often alone, in lines, or in clusters. However, they can grow into much larger clouds (cumulonimbus, for example), and their continued upward growth may bring rain showers later in the day.

Cumulonimbus clouds are often spectacular tall, dense clouds going from low level up to 12 000 metres They are often involved in thunderstorms and other intense weather. They are a result of the atmosphere being very unstable.

These can form alone or in clusters. They create lightning through the heart of the cloud. Each can contain up to 10 million tonnes of water so are often involved in dangerous flash floods when they suddenly release this water.

You may be asked to identify and describe these clouds in photographs or diagrams such as in the example below.

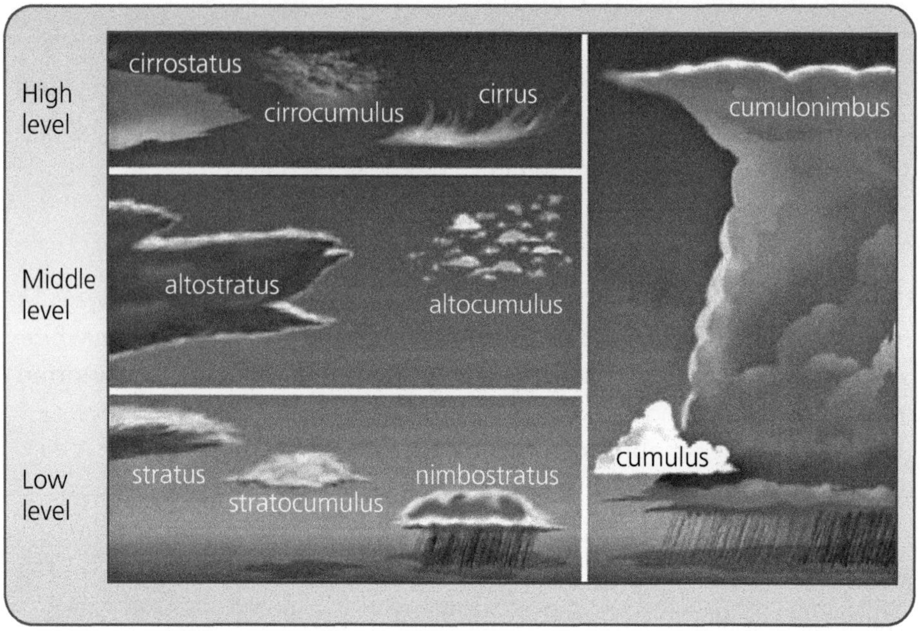

Figure 7

Cambridge 0460 Paper 1 Fig 5 Nov 2009

Tropical rainforests

An **ecosystem** is a community of living (***biotic***) and non-living things (***abiotic***) interacting with each other in an area. Tropical Rainforest ecosystems (TRFs) are usually found around the Equator between about 15° North and South of the Equator. There are three main areas where they are found.

There are several other smaller areas outside these main three areas, like Madagascar and many of the Pacific Islands.

- **Amazonia** (which includes northern South America – mainly Brazil and Central America)
- **Central Africa** (which includes both Central Africa and southern West Africa)
- **Indo-Malaysia** (which includes Indonesia, Malaysia and several other countries in SE Asia and northern Australia)

The rainforests are ***home to more species than all other ecosystems combined*** – 82 per cent of the world's known plant and animal species are found in tropical rainforests. This includes over one-third of the world's tree species. One hectare of TRF can have as many as 500 different species of tree and over 1000 plant species in it.

The trees and plants have many special adaptations to living in this wet tropical environment. The following type of graph may be used to illustrate the climate of a typical tropical rainforest.

Climate is the most important factor in determining where the vegetation of tropical rainforests can be found. The wet tropical climate has:

- A ***high rainfall*** – 1 750 and 2 500 millimetres annual rainfall, evenly distributed throughout the year. This results from the very hot temperatures during the day heating the forest and causing strong, upward convection currents. This results in the daily formation and build-up of rain bearing cumulus and cumulonimbus clouds which results in heavy convectional rainfall in the early afternoon.
- ***Constant high temperatures*** – an average (mean) monthly temperature of about 26°C with no month below 18°C. This is because these areas are close to the Equator and get high amounts of solar heating from the sun throughout the year.

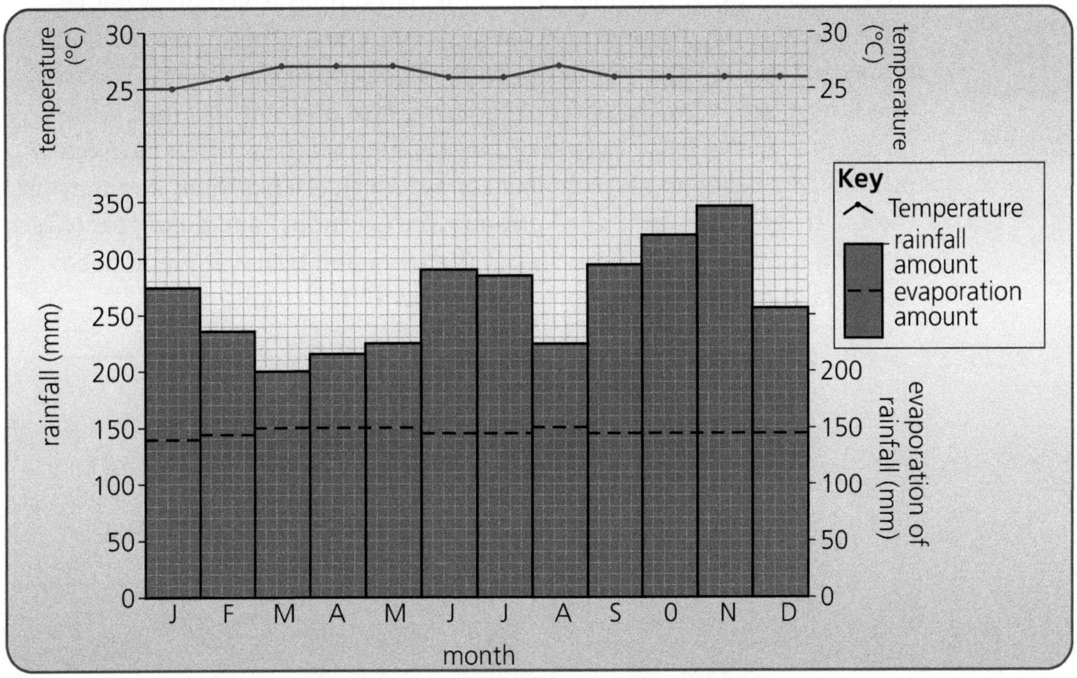

Figure 8

Cambridge 0460 Paper 23 Fig 11 Nov 2011

- A ***low range of monthly average temperatures*** – normally only a 2–3°C difference. These areas do not experience the same seasonal differences of temperature that areas further away from the Equator because the Earth's tilt does not have the same effect on them.
- ***High humidity*** – usually over 80 per cent. The high rates of evaporation and transpiration in the forests along with the large amounts of water on the ground and surfaces of the plants from the high rainfall causes the humidity to be very high.

For the tropical rainforest ecosystem to develop a number of natural/physical factors combine together with these climatic factors. For example, the constant high temperatures and rainfall results in a ***constant growing season*** which means that trees grow all year round and so drop their leaves throughout the year. This ***leaf litter rapidly decomposes*** and is ***recycled as nutrients*** for the trees and plants to grow.

The structure of the tropical rainforest

The trees, plants and animals have many special adaptations to living in this wet tropical environment. You may be asked to describe the characteristics of the natural vegetation in a tropical rainforest. Tropical rainforests have five distinct layers each with its' own characteristic features and adaptations.

The Emergent Layer: 45–55 metres in height

Eagles, other birds, butterflies, bats and certain monkeys inhabit this layer.

This contains a small number of very tall, large trees which grow above the general canopy. Their trunks are straight and, in their lower sections, branchless as they attempt to get to the light above the canopy. The trees need to be able to withstand hot temperatures and strong winds. As a result, many have large ***buttress roots*** for support. They often have many other plants growing on them like ***lianas*** (which are like vines and they use the tall trees to get up to the light above the canopy) and ***epiphytes*** (which grow on the trunks and branches of the trees and trap water and dead leaves falling from the tree or running down their trunks).

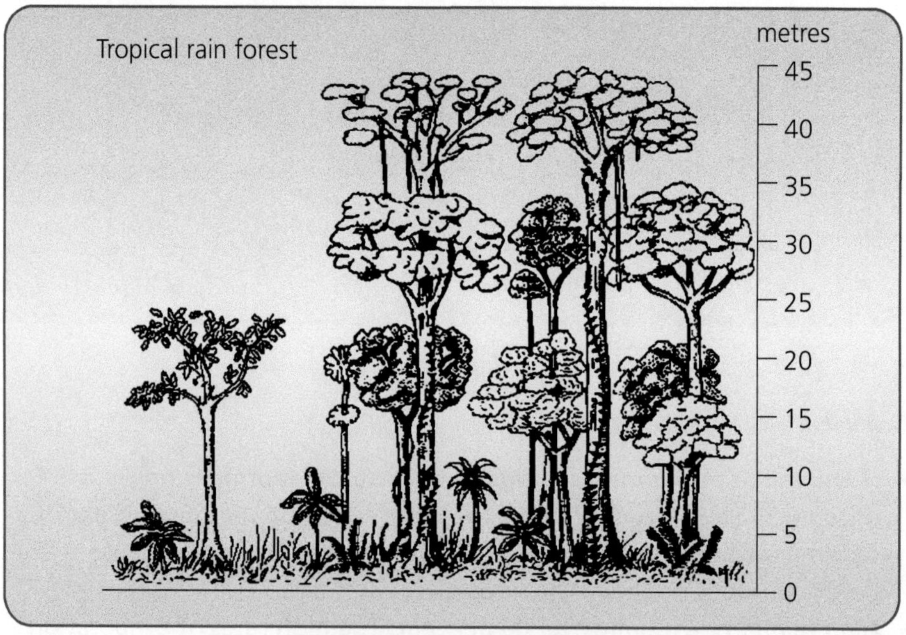

Figure 9 Tropical rain forest

Cambridge 0460 Paper 2 Fig 6 June 2003

The Canopy Layer: 30 metres

This forms a roof over the three remaining layers. Most canopy trees have smooth, oval leaves and like many of the leaves found in the rainforest they come to a point, called a ***Drip Tip***, to get rid of the rain that falls on the leaf. The canopy is a thick dense layer of leaves and branches. Very little light gets through this layer to the layers below. The canopy, by some estimates, is home to 50 per cent of the Earth's plant species. Many animals live in the canopy as food is abundant. Those animals include: snakes, parrots, toucans, sloths and tree frogs.

The canopy often supports a rich flora of epiphytes, including orchids, bromeliads, mosses, and lichens, who live attached to the branches of trees.

The Under Canopy Layer: 15 metres

Little light reaches this layer so the plants have to grow larger leaves to catch the sunlight. Many animals live here including jaguars, red-eyed tree frogs and leopards. There is also a large concentration of insects here.

Shrub Layer: 3 to 4 metres

It is very dark in this layer – only about 5 per cent of the sunlight shining on the rainforest reaches down to this layer. Tree ferns and small shrubs that grow here are able to grow in low light conditions. Many have large leaves to catch the little light that gets down to this layer.

Floor Layer

As less than 1 per cent of the sunlight makes it down to this layer, almost no plants grow here. Due to the lack of sunlight reaching the forest floor, things begin to decay quickly. A leaf that might take one year to decompose in a regular climate will disappear in 6 weeks due to the warm, humid conditions promoting rapid decay. The leaves are quickly recycled into nutrients and taken up by the trees and plants. The soil gives the impression of being extremely fertile but in fact almost all of its fertility comes from the thin layer of rapidly recycled leaf litter.

Therefore, if the rainforest is removed by the process of ***deforestation*** – the soil stops receiving dead leaves and plants and it quickly, within a couple of years, turns into infertile soil on which little will grow. Giant anteaters live in this layer.

Many forms of fungi grow here which help decay the animal and plant waste.

It takes upto 20 minutes for rain to actually touch the ground from the trees above. As the undergrowth in a rainforest is restricted by the lack of sunlight, it makes it possible for people and other animals to walk through the forest. When a huge emergent tree dies and falls down, the ground beneath is soon colonised by a dense, tangled growth of vines, shrubs and small trees trying to become a new, giant emergent tree.

Native people

The rainforest is the home for many native peoples, who are ***hunter-gatherers*** – people who hunt animals and gather food from the forest – fruit, berries, seeds and roots. These people live in, and totally depend on, the rainforests, so that complete cultures may be lost, as they are forced to migrate and start to live new lives.

Some of the indigenous people (people native to an area) are subsistence farmers as well as hunter-gatherers. They clear, and then burn, small patches of the forest to grow crops in.

Land allowed to rest is called fallow land.

They only farm these for 2-4 years as the nutrients are quickly used up by the crops or removed by the heavy rain which can now get to the ground without being intercepted by the trees. They then clear another small patch and repeat the process. Being small patches of forest, the surrounding forest can re-colonise the cleared area quite quickly. This is called ***slash and burn*** agriculture and was thought in the past to be sustainable (unlike the plantation agriculture which can only survive with addition of artificial chemical fertilisers). However, even this small scale farming causes the soil to lose its fertility over time and it does not recover fully even when left to rest for several years.

Threats to the tropical rainforests and their importance

The tropical rainforests provide most of the world's tropical hardwood timber. In the forest itself, they provide fuel wood and charcoal for cooking and heating. The indigenous peoples that inhabit them use the forests in many ways. However, they are important in many other ways as well and their existence is threatened from several activities. The three main areas of Tropical Rain Forest Amazonia, Central Africa and Indo-Malaysia are almost all in countries which have experienced rapid population growth and development. This has meant that more land is needed for settlements, for farming to feed the increasing numbers of people, to provide employment and to exploit the resources needed for development. In Amazonia, the result is that the population grew from 2 million in 1960 to 30 million in 2000.

There are many other activities that threaten the TRF's as well.

Deforestation

- Where the rainforest is ***logged for its valuable timber***, like mahogany and teak, it means that the habitat for thousands of species of plants and animals are destroyed. This destroys delicate food webs and food chains and the animals disappear often to become extinct. As mentioned, it also takes away the habitat for the indigenous peoples.

- ***Plantation agriculture*** where the forest is cleared to create huge farms for the growing of plantation crops such as sugar cane and oil palms – both now in great demand as biofuels. Malaysia has cleared large areas of TRF and is now the world's biggest exporter of palm oil.
- ***Cattle ranching*** to meet the growing demand for beef and burgers from MEDC's in particular.
- ***New settlement*** to provide land for small scale farmers. The Brazilian government has used the rainforest to provide land for some of the country's 25 million landless people. Alongside some stretches of the 12 000 kms of new roads built through the rainforest strips of land, 10 kms wide have been cleared to provide new settlers with land to farm.

The area of clearance of the forest in Amazonia has been estimated at between 20 per cent and 40 per cent – at a rate of about 15 hectares a minute! In Malaysia, 70 per cent of the Malay Peninsula was covered in rainforest in 2000 but, at present rates of clearance this could be as low as 25 per cent by 2020.

Mining

The TRF's often have important deposits of valuable minerals under them such as gold, coal, iron ore and bauxite (the ore from which aluminium is made). Many of these mines are some of the biggest in the world and are open cast – where the soil and forest are removed (called the overburden) and the minerals removed. Often, the mines are abandoned after the minerals have been removed. The area is totally destroyed by the mining activities.

Dams and reservoirs

Some of the world's largest rivers flow through TRF's and they are an important source of energy – HEP (Hydro Electric Power). Paraguay in South America, for example gets all its electricity from HEP. Some of the world's biggest dams and reservoirs now cover large areas of TRF and have a major impact on the ecology of the areas they have flooded.

Cultivated foods and spices

Many of the fruits and nuts we eat and buy in supermarkets, such as coffee, chocolate, banana, mango, papaya, macadamia nuts, avocado, and sugarcane all originally came from tropical rainforests. Many are grown on plantations in cleared areas of rainforest. However, as the forest is no longer supplying the soil nutrients, many of these crops rely on the heavy use of artificial chemical fertilisers. For example, about 40 million tons of bananas are consumed worldwide each year, along with 13 million tons of mangoes.

Central American coffee exports alone are worth $3 billion.

Much of the genetic variation used in preventing damage caused by pests still comes from resistant wild plants. Tropical forests have supplied 250 cultivated kinds of fruit, compared to only 20 from temperate forests.

Forests in Papua New Guinea in South East Asia alone contain 251 tree species with edible fruits, of which only 43 are currently grown as cultivated crops. They are also a very important ***gene pool*** due to their ***biodiversity***, much of which has yet to be fully understood and studied.

Source of medicines

TRF's are often called the 'world's largest pharmacy' because over a half of modern medicines used in the world originate from its plants. A recently discovered type of periwinkle plant has provided a cure for child leukaemia which has seen death rates fall from 80 per cent to 20 per cent.

Climate change and carbon dioxide sink

It is thought that TRF's may provide one third of the Earth's fresh oxygen supply.

Such a huge area of trees and plants play an important part in regulating climate and the gases that make up the atmosphere. Deforestation of trees means that there is less evapotranspiration so there is less water vapour in the atmosphere above rainforests. Due to this there is a reduction in rainfall in the areas of TRF and this can increase the threat of droughts. As the world produces more carbon dioxide the rainforests are responsible, through the process of photosynthesis, for turning the carbon dioxide into oxygen.

Hydroelectric power

With their high rainfall and large rivers, rainforests are potentially excellent locations for large HEP dams. The advantages of having a huge source of renewable energy have to be weighed against the loss of rainforest.

Minerals

Underneath the vast areas of many rainforests are some of the world's largest deposits of important minerals, for example, oil, coal, iron ore, bauxite (the raw material for making aluminium), copper, gold and diamonds. Their exploitation can lead to total destruction of the rainforest. Again, exploiting these resources has to be weighed against the loss of the rainforest ecosystem.

Loss of indigenous people

Many of these activities have had a great impact on the traditional societies and people of the rainforests. In Amazonia, the indigenous population before European settlers arrived, is estimated to have been 6 million. By 2003, this had fallen to 200 000.

Tropical deserts

There are both cold and hot deserts but the syllabus concentrates on the hot tropical deserts.

A desert is an area that receives very little precipitation. Deserts are defined as areas with an average annual precipitation of less than 250 mm. They are also areas where more water is lost by evapotranspiration than falls as precipitation.

A typical hot tropical desert will have the following features.

- ***Rare rainfall events*** – often less than 120 mms a year. The hot tropical deserts are found in areas of high pressure where the air is descending so that the air is warm and not cool – which means that condensation will not take place.
- Average monthly temperatures of ***over 29°C in the hot summer season*** to ***10°C in the cool winter season***.
- Daytime temperatures of ***over 38°C*** but capable of falling ***as low as 5°C at night***. There is a lack of cloud cover in deserts which means that instead of being trapped by a blanket of clouds the heat is lost to space at night and temperatures fall rapidly when the sun goes down.
- ***Low humidity*** of 25–30 per cent. This and the high temperatures mean that any surface water quickly evaporates.

Deserts make up about one third of the Earth's land surface. Hot deserts usually have a large diurnal (daily) and seasonal temperature range, with high daytime temperatures, and low night time temperatures (due to extremely low humidity). In hot deserts, the temperature in the daytime can reach 45–55°C or higher in the summer, and fall to 0°C or lower in the winter. They are also mainly found in tropical areas with high atmospheric pressure where the air is usually descending and therefore, warming (to make the water vapour in air condense into water droplets and rain, the air needs to be cooled – which is what happens when air is forced to rise).

Many deserts are a long distance from oceans, seas or large lakes which means that they receive little rainfall; other deserts have prevailing winds that blow over large areas of land and so there is no source of moisture; some deserts are in areas of rain shadow – where moist air is blocked by tall mountains. Where are they found? The map in Figure 10 shows their distribution.

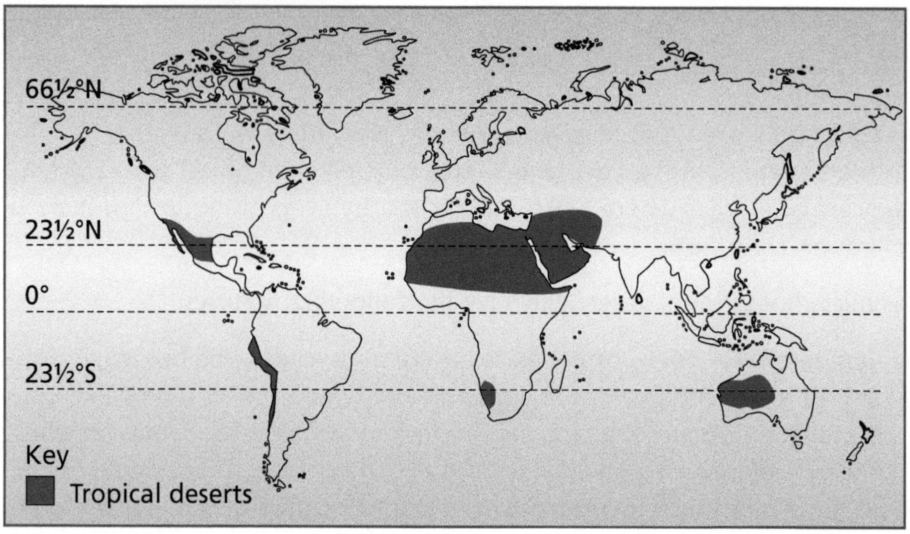

Figure 10 World's major deserts

Cambridge 0460 Paper 2 Fig 4 Nov 2003

Types of desert

Deserts make up about one third (33 per cent) of the Earth's total land surface. The largest hot desert is the Sahara in northern Africa. This desert covers about 9 million square kilometres and stretches across 12 countries.

Many people think that deserts are all sand but sand covers only about 20 per cent of the Earth's deserts. Most of the sand is in large sand seas made up of dunes which take on different shapes and forms.

Deserts are classified in two main ways.

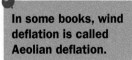

About 8 times more water could evaporate from Tucson region than what actually falls.

1. According to the ***amount of precipitation and the rates of evaporation*** (calculated as potential evaporation) they receive. In this classification there are two types:
   - ***Extremely arid areas*** have at least 12 consecutive months without rainfall, such as The Atacama Desert
   - ***Arid areas*** have less than 250 millimetres of annual rainfall.

Potential evaporation is added to the measurement of rainfall in providing a scientific measurement based definition of a desert. ***Potential evaporation is the amount of water that could evaporate if it were available.***

In some books, wind deflation is called Aeolian deflation.

As an example, Tucson in Arizona, USA receives about 300 millimetres of rain per year; however, about 2 500 millimetres of water could evaporate in a year.

2. Whether they are ***sandy*** **(Ergs)** or ***rocky*** **(Regs)**. Most people think of deserts as being vast areas of sand but, in fact sand covers only about 20 per cent of the Earth's deserts.

- A sandy desert is called an ***Erg***, the term takes its name from the Arabic word 'erg'.
- The rest are a mixture of bare rock surfaces or covered in rocks. These are called ***Regs***.
- Nearly all the Reg deserts have had their fine sand blown away. This is a process called ***wind deflation***.

Deserts often contain other common features such as river deposits – mainly small dried up deltas called alluvial fans, and dried up lakes called playas, or river channels and beds called wadis, and wetter areas where the water table comes to the surface called oases.

The oasis is normally a depression or low point in a desert which has been lowered as the lighter sand has been blown away by the process of wind deflation.

Types of sand dune

Sandy deserts, Ergs, contain several different types of sand dunes. These are as following.

- ***Barchan dunes*** are produced by strong winds blowing across a level surface and are crescent-shaped.
- ***Longitudinal or seif dunes*** are dunes that are parallel to a strong wind that blows in one general direction.
- ***Transverse dunes*** run at a right angle to the constant wind direction.
- ***Star dunes*** are star-shaped and have several ridges that spread out around a point.

Other desert features and processes

Rock pedestals/mushroom rocks

Wind Abrasion – the abrasion caused as a result of sand being carried by the wind causes any isolated rocks to be eroded at their base leaving a rock shaped like a mushroom.

Exfoliation – This process causes the surface layer of rocks to peel away. It happens as a result of the high daytime temperatures (an air temperature of 50°C may cause the surfaces of rocks to reach 90°C as they absorb the heat) causing the surface layer of a rock to expand. A few hours later, when the sun goes down, temperatures may drop to 20°C and below. This means that the surface layer of the rock contracts. This daily expansion and contraction of the surface layer causes it to peel away from the rest of the rock.

Desert vegetation

Deserts typically have a very sparse vegetation cover but it is very diverse. People often think they are covered in cactus plants, but few are! An example, though, is the giant saguaro cacti of the Sonoran Desert in

When fully grown, saguaro cacti are 15 meters tall and weigh as much as 10 tons!

Arizona, USA. It provides nest sites for desert birds and they serve as 'trees' of the desert. Saguaro grows slowly but may live up to 200 years. When 9 years old, they are about 15 cms high. After about 75 years, the cacti develop their first branches.

More typical plants are small bushes or shrubs. Most desert plants have to be drought and/or salt-tolerant. These plants are called ***Xerophytes***. They adapt in 4 main ways to the lack of water.

- Some store water in their leaves, roots, and stems – like the prickly pear cactus
- Others have long tap roots that may reach down as far as 50 metres to the water table.
- Wide-spreading shallow roots just below the ground surface to absorb water when it rains before it quickly evaporates, from a larger area of the ground.
- The development of small, spiny leaves which give off less moisture than leaves with greater surface areas.

The stems and leaves of these plants play another important role in that they reduce the speed of sand-carrying winds and therefore, protect the ground from erosion. Even small fungi and microscopic plant organisms found on the soil surface (so-called ***cryptobiotic*** soil) can be a vital link in preventing erosion and providing support for other living organisms.

Desert lakes

Desert lakes are usually very shallow, temporary, and salty. When they dry up, they leave a salt crust on the surface of the sand or soil. The flat area of clay, silt, or sand encrusted with salt that is left behind is known as a **playa**.

Human life in deserts

A desert is a hostile, potentially deadly environment for unprepared humans. In hot deserts, high temperatures cause rapid loss of water due to sweating, and the absence of water can result in dehydration and death within a few days. In addition, unprotected humans are also at risk from heatstroke. Humans may also have to adapt to ***sandstorms*** in some deserts, like Kuwait, not just in their adverse effects on breathing and eyes, but also in their potentially harmful effects on equipment such as engine filters, vehicles and communication equipment.

This process is sometimes called Onion Skin Weathering, as it resembles the different layers of an onion.

Sandstorms can last for hours, sometimes even days. This makes surviving in the desert quite difficult for humans. Despite this, some cultures have made hot deserts their home for thousands of years, including the Bedouin, the Tuareg and Pueblo people. Modern technologies, including advanced irrigation systems, desalinisation and air conditioning, have made deserts much more hospitable.

Most traditional human life in deserts is nomadic. Their life depends on finding water, surviving frequent droughts and on following infrequent rains to obtain grazing for their animals. Any permanent settlement in deserts requires permanent water and food sources and adequate shelter, or the technology and energy sources to provide it.

Larger settlements are only usually found where these conditions exist, such as in the oil rich economies of Kuwait, the Gulf States and Saudi Arabia.

Progress check

1. What is meant by the terms weather and climate?
2. What are the characteristics features of a Stevenson screen; where would one be sited and what is it used for?
3. Draw, describe and explain the use and siting of the following instruments at a weather station: rain-gauge, maximum-minimum thermometer, wet and dry bulb thermometer (hygrometer), barometer, anemometer and wind vane.
4. What are the main types of cloud and how is the extent of cloud cover estimated?
5. Describe and explain the characteristics of the climate and natural vegetation of two ecosystems:
   (i) Tropical rainforest
   (ii) Tropical desert.
6. Describe and explain the relationship between the climate and natural vegetation in these two ecosystems.

Examination style questions

1. What is meant by the term ecosystem? **[1]**

   Example answer:

   An ecosystem is a community of living and non-living things interacting with each other in an area.

2. Describe the distribution of tropical rain forests. **[2]**

   Example answer:

   Tropical rainforests are found close to the Equator, between about 15 degrees north and south of the Equator. They are found in the Amazon in South America, in South East Asia and in West Africa.

3. Name the individual weather instruments that would be used to collect data on the diurnal (daily) range of temperature, air pressure and wind direction. **[3]**

Example answer:

For measuring the daily range of temperature a maximum and minimum thermometer is used. For air pressure a barometer is used and for wind direction a wind vane is used.

4. For a named area of tropical rainforest which you have studied, describe and explain the characteristics of its climate. **[6]**

Example Answer:

A tropical rainforest like the ones in the Amazon in Brazil and in Malaysia have a very distinctive climate with high temperatures averaging about 30°C for most of the year, small annual range of temperature. There is also very little difference, about 2–3°C, in the monthly average temperatures. This is because these areas are very close to the Equator and the sun is overhead all year round.

They have a very high rainfall of about 2,000 mm spread evenly through the year. The heavy rainfall is due to them having very hot temperatures during the day, producing strong convection currents which causes the formation of rain clouds resulting in heavy rain every day.

Comment: A very good, detailed answer for the first part of the question with good use of examples in the second and fourth parts. In the fourth part, the characteristics are both described fully and the reasons given for the characteristics, with a named example.

Overall mark: 12/12

Examination style questions for you to try

1. (i) Explain the effects of climate on the natural vegetation in tropical rain forests. **[4]**

(ii) Explain how cumulonimbus clouds form and bring heavy rain in areas of tropical rain forest. **[2]**

2. (i) Explain how cloud cover is estimated and shown on a map. **[2]**

(ii) Explain how a student would use a wet and dry bulb thermometer (Hygrometer) to measure humidity. You may include a diagram to show how this weather instrument is read **[4]**

(iii) Describe two of the factors that influence the distribution of tropical deserts. **[4]**

3. Describe and explain the impacts of human activities on the natural environment of a named area of tropical rain forest which you have studied. **[7]**

Theme 3:

Economic development and use of resources

Chapter

8 Agricultural systems

Learning Summary

In this chapter you will learn about:

- ***The different types of agricultural/farming classification***
- ***The main features of an agricultural system***
- ***The combined influence of natural and human inputs on the processes and outputs of the two agricultural systems***
- ***The causes and effects of shortages of food and possible solutions to this problem***
- ***How these shortages may be related to natural problems***
- ***Economic and political factors and their effects upon food shortages***
- ***The effects of food shortages in encouraging food aid and measures such as those of the 'Green Revolution' to produce more food***

The classification of farming or agriculture

Farming/agriculture can be classified in several ways.

- By its ***specialisation*** – it can be either ***arable*** or ***pastoral*** or a combination of the two – called ***mixed*** farming. Arable farming involves the growing of crops while pastoral farming is the rearing of animals.
- By its ***economic status*** – it can either be ***commercial*** or ***subsistence***. Commercial is growing of crops or rearing animals for sale. Subsistence is where the crops or animals are grown to feed the farmer's family.
- By the ***intensity*** of its use of the land – it can either be ***extensive*** or ***intensive***.
  Extensive farming is where the farm is very large. This is usually where the land is not very productive and so large areas of land are needed to be profitable.
  Intensive farming is where the farm is smaller but the land is very intensively used either in terms of investment in the farm or the numbers of people working on the land.
- By its ***land tenure*** or ***ownership*** – whether the land is owned or rented
- By the method in which the land is used and farmed it can either be ***shifting*** (which includes ***nomadic***) or ***sedentary***. Shifting cultivation is where farmers move from one area to another. Sedentary is where the farming is located in a permanent location.

Intensive farming normally has a higher yield, more capital input and greater profit per hectare.

Farming as a system

As in industry, farming can be seen as a system which has **inputs, processes** and **outputs**.

The inputs in farming

The physical or natural inputs include the following.

Having water during the growth period of a crop is very important; less important when a crop like a cereal is ripening.

1. ***Climate*** – this includes ***temperature, precipitation*** and their impact on the ***length of the growing season***. Plant growth starts at a ***temperature*** of 6°C. As temperatures increase so does the rate of plant growth. Areas that have temperatures above 6°C for most of the year, have a long growing season. A crop such as wheat needs a growing season of 90 days. ***Precipitation*** in the form of rain needs to be high enough to provide plants with enough water to grow. The amount needed will vary according to the temperatures as more will be lost by evaporation if the temperatures are high.
2. ***Relief (also called topography)*** is a term that describes the height and shape of the land. How high the land is will affect the temperature and the amount and type of precipitation.

   Temperature drops at a rate of about 1°C for every 100 metres you go up in height. This means, therefore, that the growing season shortens with height. Precipitation also increases with height, as does the amount of snow – again this contributes to the growing season becoming shorter with height.
   The ***shape*** of the land includes whether slopes are steep or gentle. A ***steep slope*** will be difficult to farm but more importantly, will often have thin soils due to increased run off and erosion. A ***gentler slope*** will have deeper soils and less erosion. Slopes in the northern hemisphere will receive more direct sunshine.
   The ***aspect*** of the land – the direction that a slope faces is important. A south facing slope will have warmer soils which will mean that seeds will germinate and grow faster. The growing season can be six weeks longer on a south facing slope compared to a colder north facing slope at the same location.
3. ***Soils*** – some soils are deeper and more fertile than others which will affect plant growth. A thin and infertile soil will not be very productive.
4. ***Drainage*** – land needs to be well drained to allow most plants to grow and not find their roots waterlogged. Flat land is easy to plough but may become waterlogged and flooded. Gentle slopes allow water to drain away.

The human and economic inputs include the following.

- ***Investment of money/capital*** – the cost of land, buildings and machinery can be high on many farms. There is also the cost of seed and animals.

- ***Labour*** – some farms are labour intensive – they may need large numbers of people to carry out the jobs on the farm which may be impossible for machinery to do.
- ***New machinery and technology*** can help the farmer improve income and profits.
- ***Markets*** – the farmer must ensure that there is always a market for the crop or product and also look for potential new markets or new crops and animals.
- ***Transport*** can be an expensive part of farming as products need to be brought to the markets.
- The ***cost and maintenance*** of the farm buildings and machinery.
- ***Artificial inputs*** can increase yields considerably and more than pay for their costs in increased profits. Irrigation is an example and the use of artificial chemical fertilisers, pesticides and herbicides are other examples.
- ***Subsidies*** for crops and animals are now essential for some types of farming to survive in many areas of the developed world as in the EU, USA and Japan.
- ***Quotas*** – governments can put limits on the amount of crop or product, like milk, that can be produced.
- The use of ***GM*** crops and ***Genetic Engineering*** of animals' increases yields but GM crops are very controversial.

Subsidies are used to maintain farming communities in rural areas where there is little or no alternative employment.

The processes in farming

The processes include all the activities that take place on a farm.

- On an ***arable*** farm, they include: ***ploughing*** and preparing the land, ***harrowing*** the soil to prepare it for planting, ***planting*** of seeds, ***controlling weeds*** and ***pests, harvesting*** the crop.
- On a ***pastoral*** farm, they include: ***grazing, calving*** and ***lambing, milking, slaughter*** and ***shearing***, producing ***fodder crops*** like silage.

The outputs in farming

The outputs include the following.

- **Crops** – like cereals, vegetables, fruit and flowers
- **Animals** – like cattle, lambs, pigs, chickens and turkeys
- **Animal products** – like meat, milk, wool, skins, eggs.

Commercial farming and subsistence farming

Commercial farming aims to sell the produce that comes from the farm. ***Subsistence farming*** is where the produce is consumed by the family or community that grows it. Any surplus produce can be sold at local markets to obtain money or it can be traded for other products.

Subsistence farming is most common in LEDC's, it is normally small scale and may involve ***shifting cultivation***, where small areas of land, often forest, is cleared and used for crop farming, or by ***nomadic*** people who keep animals like sheep, goats, cattle and camels and move over large areas grazing their herds.

The large-scale system of commercial farming

There are several types of large scale commercial farming. ***Plantation farming*** is one of the most common and involves the growing of one crop (called ***monoculture***), often over very large areas. Examples include sugar cane, bananas, rubber, tea, coffee and pineapples. Other types of large scale commercial farming include the growing of cereals, such as wheat, maize and barley and the rearing of livestock animals such as cattle and sheep.

Case studies of commercial farming

Sheep farming in Australia

Sheep farming employs around 28 500 people on more than 60 000 farms.

Sheep are raised either as lambs for meat or as older sheep for wool. Australia is the world's biggest sheep producer. There are over 120 million sheep in Australia on 85 000 hectares of land.

Commercial sheep farming in Australia is found on very large farms in ***marginal*** areas – areas where other animals and crops would not be as successful or as profitable due to physical and human factors. Therefore, they are often found in areas of low rainfall, high temperatures and poor quality grazing where they are left to graze on grass or small bushes. Such land is also cheaper to buy.

Per hectare, sheep farming has very low inputs of ***capital*** – much of the land that is used is of relatively small value as it cannot often be used for arable farming, so it is cheap to buy. Farms may need upto 25 hectares of grazing land per animal as grazing land is poor. Rearing animals in these areas produces the smallest profits per hectare of any type of commercial farming. However, Australia has very large areas of land available for this activity, so is suited to this type of farming.

Labour – it takes very few people to look after large numbers of sheep – as they can be left out in the fields all year round, or to gather the sheep together for shearing (the actual shearing is often done by groups of skilled shearers who move from farm to farm); applying any pesticide to their fleece and antibiotics to overcome any pests.

The **output** of this industry is that it produces about 620 000 tonnes of meat and 575 000 tonnes of wool in a typical year. Of this, about 68 per cent of the wool and 39 per cent of the meat are exported. Sheep farms occupy about 85 million hectares of land. The industry is worth about $1 billion in meat products and $2.8 billion in wool products.

The industry faces several major challenges, most of them environmental, such as the following.

- **Periodic droughts** – some lasting several years have become increasingly common. A ten year drought in the south east of Australia, from 2000–2010, has had a major impact on the industry. This makes the supply of water and food for the animals very difficult and increases costs to the farmer who may have to buy food for the sheep.
- ***Weed infestation*** – a variety of non native plants have found their way into Australia and thrived, covering large areas of grazing land. These include the so called sensitive plant whose leaves curl up when touched, but which has very thorny stems making it inedible for sheep. Also, types of plant that encase their seeds in burrs that become stuck firmly in the sheep's fleece and are almost impossible to remove greatly lowering the value of the wool.
- ***Destruction of natural habitats and soil erosion*** – this is due to the grazing of sheep and in the worst cases, sheep have overgrazed destroying the natural protective vegetation cover for the soil which is then exposed and easily eroded by water and wind.
- ***Shortage of sheep shearers*** – a very tough, hard, manual job which has lost workers to other, easier jobs in the expanding Australian mining industry, for example.

Plantation farming (Rubber)

Plantations were first developed in wet tropical areas in countries such as Malaysia, Thailand, Indonesia, Southwest India and Brazil by European and North American entrepreneurs and merchants in the eighteenth and nineteenth centuries. These wet tropical locations benefit from the natural inputs of high, year round temperatures with monthly averages over 23°C, high rainfall (over 1750 mms) and fertile soils.

Plantations need high capital and labour ***input*** to firstly clear the forest and then to drain and irrigate the land. So many workers are needed that small settlements containing schools, hospitals and roads are required to be built for the workers and their families. In addition, many of these trees and bushes need several years to grow before they can be cropped and so there is no income during this period for the owners. Today, most plantations are owned either by large multinational companies or by governments who have the resources to invest in this type of farming.

The other ***inputs*** needed on a plantation crop are fertilisers, pesticides and herbicides. The ***processes*** on a ***rubber plantation*** require the application of these inputs and the harvesting of the rubber by hand. A rubber tree can be 'tapped' for its sap – called latex, five to seven years after it has been planted and this can go on typically for another thirty years. An experienced rubber tapper can tap upto 600 trees a day which involves cutting a shallow groove into the bark of the tree, which cuts into the cells of the tree emiting a white latex which drips into a collecting cup attached to the tree.

The latex, the output of this system, is then collected and coagulated in metal trays using a dilute acid. It is then washed to remove any acid and dried to be sold to rubber manufacturers.

The main threats to the rubber plantations in countries such as Malaysia have come from low prices, as 77 per cent of the world's rubber is now synthesised from oil, and oil palms which can be grown in the same environment but has lower production costs, needs less labour, has higher yields and gets higher prices than rubber.

Case studies of small scale subsistence farming

Shifting cultivation in the Amazon River basin

The most widely practised form of subsistence agriculture is shifting cultivation. It has been practised for several thousand years by many traditional societies in the tropical rainforests of the Amazon in South America, the Congo River Basin in Central Africa and in Indonesia and Malaysia.

This form of agriculture is disappearing as the rainforests are cleared to be used for plantation agriculture and cattle ranching, mining, logging, roads and new settlements.

It involves the clearing of a small (about one hectare) area of rainforest by cutting it down, letting it dry and then burning the vegetation to both clear the land and provide nutrients for the soil. It is sometimes called ***slash and burn agriculture***. Some of the larger, emergent trees are left to give some degree of protection for the soil from the heavy tropical rain.

The fertility of the rainforest soils depends on the rapid and constant recycling of the large amounts of leaf litter that falls from the trees. Once the trees have been cleared, the cycle is broken. For a short period of time the soil remains fertile from the nutrients left by the forest. This however, quickly becomes less fertile due to the heavy tropical rains which erode the soil and remove the nutrients. When this happens, a new area of forest is then cleared and the small clearings are left to recover and be re-colonised by the forest.

In some communities, this is done on an 18–25 year cycle. The crops from the land provide food for the traditional people along with other food such as fruit and nuts gathered from the forest and by fishing and the hunting of animals for meat.

Intensive subsistence farming (Rice)

Rice has a high nutritional value and is the main food crop for much of the population of South and South East Asia. The Ganges valley in northern India supports a population of over 450 million and rice can provide 90 per cent of the total diet. 'Wet' rice is grown on the fertile soils of the flood plains and 'dry' rice is grown on terraced fields cut into the valley sides of the rivers. Fields are flooded with water during the annual monsoon rains.

To produce 1 kg of rice, it requires 5 000 litres of water and this result in rice cultivation using 90 per cent of the water used in Asian agriculture. However, rice is a very high yielding crop and being quick growing in the high temperatures of south and south-east Asia, it can be ready for harvesting in 100 days.

Rice growing is very labour intensive and it takes an average of 2 000 hours to produce 1 hectare of rice. Most tasks, due to a lack of capital to buy machinery, are either done by hand or with the help of domesticated water buffalo. They include building the embankments around the fields to keep in the water; constructing and constantly maintaining the network of irrigation canals which bring the water to the fields; ploughing the fields to mix the rich soils with the water; planting the rice in small nursery fields; transplanting the rice into the main ***padi-fields***; weeding, harvesting and threshing (removing the rice seeds from the stalk) the rice crop; drying and storing the rice; planting other crops in the drier parts of the year.

Food shortages and possible solutions

From a total world population of over 7 billion people, 800 million in the LEDC countries, do not get enough food to eat and suffer from hunger. The problem is mainly concentrated in the African countries but is also seen in parts of South America and Asia. Many of these countries currently receive food aid but this is not a long term solution to the problem.

The reasons why these people are suffering from hunger is usually a ***combination*** of natural and human factors. Many of the natural factors are extreme climatic events. The following map shows the distribution of some of the areas that have experienced food shortages in recent years.

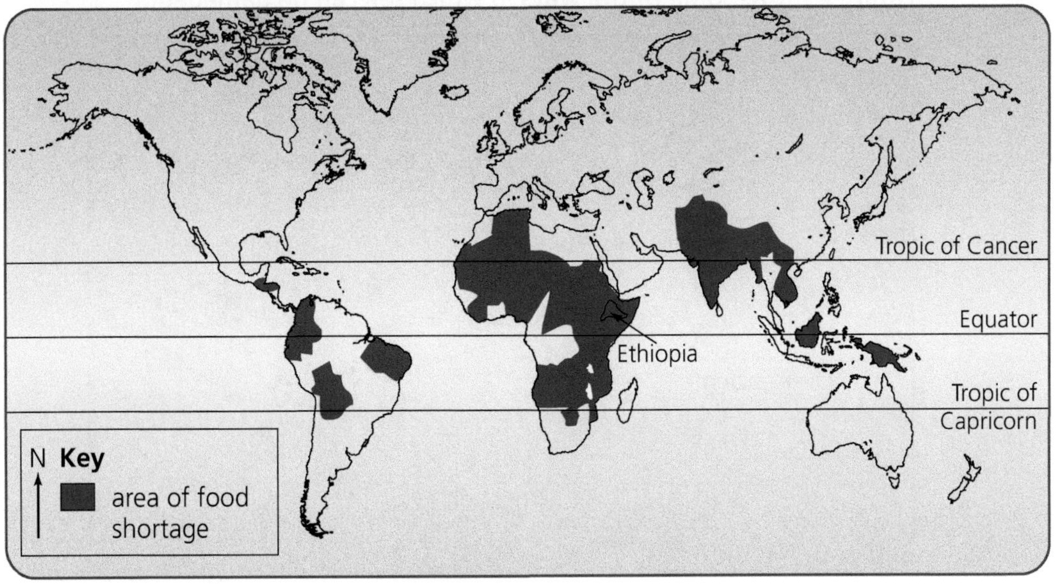

Figure 1

Cambridge 0460 Paper 23 Fig 6 June 2010

The natural factors

Crop yields can be drastically reduced without adequate rainfall.

- ***Drought and unreliable rainfall*** – much of East Africa, including the north of Kenya, Sudan, Somalia and Ethiopia has suffered from a period of drought and very low, unreliable rainfall that has lasted for over ten years. This has meant that farmers have sowns seed which has germinated but not been able to grow due to the lack of rainfall. Farmers have repeated the sowing of seed and seen it fail to grow until their seed banks have become empty and this has meant that no food has been sent to local markets and no food is available for both their families and animals.
- ***Tropical hurricanes/cyclones/typhoons*** – when these storms hit, with their high winds, torrential rainfall and storm surges (where sea levels are raised by the high winds and then surge inland flooding low lying areas like southern Bangladesh), they can devastate farm land and crops. Subsistence farmers have very little resources to recover from such events, a situation made even worse if the storm is repeated within short periods of time. The Philippines and Vietnam have suffered severe devastation from such events in 2008 and 2009.
- ***Floods*** – though often associated with Tropical hurricanes, they usually result from heavy rainfall, often associated with monsoons or El Nino events. Crops can be destroyed by flooding and they also affect whole communities who may lose their houses, belongings, animals, roads, etc.
- ***Pests and diseases*** – there are many pests and diseases which can prey on crops, for example, locusts and diseases such as mildew. Without the expensive pesticides and sprays to deal with them, poor rural communities may suffer severe crop losses.

The human factors

Figure 2 shows some of the ways in which soil can be damaged.

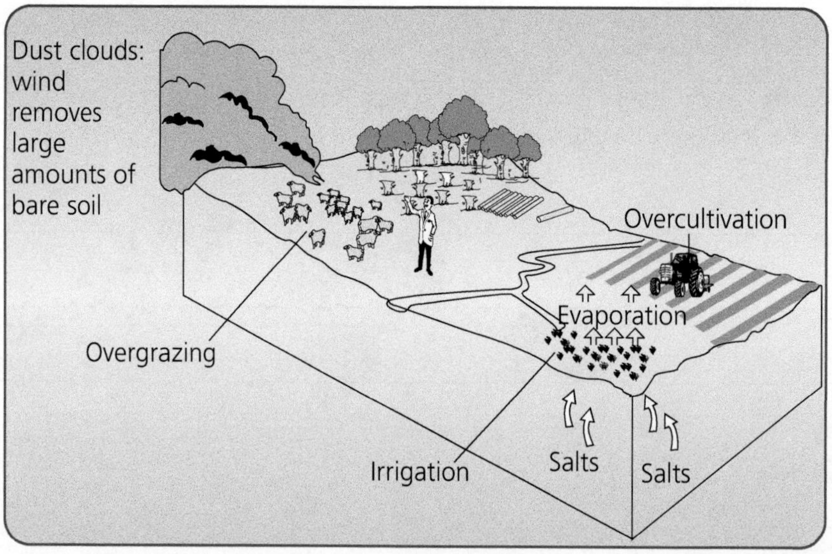

Figure 2

Cambridge 0460 Paper 11 Fig 9 June 2011

- ***Soil erosion and loss of soil fertility*** – land that has been cleared of its natural protective cover of vegetation is much more easily eroded by rainfall. Soil fertility will be lost as land is eroded and soil minerals washed out of the soil. Also, overgrazing by grazing herds of domestic animals can remove the protective vegetation cover. Without applying either natural fertiliser, dung, or expensive artificial chemical fertilisers, or allowing the soil to rest and recover (leaving the land fallow), this will lead to a loss of fertility and lower crop yields.
- ***Rural poverty*** in many LEDC's means that there is a lack of money to invest in irrigation or buy expensive fertilisers. Many farmers are still using traditional farming practices such as ploughing up and down slopes which increases soil erosion.
- ***War*** – Darfur in the south of Sudan, for example, has suffered from many years of civil war. Even with the creation of the new independent country of South Sudan, internal tribal conflicts remain. During these years of conflict, upto 2 million people have had to leave their homes and farms and it has often been impossible for farmers to grow crops and rear animals. Those that do may find their crops and animals destroyed or stolen. More than 70 000 people have died so far from a mixture of starvation and diseases often caused or made worse by malnutrition.
- ***Increasing population*** – as a result of rising population more land is having to be cleared of forest; less fertile, marginal land brought in to use, and farms divided into much smaller units amongst farmer's children as they grow up and have their own families to feed. As less land becomes available food shortages result.
- ***Inability to invest capital and improve infrastructure*** – the lack of capital available in LEDC's, particularly in rural areas, means that schemes to improve agricultural production, improve food storage, improve roads and transportation for distributing farm products are very hard to initiate and develop.

Between 2001 and 2012, the price of many globally important crops rose dramatically, as can be seen in the following table (*Source: indexmundi.com*).

Rising food prices

Crop	2001 (price in $ per tonne)	2012(price in $ per tonne)
Wheat	120	270
Rice	180	550
Maize	90	260
Barley	90	210
Sorghum	90	260

Although this should have been good news for producers and consumers especially the poor in LEDC's, it has been a very serious problem.

The impact of food shortages

People who are malnourished are unable to work as hard and an already poor situation is made worse.

Where there is a complete collapse of food supplies, ***starvation*** can result. Where there is not enough food to keep people healthy, it can lead to ***malnutrition***. When this occurs, people are less able to resist diseases and can suffer from a number of ***protein and vitamin deficiency diseases***, such as ***Kwashiorkor*** (lack of protein), ***Beriberi*** (lack of vitamin B1), ***Rickets*** (lack of vitamin D) and ***Scurvy*** (lack of vitamin C).

Solutions to food shortages

The governments of many MEDC's and the EU, often acting through agencies of the ***United Nations***, such as the ***FAO*** (Food and Agriculture Organisation) and the ***WFP*** (World Food Programme) and many ***NGOs*** (Non Government Organisations), such as ***Action Aid*** and ***Oxfam***, give assistance and food aid to areas suffering from food shortages to improve both the standard of living and quality of life of the people affected. Food aid can be given on both a short and a long term basis.

Short term food aid is delivered directly to those people affected during a crisis caused by natural events or war.

Long term food aid is often given to the government of an LEDC to sell in local markets to add to that produced by local farmers. It may also be given as part of a '***Food for Work***' programme, where communities are given food to enable them to work on long term projects that will increase local crop and animal yields in the future. This often involves introducing ***appropriate technology*** (technology which is suited to the level of wealth, knowledge and skills of local people and is developed to meet their specific needs) to rural areas. For example, in areas of the world where soil erosion is linked to over cultivation and overgrazing there are a variety of sustainable solutions to manage this. These include:

- The building of ***small earth dams*** and ***wells*** to provide water for basic irrigation projects.
- ***Simple methods of soil conservation***, such as planting trees to make ***shelter belts*** to protect soil from wind erosion in dry periods, or building ***low stone walls*** along the contours of a slope to stop the run off of rain water allowing it time to enter the soil helping to prevent soil erosion and increasing the amount of water in the soil and making it available for crops. ***Tied ridging*** where low walls of soil are built in a grid of small squares which stops rainfall run off and allows water to be drained into the soil. Crops such as potatoes and cassava are grown on the soil walls.
- ***Strip or inter cropping*** which has alternate strips of crops being grown, at different stages of growth, across a slope to limit rainfall run off as there is always a strip of crop to trap water and soil moving down the slope.
- ***Tier or layer cropping*** where several types and sizes of crops are grown in one field to provide protection from rainfall and increase food and crop yields.

For example, the top tier or layer, may be coconut trees, below this may be a tier of coffee or fruit trees, and, at ground level, vegetables or pineapples.

- ***Improved food storage*** which allows food to be kept fresh and edible for longer periods of time and protected from being eaten by rats and insects and affected by diseases.

Food Aid is not without its problems. It is very difficult and expensive to transport food from MEDCs to LEDCs. MEDC food for sale in local markets may be cheaper than food grown by local farmers making them less well off. This can be solved by providing money not food that can be used to buy local food and so increase local farmer's incomes.

Globally, the ***Green Revolution*** has had as much impact on food shortages. The Green Revolution started in the mid 1960s with the development of ***High Yielding Varieties*** **(HYV's)** of five of the world's major cereal crops – rice, wheat, maize, sorghum and millet. These new hybrid varieties of crops were:

- apart from rice, resistant to drought
- higher yielding, often by two to four times, than traditional species of these crops
- had a shorter growing season, allowing more crops to be grown in a year in some areas.

Several countries, such as India, Indonesia and the Philippines, set up research programmes to investigate how to increase rice yields. One result was a new variety of rice called IR8. This was produced by crossing a semi-dwarf variety from China with a stronger taller variety from Indonesia. The result was a stronger, shorter variety of rice which could be planted closer together, had a shorter growing season – 4 months instead of 5 months, and a much higher yield – 5 tonnes instead of 1.5 tonnes per hectare, than traditional varieties of rice. All very positive results, however, this new variety needed expensive fertilisers and more water for irrigation, which smaller farmers could not afford to buy.

IR8 also attracted more pests than the traditional varieties so that expensive pesticides had to be used.

The Green Revolution had several **positive results** as well as its share of problems and critics.

Advantages

- Farm incomes increased, increasing the standard of living of many people in rural area which, in turn, meant that families had money to pay for the education of their children; giving them access to qualifications that could allow them to get a better job in future.
- Increased yields mean that crops can now be exported.
- Stopped food shortages in some areas and improved people's diets.
- Increased employment on farms and in food processing industries.
- Paid for machinery, fertilisers, pesticides, herbicides and irrigation.

Much of the farm land is now being used for growing one HYV crop.

Disadvantages

- The HYV crops need bigger, more expensive inputs of fertiliser, pesticides and herbicides.
- The mechanisation of jobs on the farms increased unemployment, increasing poverty and forcing people to migrate to cities in search of jobs.
- There has been the following two impacts on local diets making them more deficient. Firstly, other local food crops are not being grown removing important minerals and vitamins from people's diets. Secondly, HYV crops are often lower in minerals and vitamins than the local varieties they have replaced which means that they do not provide people with the same level of nutrition compared to their traditional crop varieties.

The use of irrigation

- ***Irrigation*** is an artificial application of water to the soil usually for assisting in growing crops. In crop production, it is mainly used in dry areas and in periods of rainfall shortfalls, but also to protect plants against frost. Additionally, irrigation helps to suppress weed growing in rice fields.
- In contrast, agriculture that relies only on direct rainfall is referred to as ***rain-fed farming***.
- The various types of irrigation techniques differ in how the water obtained from the source is distributed within the field. In general, the goal is to supply the entire field uniformly with water, so that each plant has the amount of water it needs, neither too much nor too little.

Surface irrigation

Historically, this has been the most common method of irrigating agricultural land.

- In surface irrigation systems, water moves over and across the land by simple gravity flow in order to wet it and to infiltrate into the soil. Surface irrigation can be subdivided into furrow, border strip or basin irrigation. It is often called ***flood irrigation*** when the irrigation results in flooding or near flooding of the cultivated land.
- Where water levels from the irrigation source permit, the levels are controlled by dikes, usually plugged by soil. This is often seen in terraced rice fields (rice paddies), where the method is used to flood or control the level of water in each distinct field. In some cases, the water is pumped, or lifted by human or animal power to the level of the land.

Drip irrigation

- Drip irrigation, also known as trickle irrigation, is where water is delivered at or near the root zone of plants, drop by drop. This method can be the most water-efficient method of irrigation, if managed properly, since evaporation and runoff are minimised. In modern agriculture, drip irrigation and is also the means of delivery of fertilizer. The process is known as ***fertigation***.
- Modern drip irrigation has arguably become the world's most valued innovation in agriculture since the invention of the impact sprinkler in the 1930s, which replaced flood irrigation. They are generally used on tree and vine crops with wider root zones.
- ***Subsurface Drip Irrigation (SDI)*** uses a permanently or temporarily buried dripperline or a drip tape located at or below the plant roots. It is becoming popular for row crop irrigation, especially in areas where water supplies are limited or recycled water is used for irrigation.
- Careful study of all the relevant factors like land topography, soil, water, crop and agro-climatic conditions are needed to determine the most suitable drip irrigation system.

The problem of salination

Overuse and poor irrigation practices have led to increased salt content in the soil, reducing the productivity of the land. Irrigation salinity is caused by water soaking through the soil level adding to the ground water below. This causes the water table to rise, bringing dissolved salts to the surface. As the irrigated area dries, the salt remains.

Solution to the salination produced from irrigation

In New South Wales, Australia irrigation salinity is solved through a salt interception scheme that pumps saline ground water into evaporation basins, protecting approximately 50 000 hectares of farmland in the area from high water tables and salinity.

The subsequent salt has various uses including as an animal feed supplement. The programme has returned to production over 2 000 hectares of previously barren farmland and encouraged the regeneration of native eucalypts.

Other problems caused by irrigation

- There is increased competition for water, from individual farmers, communities and even countries.
- Over extraction of water can lead to the dropping and depletion of underground aquifers.

- Ground subsidence, for example, New Orleans, Louisiana, USA may occur as water is removed for irrigation from the underground aquifer.
- Under irrigation leads to increased soil salinity with the buildup of toxic salts on the soil surface in areas with high evaporation. This requires either leaching to remove these salts or a method of drainage to carry the salts away.
- Over irrigation because of poor distribution may lead to water pollution.
- Deep drainage (from over-irrigation) may result in rising water tables which in some instances will lead to problems of irrigation salinity.

Progress check

1. Name the different types of farming.
2. Describe the main features of an agricultural system: inputs, processes and outputs.
3. Describe the main influences of natural and human inputs on the processes and outputs on an example of both a large-scale system of commercial farming and a small scale system of subsistence farming.
4. The causes and effects of shortages of food and the possible solutions to this problem.
5. Describe and explain the formation of Scree.
6. Why is weathering more rapid in humid tropical regions than in temperate regions?
7. How can the rock type and structure affect the type and degree of weathering that takes place?
8. How can climate affect the type and degree of weathering that takes place?

Examination style questions

1. What is the difference between subsistence and commercial farming? **[2]**

   Example Answer:

   Subsistence farming is where crops and animals are grown for the farmer's family only. Commercial farming is where the crops and animals and their products are for sale for money.

2. Identify an input, a process and an output on a commercial farm. **[3]**

   Example Answer:

   An input could be fertilizer, a process could be applying the fertilizer and an output could be a crop such as wheat.

3. For a named area or country which you have studied which suffers from famine, explain why there is a shortage of food. **[5]**

Example Answer:

In Somalia, in 2011, many subsistence farmers suffered from famine and food shortages as a result of three years of drought which greatly reduced the amount of crops they could grow and their animals died from a lack of food and water. After these three years, they ran out of seeds and they did not have the money to buy any more seeds. Also, there was a war going on in the country which meant it was difficult for them to receive any aid or help so many had to leave their farms.

Comment: A very good answer, with a very good explanation of both subsistence and commercial farming and good examples of inputs, processes and outputs. It provides a good example of a country with a food shortage facing both natural and human problems.

Overall mark: 10/10

Examination style questions for you to try

1. (i) What is meant by the terms nomadic and sedentary farming? **[2]**

2. (i) What problems can be caused by irrigation? **[3]**

(ii) Explain the ways in which farmers in LEDCs might increase the amount of food they produce from their land. **[4]**

(iii) Explain how both natural and human factors may cause food shortages. **[6]**

3. Name an example of large-scale commercial farming. Describe the inputs, processes and outputs of this farming system. **[7]**

Chapter

9 Industrial systems

Learning Summary

In this chapter you will learn about:

- ***Classifying industries into primary, secondary and tertiary***
- ***The influence of inputs on the processes and outputs (products and waste) of industrial systems***
- ***The factors influencing the distribution and location of high technology industries***
- ***Describing and explaining how the proportions employed in primary, secondary and tertiary industries differ in LEDCs and MEDCs***

Types of industry

There are three main types of industry, which together make up the ***employment structure*** of a country or region.

- **Primary industries** – industries that extract raw materials such as mining, quarrying, farming, fishing and forestry. These primary products may be sold directly to customers or moved on to secondary industries to be processed.
- **Secondary industries** – industries that ***process and manufacture*** the products of the primary industry, the ***raw materials*** such as iron and steel making or processing food, or assemble the component parts made by other secondary industries such as car assembly.
- **Tertiary industries** – industries that provide a ***service or skill*** such as education, health care, retailing, office work, transport and entertainment.

However, since the 1980s a fourth type has been added – ***Quaternary industries*** – industries that provide information and expertise such as the microelectronics industry.

The proportions employed in each sector have changed considerably over time in many countries. This is evident in many of the MEDC's and especially in the Newly Industrialised Countries (NIC's), such as Singapore, South Korea, Taiwan and Malaysia. As seen in the following triangular graph in Figure 1 which shows the percentages of people employed in different sectors in the United Kingdom in 1900, 1940 and 1980.

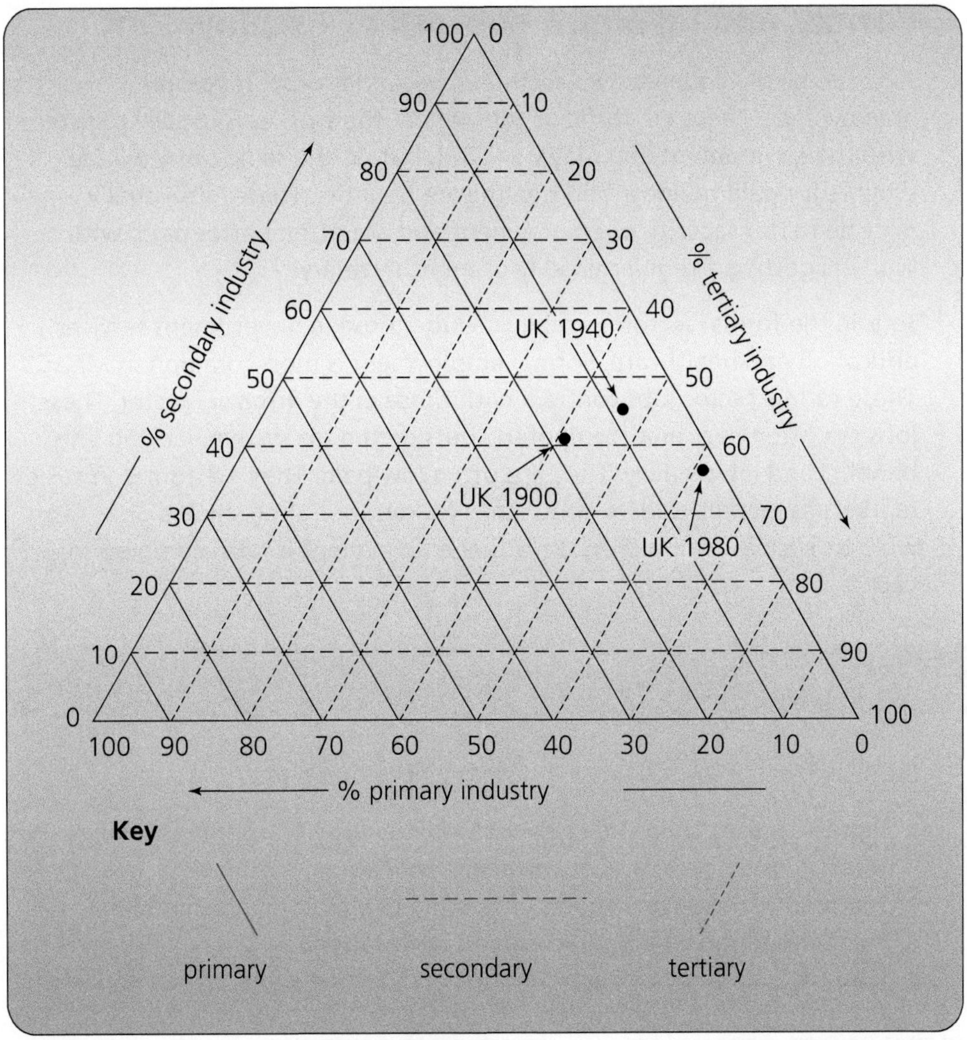

Figure 1

Cambridge 0460 Paper 23 Fig 5 June 2010

Until the 1970s, many of these economies were traditionally based on the primary industry of agriculture. However, although agriculture may still provide many jobs, the contribution that agriculture makes to their economies today has fallen steadily. In Malaysia it is now just over 12 per cent of GDP.

In the late 1960s and 1970s the governments of these countries invested heavily in expanding and developing manufacturing industry. As industry developed, so did the skills and experience of their workforces. One of the areas that developed most rapidly was the electronics industry.

Today some of the world's most important electronics industries, such as Samsung, are based in these countries. The rise in industrial production has also led to the development and expansion of their Tertiary industries, with both their governments and private firms investing in their ***service or skill based*** industries such as education, health care, retailing, transport and entertainment.

Formal and informal sectors of employment

Jobs can be divided into two sectors – those that provide ***formal*** employment. These are 'official' jobs where the worker is usually registered with the government and may be taxed, but, at the same time, will be eligible for paid holidays and health care benefits. These jobs usually provide better security of employment and are often better paid, with workers getting a regular weekly or monthly salary.

Jobs in the formal sector normally include those in government services, education and healthcare. Formal employment is most common in MEDC's. These formal sector jobs contrast with those in the ***informal*** sector. These jobs are often part time, temporary, outside the tax system, lacking any benefits and job security. They are often low paid. They are found in street markets as market traders, food stall workers, and shoe shiners or as farm workers such as fruit pickers. Informal employment is most common in LEDC's.

Industry as a system

Industry is sometimes seen as a system where there are:

- **Inputs** – these can include raw materials, energy, transport, labour, money (capital investment) and government policies.
- **Processes** – these can include processing raw materials, assembling component parts, packaging and administration.
- **Outputs** – these can include the finished products, the profits and waste.

Factors affecting the location of industry

In deciding where to build a factory a number of factors need to be taken into account. These factors can be put into two groups – ***physical*** factors and ***human*** and ***economic*** factors. All these factors combine to produce the total '***costs of production***'. These costs need to be below the price charged to customers so that a factory or business can make a ***profit*** and remain in business.

Physical factors

Easy access to raw materials

Raw materials are often very bulky, heavy and expensive to transport. An industry that uses large amounts of bulky raw materials will find it much easier to locate near the source of the raw materials or at a location where they can be cheaply transported to.

Such as a deep water port – a ***break of bulk*** location, where bulky cargo is unloaded and then processed at that location, so saving on very significant transport costs if the materials were to be transported inland by road or rail.

Easy access to cheap sources of power

Many industries need large amounts of power and therefore a location, beside a cheap source of power such as fast flowing water for mills or a coalfield, is both useful and often much cheaper. In the past one of the major sources of power was coal and therefore, a location on or near a major coalfield was a perfect location. Such as South Wales, in the UK and the Ruhr, in Germany. Hydro Electric Power (HEP) is a cheap source of electricity and so is often used by power hungry industries – such as an aluminium smelter.

A site that is cheap to buy or rent and is easy to build and expand on

A large, flat site is easier to build on and for a factory to expand on in the future. A large site may be expensive to buy so cheaper land is also an advantage. As a result a large, flat floodplain or a coastal plain are popular sites for factories. The site does need to be well drained; though choosing either a river floodplain or a coastal plain needs careful thought.

A situation that allows easy transport routes to be set up

A good natural route way, such as where valleys meet (called a confluence), rivers meet or a port, provide the ways in which raw materials, component parts or finished goods can be transported easily to and from factories. Valleys can carry roads, railways and canals so that where they meet in a confluence or where they link to the coast gives that location an advantage over others.

Large industrial complexes can often be found near important ports, such as Europort in the Netherlands.

Human and economic factors

Availability of labour

Different industries need different types of workers. Some industries need large numbers of relatively ***unskilled*** workers – for example, shoe factories. These are called ***labour intensive industries***. Other industries need relatively few workers but they must be ***highly skilled*** – such as the IT industry, often called mechanised industries.

Availability of capital (money) to invest in the factory

New factories are often highly expensive to build and bring online. The new Volkswagen Phaeton car factory cost 186 million Euros (roughly $208 million) in Dresden, Germany.

A new oil refinery, for example, can cost between $1–4 billion!

Toyota plans to set up a small-car assembly factory in Bangalore, southern India, at a cost of more than $100 million. This means that for both companies and governments finding the optimum location for a factory is therefore very important.

A market where the products of the factory can be sold

The size and the location of a market have now become more important than raw materials. Large MEDC cities like New York, Paris and London provide very large markets for many products.

Locating near these cities or with an easy, fast form of transport like a motorway, is a prime location. Also locating near a factory that uses your products reduces transport costs – for example car component factories beside car assembly plants.

Availability of cheap transport

It now costs $1 700 to fill up a lorry's diesel tank lasting one week in the UK!

Transport costs can make up a larger proportion of production costs, therefore finding the cheapest forms of transport for moving raw materials and finished goods is very important. This has been made even more important with the global rise in oil prices. Bulky raw materials like crude oil, iron ore and wheat can be most cheaply moved by bulk carriers. Container ships can carry other goods relatively cheaply and efficiently as they are easy to transfer in comparison to road or rail.

Government policies affecting the location of industry

Many national governments and the EU have a wide range of policies which they can use to encourage industries to move to particular locations. A common policy is to decentralise their government departments. In the UK, the government has moved the Royal Mint and the Passport Office away from London to South Wales and parts of the Foreign Office to Milton Keynes and the Pensions Department to Newcastle. Governments can also provide incentives such as lower company taxes, subsidised wages, lower rents and improved infrastructures like better roads and railways.

Economies of scale

A business with many small factories may not be very profitable compared to those which have just one large factory location. Therefore, many businesses have closed their smaller plants and built larger ones to put all the industrial processes in one site.

Fully integrated iron and steel works, such as the Llanwern iron and steel works in South Wales, is an example where all the iron and steel making processes are put on one site, from the blast furnace to the rolling mill. This has now become the normal practise for car assembly factories, such as the Nissan car factory at Washington in the N.E. of England.

Changes in technology

The use of robotic machines run with computer software to do repetitive jobs has transformed many factories, for example car assembly plants. The internet, video conferencing and fax machines have released workers from their normal workplace. This means that many workers in tertiary industries can work from home. IT software companies, banks and insurance companies have been able to close offices in MEDCs where labour costs are high and open up in India where labour costs are much lower. For example, Universal moving to New Delhi from London.

This has also led to the practise of outsourcing.

Living environment

Many businesses now look at attracting workers by offering them better living environments. This often involves moving out of large urban, city areas to suburban and rural environments. This offers workers a number of opportunities to improve their quality of life. This may include a cleaner, less polluted, quieter environment, lower rates of crime, cheaper housing costs, less time spent commuting to work and better schools.

The changing location and nature of industry

There are many reasons why businesses may fail and industries close, or move location within a country or to another part of the world. Most of these reasons are due to the factors previously discussed. Many primary industries will close or suffer because of the following.

The information that follows will illustrate some of these changes.

1. Resources or raw materials they depend on may become exhausted or too expensive to get out of the ground. For example, the exhaustion of a coalfield or an iron ore deposits or the over exploitation of a fish stock – such as the cod fishing industry in the North Sea in Europe and off the coast of Labrador in North America.
2. The replacement of manual workers with mechanisation. Car assembly plants have replaced most of the manual jobs, like paint spraying and welding, with robots.
3. A fall in demand for a product. Products as diverse as car models, trainers, food products, mobile phones, TV sets and clothing all change rapidly and customers stop buying older models. This may result in the closure of a factory. For example, the LG factory in Newport in South Wales.
4. Increases in production costs. Increases in wages, transport costs and the cost of raw materials can all make a factory uncompetitive. The minimum wage law in the EU has seen many industries move out to LEDCs where labour costs are much lower – going from $10 an hour in the EU to $2 a day in Vietnam, China and India.

5. Foreign competition. Countries with lower costs of production can undercut the prices of their competitors and cause the collapse of some industry. For example, the textile industry in the UK could not compete with the lower costs of factories in India and Bangladesh. The ship building industry in Europe found it very difficult to compete with lower cost producers in Japan and South Korea.
6. Lack of money for new investment. Industries facing competition may find it hard to find the money to pay for new factories and machinery to make them more competitive. They often have to close and sell the brand name to foreign competitors – such as selling Jaguar, Land Rover and Range Rover to Ford in the US, Rolls Royce and the Mini to the German BMW group, Bentley to Volkswagen. The Swedish Volvo group was also sold to Ford.

The UK car industry found lack of money a real problem in the 1970s and 80s.

Case study – The iron and steel industry in South Wales, UK

The early location of the industry

In the early nineteenth century, the industry was located where it could find its three essential raw materials – iron ore, coal and limestone. In several places in the UK, these were found in almost the same location – South Wales was such an area. By 1850, there were 35 iron works dotted around the South Wales coalfield as a result of these raw materials being located together. Another factor in favour of their location was the fact that the valleys in which they were located led to the coast where iron products could be transported and then exported easily.

As technology improved, the process of steel making was introduced. These replaced the early iron works which produced a very brittle iron that had limited use.

The twentieth century

A hundred years later, South Wales only had two iron and steel works. There were several reasons which caused this enormous change.

- The raw materials became exhausted – the iron ore deposits and the easily accessible coal deposits were used up and so these now had to be imported.
- The works inland suddenly found themselves at a real disadvantage as the iron ore and coal had to be unloaded at the coast and put on trains to be transported to the works.

- This added enormously to the production costs and made inland works non-competitive as their products became much more expensive than those at coastal works.

The twenty first century

Two huge, fully integrated sites were set up on the South Wales coast – at Port Talbot and Llanwern. These were on large, flat sites to accommodate the very large buildings, over 1 km long and to give plenty of room for future expansion. The main factor governing the future of both plants is the world price and the demand for steel. However, the period since 2001 has seen an increased demand for steel as the Chinese economy has expanded making Port Talbot very profitable.

In 2001, the demand for steel fell and as a result the Llanwern plant closed.

Then again, the Credit Crunch of late 2008 and 2009 saw a slowdown in the global economy and some MEDCs actually went into recession which dropped the demand for steel. The largest market for South Wales steel is the car industry and sales of cars dropped in the last half of 2008 and 2009 – so the future remains uncertain for the industry!

Multinational or Transnational Companies (TNCs)

In the past, many companies were small to medium sized and manufactured in only one country. However, many companies have decided to take control of all stages of their business from the sourcing of their raw materials and component parts, through manufacturing and processing to transportation and marketing. This has often meant operating in several countries because of which they become ***Multinational or Transnational Companies*** (***TNCs***).

These companies have become some of the biggest and most powerful companies in the world with operating budgets and profits exceeding that of many countries. They include the large car manufacturing companies such as Volkswagen of Germany, Toyota of Japan and General Motors of the US, and also include large clothing manufacturers such as Nike of USA and Adidas of Germany, pharmaceutical companies such as Glaxo Smith Kline of the UK and Pfizer of the US, or food companies such as Nestle of Switzerland and Del Monte of USA.

Volkswagen, for example, accounts for almost one quarter of Slovakia's, in Eastern Europe, total exports.

Slovakia's success with Volkswagen has led to ***cumulative causation*** – where the success of this car company has attracted other car manufacturers to the country such as Hyundai of Korea and Peugeot Citroen of France. This has made the country the largest per capita car manufacturer in the world. With these companies, their headquarters and Research and Development activities are often in the MEDC country of origin, while their manufacturing is often carried out in LEDCs.

High technology or Hi tech industries

Hi tech industries

The Hi tech industries have several characteristics which make them different from many of the older traditional industries.

- They have been set up in the last 25 years.
- They have processing techniques which normally involve the use of microelectronics.
- They normally produce high value products such as computers, microchips, electronic equipment or medical products.
- They use the most advanced manufacturing techniques.
- They employ a highly skilled workforce and carry out a lot of research and development.

Many Hi tech industries are divided into two sections.

1. Research and product development
2. The manufacturing of the product which normally involves the assembly of small easily transported component parts.

Because they can transport their component parts easily, the Hi tech industries are normally put into the footloose group of industries.

Footloose industries

A footloose industry is one which is not dependent on a particular location, unlike many other types of industry which need to be beside their raw materials, ports, fast and easy transport, etc.

The reasons for them being footloose are that they:

- use small light component parts
- their products tend to be small and light
- they use electricity as their power source
- they need a small skilled labour force
- they are non-polluting and so can locate in or near residential areas.

Do they favour any particular location?

They need to attract a highly skilled workforce, therefore they often locate in areas with a pleasant living and working environment. Locations which have good communications – such as access to the M4 motorway and Heathrow Airport in London and centres of research in universities are also attractive to Hi Tech firms.

There are several areas around the world which have become particularly popular, these include the following.

- 'Silicon Valley' in Santa Clara valley near San Francisco, California
- 'Silicon Valley North' in Ottawa, Canada
- 'Silicon Glen' in Scotland
- 'Silicon Island' in Penang, Malaysia
- Electronic City in Bangalore, India
- 'Silicon Fen' near Cambridge in England
- 'Sunrise Strip' along the M4 motorway in England
- Near the city of Nice in the south of France
- Tsukuba Science City near Tokyo, Japan.

Figure 2 shows the location of Silicon Valley, an important centre for high technology industries in the USA. Silicon Valley has many companies making and using silicon chips, computers, semi-conductor devices and computer-controlled machinery.

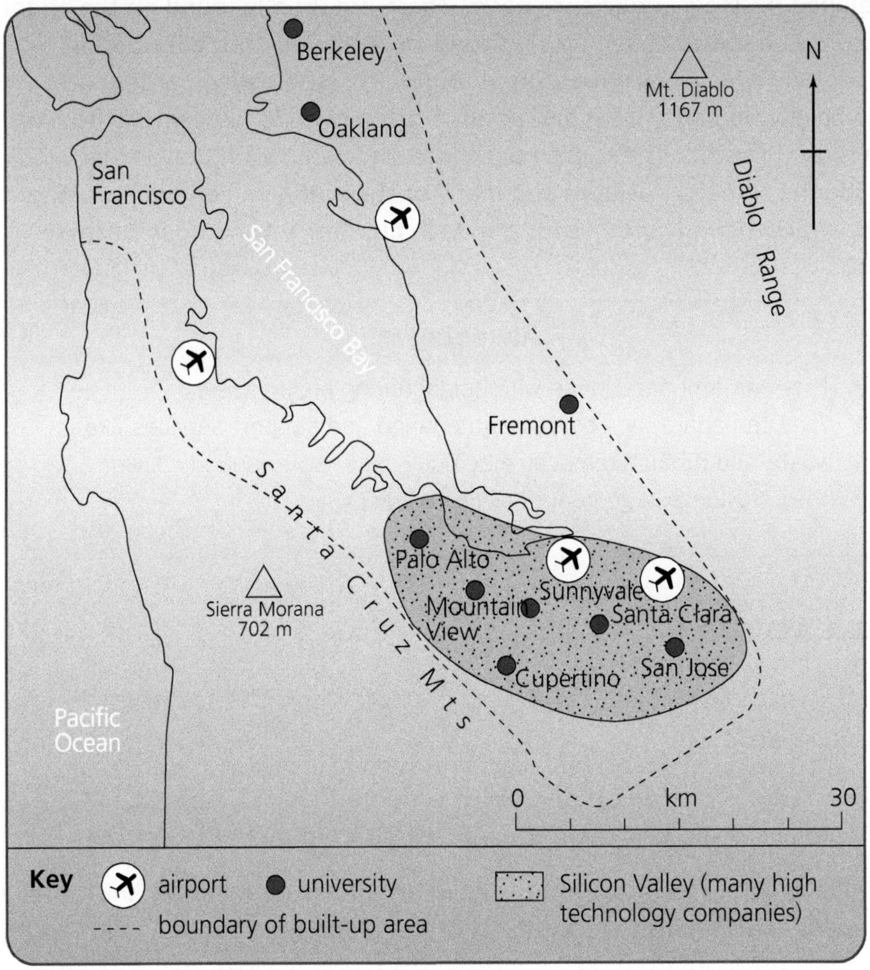

Figure 2

Cambridge 0460 Paper 2 Fig 8 June 2008

The location of these companies on the map illustrates the important factors that include:

- A highly educated, specialised labour force, many provided by the universities close by which also provide research facilities.
- They are close to other high-tech industries so that ideas, staff and equipment can be shared.
- They are near to large urban markets of the cities surrounding San Francisco Bay, but as they mainly produce high-value, low-bulk goods, these can be transported to global markets from the four nearby airports as the cost of transport is a relatively small percentage of their cost.
- Silicon Valley provides a pleasant environment for the workers to live in with close proximity to the coast and mountains.

Business and science parks

Many of the parks now also include large supermarkets and leisure facilities like cinemas.

Within these areas, Hi tech industries often group together in newly developed business and science parks. These are usually found on the edges of towns in a spacious, semi-rural situation, surrounded by countryside – Greenfield sites. They have modern buildings, landscaped gardens and some have woodland, lakes and ponds – often over 70 per cent of the park area is used for this. The science parks are associated with universities who provide the research facilities and many of the highly skilled workers. There are several other advantages for a Hi tech business setting up in of these parks.

Advantages

- They can exchange ideas with neighbouring businesses.
- They can share the cost of maintenance and support services like waste and rubbish removal, electricity lines, water and gas links.
- They provide a large pool of skilled workers.

Case studies

Silicon strip

Silicon strip is located to the west of London in the UK along the M4 motorway. Listed below are the reasons for locating beside the M4.

- Being close to the M4, industries will have a fast motorway link between the cities of London, Bristol and Cardiff.
- The busiest international airport in the world at Heathrow is just to the west of London and beside the M4.

- It is the location of several government research establishments – many have been sold by the government and are now in the private sector.
- A large, skilled labour force nearby, so that they benefit from 'agglomeration economies' by being so close together.
- Due to this they can swap both workers and ideas easily – and the large population of this part of England is within easy commuting distance.
- Close to universities which provide potential new highly qualified graduate workers, research facilities and expertise.
- An attractive working and living environment – less pollution – air, noise, visual.

Bangalore

Bangalore has become India's most important centre for Hi tech industry. It has a pleasant climate and the Indian government has provided capital for investment in the city for over a long period of time now.

It is now a major centre for ICT, biotechnology and aerospace industries. It has benefited from European and North American companies out sourcing their ICT activities to Bangalore due to its low labour costs and large, English speaking, skilled workforce – it has over 80 000 ICT workers.

There are a number of reasons as to why many large companies have located High technology industries in NICs, such as South Korea.

- The large and expanding market for goods in many NICs and LEDCs.
- There is a large and educated workforce available.
- The labour supply is relatively cheap compared to MEDCs.
- The low cost of land for building on.
- There are few labour laws and restrictions and there is very limited organised trade union activity in many LEDCs.
- The increasing ease in the global transport of components, parts and products by both air and sea.
- Government help and assistance in the setting up of new industries such as subsidies, low taxes and development grants.
- There is often a lack of environmental restrictions on the activities of many industries in comparison to many MEDCs.

There are both advantages and disadvantages, for the people who live in LEDCs, of foreign companies setting up and building factories.

Advantages

- More people will be employed.
- They will receive higher wages than in their existing work.
- An improvement in skills.
- Improvements in transport infrastructure – to roads and railways.
- Improvements in service infrastructure electricity, water supply, and sanitation. Rise in the standard of living.
- Improvements in public services such as health care and education.
- The multiplier effect/cumulative causation – there will be positive effects on other areas of the economy.
- People will be able to buy more goods in the shops; they may want to extend and improve their houses, they can afford to send their children to school.

Disadvantages

- Exploitation of the labour force.
- Comparitively low wages for workers and long hours at work.
- Long hours at work for workers.
- Poor working conditions in many factories.
- Loss of rural land/farmland for the building of new factories.
- Increased pollution to the local area from some factories example air, water, noise and visual pollution.

Progress check

1. What are the four types of industry? Give an example of each.
2. Using examples explain what is meant by inputs, processes and outputs in an industrial system.
3. Using examples describe and explain the factors influencing the distribution and location of manufacturing/ processing industries?
4. Using examples describe and explain the factors influencing the distribution and location of high technology industries?
5. Describe and explain how the proportions employed in primary, secondary and tertiary industries differ in LEDCs and MEDCs.
6. Describe and explain how these proportions may change with time and level of development, including Newly Industrialised Countries (NICs).

Examination style questions

1. What is meant by high technology industry? **[1]**

Example Answer:

A high technology industry is a science based industry that uses the most advanced techniques in its production methods. This may often mean the manufacturing of silicon processing chips and other types of micro-electronics.

2. What factors attract high technology industries to an area? **[4]**

Example Answer:

The factors that may attract high technology industries to an area may include the fact that an area might have a very skilled and highly qualified labour force.

An area like this may have a university nearby producing highly qualified work force or that there may be a lot of high tech industries there already.

It should have very good transport links by both good roads and an international airport. It should also be a nice place to work – possibly out in the countryside with good views. Lastly, the land on which the factory is going to be built should be cheap to buy, should be flat so that it is easy to build on and have plenty of room to expand.

3. Explain why a large percentage of the population in many LEDCs is employed in the primary sector. **[3]**

Example Answer:

In many poor LEDCs people work in farming because they are subsistence farmers who have to grow the food that their families eat. They cannot afford machines to do the work on their farms so much of the work is done by the family itself. Also, many people do not have the chance to go to school so have not been able to get an education. This means that they cannot get jobs that need them to read and write. The governments are very poor which means that there is not much money to set up new industries.

Comment: An excellent answer, it gives a very good definition of hi tech industry and good list of location factors. Also gives several valid reasons as to why some LEDCs have such a large number of their workers in primary industries.

Overall mark: 8/8

Examination style questions for you to try

1. (i) Give one example of primary employment and tertiary employment. **[2]**

   (ii) What is a meant by the term footloose industry? **[3]**

2. How may the growth of high technology industries in NICs, such as Thailand and Malaysia, benefit both the people and the economy of the country? **[5]**

3. (i) Using an example that you have studied, describe how a national government can influence the location of a new factory? **[4]**

   (ii) Describe the problems which some types of manufacturing industries, such as an iron and steel works, might cause for the natural environment that surrounds the factory. **[5]**

Chapter

10 Leisure activities and tourism

Learning Summary

In this chapter you will learn about:

- ***The growth of leisure facilities and tourism in relation to the main attractions of the physical and human landscape in an area***
- ***The effects of growth in tourism***
- ***The advantages and disadvantages of tourism***
- ***Examples of tourism to illustrate both the benefits and disadvantages associated with the growth of tourism***

Tourism

Tourism can be defined in many ways. A simple definition is that it is '*travel away from home for recreation and pleasure that involves at least one overnight stay.*'

The World Tourism Organisation defines ***tourists*** as people who '*travel to and stay in places outside their usual environment for not more than one consecutive year for leisure, business and other purposes not related to the exercise of an activity remunerated from within the place visited.*'

These definitions place it apart from the term ***recreation*** which can be defined as '*the use of a person's leisure time for relaxation and enjoyment that does not involve travelling away from their home.*'

Tourism has become the most popular global leisure activity.

- In 2010, there were over 940 million international tourist arrivals and international tourist income was worth $919 billion.
- During 2000–2012, it has grown at a rate of between 4 and 5 per cent per year.
- Tourism's contribution to worldwide Gross Domestic Product (GDP) is estimated to be at about 5 per cent.
- Tourism's contribution to employment is slightly higher and is estimated to be 6–7 per cent of the overall number of jobs worldwide (direct and indirect).
- Total receipts from international tourism, including international passenger transport, reached almost US$1.1 trillion in 2010.
- In other words, international tourism contributes close to US$ 3 billion a day to global export earnings.

Over 70 of the world's 196 countries now earn more than $1 billion annually from international tourists.

Tourism is the world's biggest service industry. Over the last decade, it has also been the world's fastest growing industry. Tourism is vital for the economy and employment in many countries, such as the UAE, Egypt, Greece and Thailand, and many island nations, such as The Bahamas, Fiji, the Maldives and the Seychelles, due to the large intake of money and the opportunity for employment in the service industries associated with tourism.

These service industries for tourism include transportation services, such as airlines, cruise ships and taxis; hospitality services such as accommodation, including hotels and resorts; and entertainment venues, such as amusement parks, casinos, shopping malls, various music venues and the theatre.

The growth of leisure facilities and tourism

Tourism has been in existence for over 400 years when rich Europeans, Japanese and North Americans visited spas to benefit from the mineral waters that they contained, followed by bathing in the sea from the mid-1700s. Until the late 1800s though, it was only the very rich in the upper class of society who could afford to take time off work to travel and stay away from their homes. The early 1900s though saw social, economic and cultural changes which led to the emergence of a larger middle class population. These people could afford to take one or more days off work and take advantage of an improved transport network, particularly the railways.

These changes became very significant after 1945 which saw the end of the Second World War and they have included the following.

- A ***rise in incomes*** which gave people, after they had paid for their basic needs, spare 'disposable' money that they could spend on leisure activities and tourism.
- ***Increased leisure time*** caused by a shorter working week, flexitime, paid annual holidays, earlier retirement with a pension.
- ***Increased mobility*** as a result of private car ownership, improved roads; a decrease in the cost of air travel combined with greater numbers of airports, the expansion of budget airlines like Air Asia, Ryanair, Jazeera, Jet, Air Dubai and Easy jet and the increased numbers of flights to a wider range of destinations. In 1970, there were 307 million airline passengers; by 2011 this had reached 2.75 billion.
- ***Increased media coverage*** by television, magazines and the internet of different holiday destinations and types of holiday.
- Governments have used ***major sporting events*** such as Winter and Summer Olympic Games, World Championship Athletics, Football, Rugby and Cricket World Cups to advertise tourist opportunities.
- ***Increased international migration*** encouraging more people to visit relatives and friends abroad.

The result of this has been a very large increase in international tourist arrivals.

This could rise to 1.6 billion by 2020.

Year	Tourist arrivals
1950	25 million
1980	277 million
2000	675 million
2005	800 million
2010	940 million

With tourism income reaching $919 billion in 2011, over 70 of the world's 196 countries are now earning more than $1 billion annually from tourism.

The advantages of tourism

There are many economic, social and cultural advantages, they include the following.

Economic

- A growth in income which will have an impact at both national and local level as it will provide extra finance for new developments in infrastructure, education, healthcare, etc. Both the tourist industries and the employed workers will usually pay taxes to their governments which increases government income. This helps pay for major infrastructure developments such as in health care, education, water and energy supply and roads. All of which may be used by the local populations.
- An increase in foreign currency which helps pay for goods and services imported from abroad.
- Increased employment opportunities in the many jobs created directly and indirectly by tourism.
- It can encourage other developments to take place in an area – Cumulative Causation.
- By increasing employment opportunities it can help reduce migration, especially from rural areas. This employment can be in small cafes, hotels, souvenir shops, tour guides, local taxis, etc. Many of these jobs will be in the ***informal*** sector which helps the people of LEDCs in particular.

A tourist development can act as a catalyst for further economic growth.

Social and cultural

- An increased understanding of different peoples, cultures and customs.
- Increased cultural links with other countries.
- Increased foreign language skills for both visitors and hosts.
- Increased social and recreational facilities for local people.
- The preservation of traditional heritage sites and customs.

The disadvantages of tourism

There are many economic, social and cultural disadvantages, they include the following.

Economic

- Seasonal unemployment – if people come for summer sun or winter skiing the rest of the year may mean few or no tourists and therefore, little or no employment.
- Leakage of tourist income – airlines, hotels and tourist activities in LEDCs are often foreign owned which can mean that 60–75 per cent of tourist income may either never come to, or may leave, an LEDC.
- Many tourists may spend most of their money in, have most of their meals in, and do trips organised by their hotels so they have little impact on the wider local economy.
- Many of the jobs provided by tourism in an LEDC are low paid and low skilled. Many of the higher skilled and better paid jobs are taken by foreigners.
- Some locations may become over dependent on tourism. Should a natural or human disaster occur, they may have little alternative income. Tunisia and Egypt witnessed a dramatic fall in tourist numbers in 2011 and 2012 as a result of political changes and turmoil.
- Water shortages caused by tourist complexes, hotels and golf courses using large amounts – up to 500 litres per tourist per day – may lead to local farms and villages not having enough.
- Traffic congestion and pollution from litter, increased sewage, etc. especially at '**Honeypot**' sites where there are large numbers of tourists in one location.
- Damage to the physical landscape – ranging from ski areas increasing soil erosion to damage to coral reefs.
- Increasing competition from other new tourist destinations.

The possibility of terrorist attacks in the coastal areas of Kenya in 2012 has also led to a fall in tourist numbers.

Social and cultural

- The **Demonstration effect** – local people may copy the actions of some tourists in terms of dress, diets, habits, and, possibly, alcohol and drug abuse. Their traditional values may be abandoned.
- An increase in prostitution and the development of 'sex tourism'.
- Young people may drop out from school to work in the informal tourist industry and earn money as unofficial guides or selling souvenirs.
- People leave family farms to work in the tourist industry and this makes it more difficult to run the farms without their help.
- People may be moved from their houses and land to make way for tourist developments.

- Local landowners may sell large areas of land and coastline to non-local or foreign buyers who may then deny access to local people.
- House and land prices may rise as non-locals buy them and put them out of the reach of local people.

Case study – Tourism in Kenya

How did the tourism industry develop in Kenya

Approximately 180 000 Kenyans are directly employed in the tourist industry, working in hotels, restaurants and as tourist guides; while another 380 000 are indirectly employed in support industries supplying food and transport to the hotels or selling souvenirs.

Kenyan tourism has developed by using the following.

- Its beautiful natural landscapes and ecosystems, its warm tropical climate, palm fringed beaches, many of which have coral reefs close to the shore which it has tried to carefully conserve. This has given rise to an eco-tourism industry.
- It has several different cultures from the coastal Swahili people to inland tribal peoples like the Maasai.

Tourism is Kenya's second largest source of foreign exchange revenue after agriculture. The main tourist attractions are the 19 National Parks and Game Preserves where tourists take photo safaris. Amboseli National Park is the largest park and it is 390 km² (150 mi2) in size and is at the centre of an 8 000 km² ecosystem that spreads across the Kenya-Tanzania border.

The local people who live in the Park are mainly Maasai, but people from other parts of the country have also settled there. They have been attracted by the prospect of getting jobs in the successful tourist industry and in the farms that have sprung up along the system of swamps that makes this low-rainfall area (average 350 mm) one of the best wildlife-viewing experiences in the world. Many animals arrive daily to drink water in these swamps. One of the major attractions to tourists, who are interested in Cultural Tourism (visiting and learning about different cultures), is the Maasai people who live in this and other Kenyan Parks.

The Maasai are an indigenous (native) African group of semi-nomadic people located in Kenya and its neighbour Tanzania. Due to their distinctive customs and dress and their location near the many game parks of East Africa, they are among the most well-known African ethnic groups internationally.

There are about 900 000 Maasai in the two countries and Amboseli National Park contains a large number of this total.

Traditional Maasai lifestyle centres around their cattle which are also their main source of food. In the Maasai culture, the measure of a man's wealth is in terms of the number of cattle they own and number of children. They have many interesting views on life, often very different from our own.

For example, the Maasai have suffered from living in such a harsh environment i.e., from a high infant mortality rate which has led to babies not truly being recognised until they reach an age of 3 moons – about 3 months old. Also, in the Maasai culture the end of life is almost without any ceremony, and the dead are left out for scavengers. Burial was in the past reserved only for great chiefs, since it is believed to be harmful to the soil.

Government policies, such as the preservation of the National Parks and reserves, often mean keeping the Maasai out of their traditional grazing areas. Along with an increasing population of Maasai, this has made the traditional Maasai way of life increasingly difficult to maintain.

To overcome these problems many projects and new forms of employment in tourism for the Maasai people have been introduced. This includes employment as security guards, waiters, tourist guides and help in establishing small business, such as small shops selling Maasai made bracelets, clothing, etc.

The impact of tourism on the Kenyan environment

Tourism can have a major impact on the natural environment. The Kenyan National Park environments are fragile and sensitive – both the natural landscapes and the animals that live in them. As a result, they can be changed and damaged by the thousands of tourists who visit them every year.

When visiting the Park, as part of a Safari (meaning journey), most tourists will take one of the many tourist buses to get into the park and close to the animals. Minibuses are meant to keep to well defined trails but sometimes drivers may go off the tracks to get closer to animals so that tourists can get better views and photos. This can increase the driver's tips and their incomes. During the wet season, the tracks can also get very muddy so drivers drive outside them and widen them, some end up 50-60 metres wide as a result. Tourism has brought great advantages to Kenya but it has also brought disadvantages.

On the ***positive*** side, it provides jobs in areas where employment would be very limited and the income from tourism helps raise the standard of living of the local people and improve their quality of life.

The National Parks and Game Reserves are often part of the traditional grazing areas of the nomadic tribes. These tribes move their animals over very large areas so that they do not overgraze any area.

The Park boundaries stop the tribes using quite large areas of land which means that they have smaller areas to put their animals on and the land is overgrazed as a result. This means that the tribal people lose income and see their traditional environment become degraded.

Many tribal people therefore have to live in more permanent settlements earning money from selling products they make or from putting on dance performances for tourists. Recently the Kenyan government has worked more closely with the tribal people to give them a share of the tourist income.

The Kenyan coast

The beautiful natural coastal environment of Kenya is also a very sensitive and fragile environment. Tourists are attracted by the beautiful beaches, fringed by coconut palms, blue skies and warm climate. In addition to the beaches, Kenya has tropical coral reefs which are a major attraction. The thousands of tourists who visit the coral reef coastlines every year can have a major impact on the local area and population.

- One of the main impacts has been the building of hotels and tourist facilities on the coast. Some of these developments are very large and make a major impact on the coast – there is pollution of the air, water and also noise, as well as visual pollution.
- Leakage of money from tourism – many of the tourist companies are foreign owned and so the profits disappear abroad – only 10–20 per cent of the money may stay in Kenya.
- New social problems may occur such as prostitution, crime, drugs and alcohol abuse.
- Local children may skip school to work in the tourist areas.
- Tourist developments also produce a lot of waste from rubbish to waste water and sewage. Unfortunately, this has not always been properly dealt with in the past and much of it was put into the sea where it polluted the beaches and reefs – destroying the very things the tourists had come to see!
- The jobs in tourism are often much easier than working on the family farm and earn the children more money.
- Unfortunately, family farms may be left short of labour which is particularly a problem at harvest time.
- The building of hotels may mean that local people lose their homes and jobs – many of the hotels are built on the coast where the local people have their houses, settlements and their jobs. It also affects the fishing industry.

Many of these problems can be solved by careful management and educating and guiding tourists, as well as the operators who take people onto the reefs. Boats may ground themselves on the delicate reefs so that tourists can walk on the reefs. This and the damage caused by their anchors being dragged across the reefs can quickly destroy this fragile ecosystem. Leaked fuel from these boats and suntan cream coming off swimmers are all toxic to the corals.

Number of boats and tourists can be controlled and rules made up to protect the reef – such as not allowing corals and shells to be taken from the reefs either by tourists or by local people to sell in shops. Some areas can be cordoned off to maintain pristine reef areas and mooring buoys can be constructed so that boats can tie up to them rather than drop their anchors on to the reefs.

They also have a whole new market for what they catch in the new hotels and restaurants.

Advantages

- Most of the people who live on the coast depend on the coral reefs for fishing as a source of food and to sell the fish as an income.
- The fishermen can greatly increase the income by using their boats to take people on trips to see and dive on the reefs.
- The hotels, restaurants and other facilities also provide hundreds of new jobs, from building to maintenance, cleaning and cooking, making furniture, etc.
- The jobs in cleaning and looking after tourists can add enormously to the local people's incomes.
- The wide range of water activities provide many new jobs.
- The opportunities are wide ranging as tourists have a wide range of tastes and demands.
- Tourists can be quite demanding in wanting the best facilities, like satellite TV and so there is a lot of competition to provide these.
- Local crafts people also have a much bigger market for their goods as well as local farmers who can provide the food for the hotels and restaurants.
- Shops now provide a wide range of goods which greatly increase local incomes.
- Transport also provides many jobs with coach and bus companies needing drivers, engineers and cleaners.

Disadvantages

- The local people who live on the coast follow a particular way of life. This can lead to problems when tourists are unaware of the local culture, customs and values and can offend local people by their dress and activities.
- Young local people can be influenced by the behaviour of tourists and copy them, such as in their clothes – in the worst cases, by drinking alcohol and taking drugs – the Demonstration Effect.
- Contact with the tourists has led to prostitution and the introduction of diseases like HIV/Aids.
- The coral reefs are really sensitive to any pollution – they are easily killed by any pollution – even sun tan cream coming off swimmers bodies, or by being touched or walked on.

This has been realised too late in many areas.

However, many of these problems can be overcome by thoughtful, sensitive management and careful control of tourist numbers so that a sustainable carrying capacity is observed. Coral reef pollution can be managed with guidelines, rules and regulation. Numbers of visitors and how they conduct themselves can be regulated to ensure that the reefs provide a long term income for local people and businesses. The major parks such as the Masai Mara and Amboseli and the Marine Parks near Mombasa have all introduced laws, rules, regulations and advice to increase their sustainability.

Most areas of the world who are developing tourism, are working towards ensuring that the industry will be there in the long term, in other words, that it remains sustainable.

Sustainable tourism

The global tourist industry is now aware that it is essential to develop in a sustainable manner. This does require very careful planning and a commitment by all people involved in the industry to the conservation of both natural landscapes and traditional cultures.

Ecotourism is a sustainable form of tourism which allows people to visit natural environments and traditional cultures while enabling local people to share in the economic and social benefits of tourism. At the same time, however, measures are taken to protect the natural environment, the local way of life and the traditional culture. Ecotourism is encouraged in the National Parks in Kenya and the protection of the environment is carried out in several ways.

- Restricting tourist numbers in both the parks and in certain areas of it.
- A limited number of tourist firms are licensed to use the parks and their activities are regulated in several ways. For example, minibuses are not allowed within 25 metres of animals. It can prevent animals from hunting, mating, separating from their young or resting.
- Limiting or preventing the destruction of natural vegetation and habitat which is cleared for tourist development.
- Ensure that any building developments are of low level and made out of local materials and in local styles.
- Use local labour in as many activities as possible and provide training for local people.
- Educating tourists with regard to the environmental and conservation issues in the parks.
- Restricting access to sensitive areas of the parks and at certain times of the year. Ban tourists from any hunting activities.
- Employing local people to check and to clear up any tourist rubbish regularly.

All this is essential if they are to survive in a hostile environment.

National Parks

A National Park is an area of countryside where the natural scenery and traditional way of life are protected by law, so that people may visit to enjoy and appreciate them. In the UK, they were set up in England and Wales in 1949. This process has continued to the present day, as there are now 13 National Parks, with the latest addition being the South Downs N.P.

There are two main aims in setting up National Parks and these apply to most of the National Parks worldwide.

- To preserve and enhance the natural and traditional human landscapes.
- To give public access to the parks for recreation and enjoyment.

With improvements in transport and people having increased leisure time the parks have become very popular. The Lake District N.P. is the largest and most popular. Over 23 million people live within a 3 hour drive of the Park and it receives over 14 million visitors every year.

Over 42 000 people live within the park and many of these depend on the visitors for their employment and income. About one third of the jobs in the park are tourism related and dependent, either directly – in running hotels, for example, or indirectly – in village shops, for example.

Having so many visitors generates several challenges for the National Parks Authority which manages the park.

Traffic congestion

The park is a rural area with a small population and so roads are small and narrow and unsuitable for heavy traffic. However, nearly 90 per cent of visitors arrive by private car and certain popular locations (called Honeypot sites as they attract large numbers of people) in the park suffer badly from traffic congestion, parking problems, as well as the problems associated with air and noise pollution. The possible solutions for this problem include:

- encourage people to leave their cars at home and take public transport
- set up Park and Ride Schemes – where people leave their cars in car parks and take frequent buses to a variety of locations in the park
- restrict 'On Road' parking
- produce a Road Hierarchy where certain road users can use certain roads
- make some roads 'Access only' so that only local people and businesses can use them
- put speed and weight limits on certain roads.

Footpath erosion

The very large numbers of people who go walking in the scenic countryside of the Park have caused very severe erosion of some footpaths and locations. The possible solutions for this problem include repairing eroded footpaths and covering them in resistant materials; encouraging people to take alternative routes and paths so that foot fall on some paths is reduced.

Over 4 million people now walk at least 6 kms on their visits to the park.

Second homes, retirement homes and holiday lets

Sixteen per cent of the homes in the park are now either second homes for people who live outside the park or are let out (hired out) to visitors on a week or weekend basis.

Many people have also decided to move and retire to this beautiful, scenic area. This means that when a house comes up for sale in the park, there is a lot of competition for buying it. This raises the price of the house making it too expensive for local people to buy, forcing them to move away from the area. The possible solutions for this problem include building houses that are for local people only; including starter homes for younger people who are buying houses for the first time and have a limited income.

Conflict between certain users and interests

Conflict can occur between local residents, farmers, for example, and tourists. The lakes themselves are a good example where different people want to carry out different often conflicting, activities, such as sailing, jet skiing, water skiing, power boating, fishing, swimming and bird watching. The possible solutions for this problem include designating certain lakes for certain activities, restricting power boat and jet ski use by limiting it to certain areas and having speed limits.

Progress check

1. What are the reasons for the growth of leisure facilities and tourism?
2. What are the advantages of tourism?
3. What are the disadvantages of tourism?
4. What are the advantages and disadvantages of tourism in an LEDC?
5. What is meant by the terms sustainable tourism and ecotourism?

Examination style questions

1. What is meant by the term ecotourism? **[2]**

   Example Answer:

   Ecotourism is a type of tourism which lets people visit natural environments without damaging the environment. There will be laws to protect the place from being damaged. It also helps local people to get jobs looking after and being guides for the tourists so that they benefit from the tourism.

2. State three benefits which tourism brings to an LEDC. **[3]**

   Example Answer:

   Tourism can bring many benefits to an LEDC. They include tourists bringing in valuable foreign exchange. This allows people in the LEDC to spend money on building school and hospitals. The money from tourism can also be used to build roads and water and electricity systems. Local farmers will have a bigger market for their crops as hotels will need food for the tourists. Local people will be able to sell craft items as souvenirs to the tourists.

3. Suggest reasons why some people are worried about the continued growth of the tourist industry in some areas of the world. **[4]**

   Example Answer:

   People may be worried about the growth of tourism because it may have a bad effect on the natural landscape and animals in many ways.

   For example, tourism can cause the pollution of the sea and rivers through sewage coming out of hotels and tourist areas. They leave a lot of litter and rubbish behind which may get eaten by animals and make them ill. There may be a lot of traffic congestion on local roads and the cars can cause a lot of air pollution. Tourists may be badly behaved and noisy and use a lot of water for their showers and baths.

Comment: A good answer, a good definition of ecotourism and mentions both protecting the natural environment and the fact that locals can get jobs from tourist activities. Also gives several valid benefits of tourism for LEDCs and a good list of worries that people may have about a growing tourist industry.

Overall mark: 9/9

Examination style questions for you to try

1. (i) Suggest reasons why there has been an increase in international tourism. **[3]**

   (ii) Tourism is important in many countries. How can it be developed so that it is sustainable? **[5]**

2. (i) How might the growth of tourism be likely to improve the lives of people who live in LEDCs? **[5]**

   (ii) Describe the possible disadvantages of tourism for people who live in LEDCs. **[5]**

3. For a named area which you have studied, explain why the tourist industry has developed there. You should refer to the area's physical and human attractions. **[7]**

Chapter

11 Energy and water resources

Learning Summary

In this chapter you will learn about:

- ***The advantages and disadvantages of different sources of power***
- ***The factors influencing the development and siting of power stations***
- ***The uses, provision and competition for water resources and the impact of water shortages***

Non-renewable and renewable energy resources

Resources are features of the natural and human environment that can be used by people.

A ***non-renewable energy resource*** is one that is either finite or ***non-sustainable***. This is because their use will eventually lead to their exhaustion. ***Fossil fuels*** such as coal, oil, natural gas and peat are examples.

A ***renewable energy resource*** is one that can be used continually without the fear of it running out – it is a ***sustainable*** resource. Wind, water, geothermal, wave, tidal, biogas, biofuels (like ethanol) and solar energy are examples.

Non-renewable energy resources

Some would argue that uranium, the raw material that fuels nuclear power, is a non-renewable resource this could be added to the fossil fuels!

Fossil fuels in 2010 supplied 86 per cent of the world's energy. Of the three main fossil fuels, ***oil*** provides 36 per cent of world energy, ***coal*** 28 per cent and ***natural gas*** 24 per cent. Of the remaining 11 per cent, ***nuclear energy*** provides 4.5 per cent. ***Hydro Electric Power (HEP)*** provides 5.5 per cent and all the other non-renewable energy resources combined to provide less than 1 per cent.

The use of these energy resources is not evenly spread across the countries of the world – there is a very uneven distribution. Currently, the richest 25 per cent of the world's population in the MEDCs use over 75 per cent of the world's available energy resources.

The huge contrast between LEDC and MEDC use of energy can be seen in the following energy consumption figures in terms of tonnes of coal equivalent per person.

Country	Consumption/person
Bangladesh	0.08
India	0.35
UK	5.43
USA	10.74

USA consumes 134 times that of Bangladesh, 31 times that of India and 2 times that of UK figures.

Coal

The use of coal as an energy resource in the world has increased by 48 per cent from 2000 to 2009. Most coal is used for producing electricity in thermal power stations. China produces and consumes 40 per cent of the world's total; the US produces 50 per cent of its electricity from coal.

Advantages

- Globally it is found in many politically stable countries so that supplies are relatively safe and guaranteed.
- World reserves of coal will last at least 118 years at the rate they were consumed in 2010.
- Improved technology has improved output per miner making it cheaper.
- It has also improved the efficiency and the cleanliness of emissions of coal fired power stations.
- Apart from generating electricity, it has other uses and can be used for heating and making coking coal (used in the iron and steel industry).

Disadvantages

- The cheapest and most accessible sources of coal have been used up and the cost of production has risen as a result in many areas.
- It causes air pollution through its production of ***Carbon Dioxide*** (a ***Greenhouse gas***) and ***Sulphur Dioxide*** which produces ***acid rain***. Acid rain from coal fired power stations in the UK has been responsible for killing forests and the aquatic life in the rivers and lakes of Norway and Sweden.
- The Greenhouse gases it produces contributes towards the ***EGE – the Enhanced Greenhouse Effect*** – leading to an increase in global warming, the melting of ice caps, a rise in sea level which cause areas of coastal lowland to flood.
- ***Open cast mining*** harms the natural environment and deep coal mining is dangerous for miners.
- Coal is heavy and bulky to transport so most thermal power stations have to be on or beside coal fields or near a deep water port, as a ***break of bulk*** location, which can import the coal in bulk ore carriers.

Oil and natural gas

These are the main sources of energy for many MEDCs and most of it has to be imported.

Advantages

- More efficient to burn, transport and distribute by pipelines and tankers.
- Less harmful to the environment than coal – gas is even cheaper and cleaner than oil.
- Can be used for generating electricity – gas is a very popular fuel for thermal power stations.
- Oil provides the raw material for the petrochemical industry.

Disadvantages

- ***World reserves*** of oil may only last 46 years and gas 57 years at the rate they were being consumed in 2010.
- '***Peak Oil***' has been reached – the world has now passed the point where it finds more oil fields than it consumes – the world now consumes more oil than it finds new oil fields.
- Danger of ***pollution through oil spills*** – example the Gulf War in Kuwait in 1990 when several hundred oil wells were set alight causing massive air pollution; while oil spillages at sea kills aquatic life and may have a massive impact on fishing industries as in the Gulf of Mexico oil spill in 2010.
- When burnt, gas and oil give off ***Nitrogen Oxide*** and ***Sulphur Dioxide***, respectively which contribute to ***acid rain***.
- Prices can fluctuate widely – for example from $150 to $40 a barrel between 2008–2009. In 2011, it stabilised at around $100 / barrel.
- Oil and gas pipelines are ***targets for terrorism***.
- ***Political decisions*** can cause supply problems example, the turning off of gas supplies to Europe by Russia in 2008 and 2009.

Renewable energy resources

In 2010, renewable forms of energy accounted for 3.3 per cent of global power generation, with the highest share (5.8 per cent) in Europe and Eurasia. The ***growth*** in renewable energy remains concentrated in the leading energy consuming countries in Europe and Eurasia, Asia Pacific, and North America.

However, many of the most pressing energy problems are in LEDCs and these problems are both serious and widespread.

Over 90 per cent of the population of many LEDCs, which amounts to over two billion people, do not have access to electricity which most people in MEDCs take for granted. A similar number of people depend on fuels such as wood and charcoal which they have to cut and gather or use the dung of their animals to cook their daily meals.

A growing population means that it is becoming increasingly difficult for many people to find sufficient and sustainable supplies of energy.

The development of sustainable and renewable energy resources would greatly help both these people and provide an alternative to the finite non-renewable fossil fuels that so much of the world depends on for its energy. However, these newer energy sources cannot yet meet even our current demands and some are in the very early stages of development. Besides, many LEDCs have very limited technology and would find it hard to set up and run these new forms of energy production.

The major forms of renewable energy will now be looked at, as well as their relative advantages and disadvantages.

Hydro Electric Power (HEP)

HEP generates the highest proportion of renewable energy – and 6.5 per cent of the world's total energy. In some countries, though, it is a very high proportion of their total energy use – in Norway 96 per cent of electricity, Paraguay 93 per cent and Brazil 86 per cent.

The major producers of HEP are China, Canada, Brazil and the US.

The Three Gorges Dam spans the Yangtze River, China and is now the largest power station in the world. It was completed in 2008 and it contained 26 generators. Six additional generators were installed for completion in 2011. With these, the total electric generating capacity of the dam is 22 500 Megawatts (a typical Nuclear power station generates about 650 Megawatts).

The dam is also used for controlling flood, improving the navigation of the river, as well as providing a vast amount of clean electricity. However, the disadvantages of this dam are that it has also flooded archaeological and cultural sites, displaced some 1.3 million people who have had to be rehoused and settled, and is causing some dramatic ecological changes. The decision to build the dam has always been deeply controversial.

Advantages

- HEP is renewable, clean and non-polluting.
- It is cheap (after the initial cost of the dam).
- Dams also help with flood control.
- Provide water for the local population and for farming (irrigation) and industry.
- They can also be stocked with fish and support a local fishery.
- They can be used for recreation and attract tourists.
- The new source of electricity may attract manufacturing industry and new jobs will be created.

Disadvantages

- Dams are expensive to build.
- The lakes take large areas of natural habitats and farmland.
- Destroys wildlife habitats.
- People may have to move and whole towns and communities may disappear along with historical and archaeological remains.
- They may trap sediment carried by the river and gradually fill up; some Californian dams last only 25 years as a result. The Aswan Dam in Egypt prevents fertile alluvium flooding over the floodplain of the Nile and this affects farming below the dam.
- The dams may collapse – though this is rare, a dam collapsed in Indonesia in March 2009 killing 55 people.
- A long period of drought may mean that they do not have enough water to power their turbines – Venezuela suffered power shortages due to a severe drought in 2009 and 2010.
- The reservoirs behind dams create large areas of still water, ideal for mosquitoes to breed. They are also ideal for the bilharzia snail to breed and so bring a new problem of disease in to an area.
- The visual impact of dams and their reservoirs may change the look of a natural landscape.

Geothermal energy

In Iceland, geothermal energy heats 95 per cent of the buildings in the capital city of Reykjavik.

Geothermal energy is used commercially in over 70 countries. In volcanic areas, heat comes close to the Earth's surface from the magma beneath the surface. Rainwater infiltrating the ground becomes heated and may rise to the surface as steam or as hot springs. It can then be used to heat buildings or in the production of electricity. Alternatively, water can be pumped underground, where it is heated and then brought back to the surface to be used in the same way.

The largest group of geothermal power plants in the world is located at The Geysers, a geothermal field in California, USA. The Philippines and Iceland are the only countries to generate a significant percentage of their electricity from geothermal sources. In both countries 15–20 per cent of their power comes from geothermal plants. In 2008, geothermal power supplied less than 1 per cent of the world's energy, but this is increasing and 46 countries are now developing its use.

Advantages

- Renewable, clean and non-polluting as well as cheap.
- Geothermal plants use very small areas of land – existing geothermal plants use 1–8 acres per megawatt (MW) produced, compared to 5–10 acres per MW for nuclear stations and 19 acres per MW for coal power stations.

Advantages

- It can be used at a variety of scales; a large geothermal plant can power an entire city while smaller power plants can supply more remote sites, such as rural villages.

Disadvantages

- High cost of construction and maintenance.
- The steam contains sulphuric gases.
- Although geothermal sites are capable of providing heat for many decades, locations may eventually cool down.

Wind power

Wind power is the conversion of wind energy into a useful form, such as electricity, using wind turbines. At the end of 2008, worldwide capacity of wind-powered generators was 121.2 gigawatts. Although wind produces only about 1.5 per cent of worldwide electricity use, it is growing rapidly, having doubled in the three years between 2005 and 2008. In several countries it is now very important, accounting for approximately 19 per cent of electricity production in Denmark, 11 per cent in Spain and Portugal, and 7 per cent in Germany and the Republic of Ireland in 2008.

Advantages

- Clean, renewable, sustainable and pollution free.
- It is cheap.
- Provides an income for the landowner on whose land the wind turbines are located.

Disadvantages

- Wind does not blow all the time and so needs to have a backup power source.
- Large turbines can cause visual pollution (as a result many are now being put offshore).
- Expensive to build and many are needed to replace conventional power stations.
- Can be noisy and can also cause bird kills.
- Can also disrupt radio and TV signals.

It is now becoming common for current wind farms to be repowered which is where smaller less efficient wind turbines are being replaced with larger, more efficient turbines.

Solar energy

Solar power can provide electricity by either generating it by providing heated water for a thermal generator or by using photovoltaic cells which convert sunlight to electricity. It is commonly used to provide hot water and thermal energy for cooking.

Advantages

- Clean, renewable, sustainable and non-polluting.
- Many LEDCs are in the tropics and have a lot of sunshine and therefore a lot of potential for using solar power.
- Can be used in remote locations where it would be expensive to build a network of electricity lines.

Disadvantages

- Expensive to produce the stations and the photovoltaic cells.
- The weather – it needs long hours of sunshine which is not always possible in many parts of the Earth.

Biomass

Biomass refers to plant matter that is grown to generate electricity. Biomass may also include biodegradable wastes that can be burnt as fuel.

Production of biomass is a growing industry as interest in sustainable fuel sources is growing.

Industrial biomass can be grown from numerous types of plants, including miscanthus, switchgrass, hemp, corn, poplar, willow, sorghum, sugarcane, and a variety of tree species, ranging from eucalyptus to oil palm (palm oil).

As it is cheap and easy to construct and maintain it has a great deal of potential for use in rural areas of LEDCs. For example, the Deenabandhu Model is popular in India where it is subsidised by the Government. The word means 'Helpful for the Poor'. The unit usually has a gas capacity of 2 to 3 cubic metres. It can be constructed very cheaply using bricks or cement.

The *Gobar* gas model is used in both India and Pakistan and generates biogas from cow dung. The Government of Pakistan provides 50 per cent of the cost for the construction of these moveable gas chamber biogas plants. It consists of an airtight circular pit made of concrete with a pipe connection. The manure is put in to the pit, usually directly from a cattle shed. The pit is then filled with a required quantity of water or wastewater. A gas pipe is connected to the kitchen fire place through control valves. The flammable methane gas generated out of this is largely odourless and smokeless. The residue left in the pit after the extraction of the gas is used as fertiliser. Owing to its simplicity in construction and its use of cheap raw materials in the villages, it is seen as one of the most environmentally sound energy sources for the rural needs of LEDCs.

Advantages

- It is cheap.
- Renewable and sustainable – the animals are constantly producing dung.
- Replaces fuel wood and so helps prevent deforestation.

Disadvantages

- Methane is a greenhouse gas.
- The dung that is used for some bio-digesters sometimes cannot be used for fertiliser afterwards.

Biofuels

World biofuels production grew by 14 per cent in 2010 and biofuels accounted for 0.5 per cent of global primary energy consumption. Most of this growth has been in North America (+18 per cent) and South and Central America (+14 per cent). These two regions accounted for three-quarters of global biofuels production.

Globally, biofuels are most commonly used to power vehicles, heat homes, and for cooking. ***Agro fuels*** are biofuels which are produced from crops.

There are two common ways of producing liquid and gas Agro fuels. One is to grow crops high in sugar content (such as sugar cane, sugar beet, and sweet sorghum) or starch content (such as corn/maize), to produce ethyl alcohol (ethanol). Ethanol accounts for nearly three-quarters of global biofuels production, and is dominant in North America and South and Central America. In Brazil, the fuel sold at filling stations for vehicles is 22–26 per cent ethanol, but newer vehicles can run on ethanol alone.

The second is to grow plants that contain high amounts of vegetable oil, such as oil palm, soybean, algae, jatropha, or pongamia pinnata. These oils can be burned directly in a diesel engine, or they can be chemically processed to produce fuels such as biodiesel.

Biodiesel is most important in Europe and Eurasia.

Advantages

- Renewable and sustainable.
- Jatropha can be grown on infertile, marginal land that crops cannot be grown on and it is drought resistant.

Disadvantages

- The effect of a drop in oil prices – as oil prices drop biofuel may become a more expensive option.
- The 'food versus fuel' debate – many farmers are now growing biofuel crops instead of food crops as they are being paid more money for the biofuel crops.
- Increased carbon emissions from burning biofuels.
- The deforestation of land to plant biofuel crops, especially oil palms, as in Indonesia, and the soil erosion that may result as well as the impact on soil being washed in to rivers and lakes.
- Human rights issues as people are moved off their land and farms by big landowners.

Fuel wood

In LEDCs, between 2.5 and 3 billion people worldwide rely on fuel wood for cooking and heating. It is sometimes burnt directly or used to produce charcoal which is then burnt. In Africa, trees are often called the ***'staff of life'*** as they provide many communities with many of their basic needs – fuel, shelter, food and shade.

However, demand is now outstripping supply in many areas of LEDCs where it is the main fuel source. In Mali in West Africa, with a population of 12 million, 50 million tonnes of wood are cut from forests every year, which is greater than the rate of regrowth and replanting. Consequently, fuel wood may or may not be regarded as a renewable energy source depending on whether the rates of replanting of those forests cut down for fuel wood matches the rate at which they are being cut down.

It also now needs to be cut and collected from many kms away from where many people live and therefore, this can take up many hours of the day, for women especially, who have to cut and bring it back.

Much of it is usually burnt inside or close to houses and it is not properly vented so that it is a major air pollutant for many families and currently accounts for 1.5 million deaths from respiratory illnesses in LEDCs every year.

Deforestation also leads to increased soil erosion and a decrease in water quality as soil gets into river streams and lakes. In turn, this can increase flood events in both size and number as there is a lack of interception of water on the valley sides. The surface run off reaches the rivers more quickly and in larger amounts. Plus, river channels become filled with sediment so that they cannot contain as much floodwater and so flood more easily.

Development and siting of power stations

Thermal power stations normally burn fossil fuels to produce steam that drives turbines and this affects their location.

- Coal is very heavy and bulky, so coal fired power stations need to be located on or near a coalfield or at a 'break of bulk' location – where the coal can be unloaded and transferred onto another form of transportation. This is a costly and time consuming process and adds to the cost of the coal. Therefore, coal fired power stations tend to be located near deep water ports or on a rail network. In the case of oil and gas, they need to be on a pipeline network.
- They need to be beside large sources of water to cool the steam that drives the turbines.
- A large, flat site is needed to build the station and store the fuel.
- The need to be near a large centre of population and industry to minimise the loss of electricity as it passes along power transmission lines and they need to be able to connect easily to feed their power into a National Grid network.

Hydroelectric power stations require the following.

- A major river with a large, reliable discharge for most, if not all, of the year to fill the reservoir created by the dam.
- A relatively narrow steep sided valley made of hard, impermeable rock to provide a solid foundation for the building of a large dam.
- A large upstream area, with few people that need to be moved, which can be flooded to provide the reservoir of water.
- Access to electricity transmission lines to transmit the electricity to centres of population and industry.

Nuclear power stations require the following.

- A large source of water for cooling – a coastal location is common.
- Solid hard rock for a solid foundation.
- A geologically stable area to construct the station, away from the threat of large earthquakes.
- Away from large centres of population for safety, but not too far away that too much electricity is lost in transmission.
- A supply of labour nearby.

Water resources and the impact of water shortages

As the world's population grows, so does the demand for water. Not only does the demand for domestic water grows, so does the demand from industry as countries develop, and from agriculture as the area of irrigated farm land increases.

The following map shows areas of the world which have a water surplus (more water than they need) and those where there is a water shortage (less water than they need).

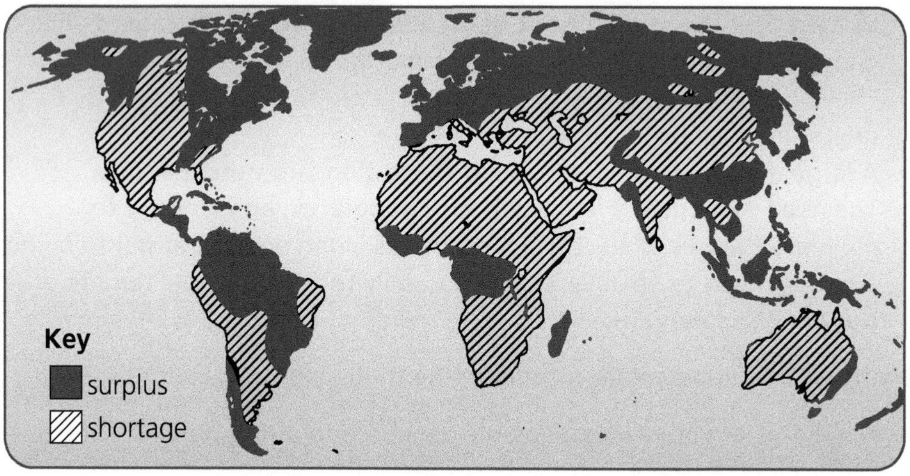

Figure 1

Cambridge 0460 Paper 1 Fig 10 June 2005

In many areas, such as near large conurbations or in semi-arid areas, the demand for water far exceeds supply. This can lead to water shortages which can have a severe impact on the local population and restrict the development of industry, agriculture and urbanisation.

Where river catchments flow through several countries it can lead to conflict and argument over the use of a finite supply of water; as in the Nile and Jordan rivers where countries up stream of Egypt (such as Kenya, Sudan, Ethiopia and Tanzania) and Jordan (Lebanon, Syria and Israel) would like to further develop their agriculture, industry and urban areas to improve standards of living and improve the quality of life.

Such an example illustrates why careful management of this finite resource will be essential in the future.

An example of the scale of problem is 1929 River Nile Agreement. Egypt has the largest share of water from the Nile, which is now being questioned by the upstream countries. Kenya wishes to withdraw from the agreement but the water minister for Egypt describes such a move as an act of war.

Worldwide water consumption is not equal. The populations of MEDC countries use much more water than those in LEDCs. The average person in North America uses over 1 600 cubic metres of water a year compared to less than 200 cubic metres for a person in Sub Saharan Africa.

MEDCs have the money and resources to transfer large quantities of water to long distances which has enabled them to develop areas with water shortages, for example, in the South West of USA. Southern California has developed enormously and it could not have done this without transferring water from the north of the state to the south with the development of the ***California State Water Project***. The northern third of California has 70 per cent of the state's water but 80 per cent of the demand for water is from the southern two thirds of the state. The demand is mainly from agriculture, which uses 80 per cent of the state's water, but the expansion of Los Angeles and San Diego, has further increased demand so that the state has looked further away for its water – to the Colorado River.

The Colorado runs through seven states after starting at the state of Colorado, in the Rocky Mountains, and finishing in California before it crosses into Mexico. In 1922, the water in the river was divided between the states, which were divided into an upper and a lower group, as part of the ***Colorado River Compact***. Each group was allocated 9.25 trillion litres of water a year and later, a treaty in 1944 brought Mexico into the agreement by guaranteeing it 1.85 trillion litres a year.

Since that time though, water demands have increased enormously. Firstly, although it has been committed to deliver 20.35 million litres annually, the annual flow of the Colorado River has only averaged 17.25 trillion litres since 1930!

Added to this, ***evaporation*** from the many reservoirs created by dams built along its course has meant that there is a further loss of 2.45 trillion litres annually. Periodic droughts in the South West of the US have also meant that it has fallen well below its average flow from its previous years. Since the compact was drawn up, demand has also increased enormously, both through an increasing population (from 1970–1990, the population of the seven states increased from 23 to 36 million) and an increase in the area of irrigated farm land (now 820 000 hectares in the US and Mexico).

The increase in demand has also been due to the ***Central Arizona Project (CAP),*** costing $4 billion. This was completed in 1992 and involved diverting water away to central Arizona including two of the fastest growing cities in USA, Phoenix and Tucson. 1.85 trillion litres of water is now delivered annually to farms, cities and native American Indian reservations over a distance of 570 kms.

In the past, Arizona never took up its full allocation from the Colorado and it was used by the other states, especially California. Now that Arizona is taking more water, California has to find a way to make up for the shortfall between what it is now allowed – 5 427 million cubic metres and what it was taking in the past – 6 416 million cubic metres.

As with many other areas of the world, California and the South west of USA, now has to carefully look at its future options and develop careful resource management strategies. This may produce a sustainable future. In this particular example of water resources there are several strategies that can be put in place for California and elsewhere, they include the following.

- ***Reduce the leakage of water*** from pipes and aqueducts as well as the loss of water by evaporation from aqueducts. This would stop up to 25 per cent of losses.
- ***Recycle water*** that is used in industry and from sewage. This does not have to be treated to the same standard as drinking water. It is termed grey water, and can be used to irrigate gardens and golf courses and flush toilets.
- ***Reduce water subsidies,*** as at the present time, farmers in the south west of USA only pay 10 per cent of the actual cost of the water they use for irrigation. The federal government subsidises the rest of the cost. Farmers need to use irrigation water more efficiently – such as using drip irrigation systems which are 100 times more efficient than flood irrigation. LEDC farmers also point out that US farmers have an unfair advantage in markets as their products are heavily subsidised and can make LEDC products uncompetitive.
- ***Grow less water dependent crops*** rather than rice and the fodder crop, alfalfa.
- Several cities in California are looking at using ***desalination plants*** to produce water – Santa Barbara has one costing $37 million.

At an individual level, much less water can be used to flush toilets – 6 litres in a more efficient toilet instead of the 26 litres used in most conventional toilets.

Increasing demand on Earth's resources

Globally, there are four important reasons behind the increasing demand of the Earth's resources.

1. Population growth
2. Economic development
3. Increasing wealth
4. Advances in technology.

As a result, many people believe that we are using the world's resources in an unsustainable way and want the world to sustainably manage its resources. Five main areas have been highlighted which could combine to provide this sustainable management of our resources, including water.

- Increase our use of renewable resources such as wind, water, solar energy.
- Recycle resources that are often ending up as waste, such as recycling paper, glass, aluminium and steel, water etc.

- Increase efficiency by using resources in a less wasteful way, by increasing the efficiency of car engines, low energy light bulbs, etc.
- Controlling pollution by controlling the emissions from thermal power stations and vehicles.
- Conservation of the Earth's natural resources and ecosystems and maintaining biodiversity as a result.

Progress check

1. What are the advantages and disadvantages of different sources of non-renewable energy (coal, oil and natural gas)?
2. What are the advantages and disadvantages of the different forms of renewable energy (geothermal, wind, water, solar, biofuels, biomass and fuel wood)?
3. What are the factors influencing the development and siting of power stations (thermal, hydro-electric and nuclear)?
4. What are the uses, provision and competition for water resources and the impact of water shortages?

Examination style questions

1. What is meant by the term 'renewable energy'? **[1]**

Example Answer:

The term 'renewable energy' means a type of energy which can be used over and over again and will not run out. For example, the wind.

2. Give two advantages that using a renewable form of energy to generate electricity has instead of using a non-renewable form of energy. **[2]**

Example Answer:

Two advantages that using a renewable form of energy to generate electricity has is that it will usually be environmentally friendly and not pollute the environment. It will also never run out unlike a non-renewable type of energy like coal.

3. Describe and explain the factors which influence the location of one type of electricity generating station. **[7]**

Example Answer:

Coal fired power stations are a very common type of power station which are used in many countries. There are a number of factors which affect where a power station is built.

A coal fired power station uses a very bulky raw material – coal – which means that it needs to be located very near to a coalfield or very close to a big port which can import the coal very cheaply. Power stations need very large sites to build on as they are big buildings and they need somewhere to store the coal that they will use in the power station. Being such a large area they will try to find relatively cheap land they also need the large area to be on flat land to build the large buildings and store the coal, such as on the flood plain of a large river or on the coast beside a big port. Power stations use large amounts of water for cooling so they need to be beside a large river or lake. They will probably be put near a large population of people, like a large city, which need lots of electricity and so there will always be a big demand for the electricity from the power station. Finally, they do need to be able to connect easily to feed their power into a National Grid.

Comment: A very good answer in all sections of the question. In the third part of the question the factors of location is explained in detail. Although not asked directly in this question, it would have been useful to have named an example of a location or a power station to gain the full 7 marks.

Overall mark: 9/10

Examination style questions for you to try

1. (i) What is meant by fossil fuel? Give an example. **[2]**

(ii) Briefly describe the factors determining the location of an HEP dam. **[2]**

(iii) Describe the advantages of using hydro-electric power (HEP), rather than other sources of energy. **[4]**

2. Explain the positive and negative effects of a water development project like the Central Arizona Project **[5]**

3. For a country or area which you have studied, describe the ways in which renewable energy supplies are being developed. **[7]**

Geographical skills for examination

Geographical skills for examination

Geographical skills are important for geographers and therefore they will be tested in the examination. You may need to demonstrate your skills of analysis and interpretation of topographical maps, other maps, diagrams, graphs, tables of data, written material and photographs and your application of graphical and other techniques.

Equipment

Check which equipment you should have for the examination – usually the following will be required.

- A pencil, eraser, ruler and a protractor, preferably 360°.
- It is also advisable that you should use a ruler, and/or a straight edged piece of paper for measuring distance on the large scale topographic map.

The scale of the maps and measuring distances

The maps are likely to be on a scale of **1:25 000** or **1:50 000**. This means that **1 centimetre** on the maps will be either **250** or **500 metres** on the ground. This makes the calculation of distances relatively easy.

For example, a distance of 4 centimetres on a 1:25 000 map will equal 1000 metres (or 1 kilometre) and on a 1:50 000 map, 4 centimetres will be 2 000 metres (or 2 kilometres).

The distances you are asked to measure will normally be straight along roads, or with easy to measure distances, along fairly straight roads. You can either measure the distances with your ruler or the edge of a straight piece of paper.

All the maps will have a full ***key*** which you will need to refer to for answering some of the questions.

Before answering the question, you should familiarise yourself with the ***map***, the ***scale*** and the ***key***. Look at the key and look at how features have been grouped together – types of roads, types of land use and vegetation, for example.

Grid references

You need to be able to both give and to read ***4 figure*** and ***6 figure grid references*** so that you can locate places on the map. There may be questions that give you a grid reference and ask you to locate a feature, either a name or a conventional sign that you need to look up on the key provided with the map.

A ***4 figure grid reference*** will locate a ***grid square***. These are used to locate a fairly large feature like a town, a river valley, a coastline or a land use like a sugar plantation.

A ***6 figure grid reference*** will ***locate an exact point,*** for example you may be asked to find a conventional sign or a building, such as a power station, and you will need to search the key to find out what it is.

To find a ***4 figure grid reference*** you use the first two figures/numbers to go along the ***bottom*** of the map ***from left to right***. You use the second two figures/numbers to go ***up*** the side of the map. To minimise the possibility of you making a basic mistake on this when under exam conditions there are two practical techniques.

In the first method, you can move a finger from one hand along the bottom line until you find the correct vertical line, Easting, and ***keep this finger to the right of this*** line; then move the finger from your other hand up left side of the map until you find the correct horizontal line, Northing, and ***keep this finger above this line***. Then bring your fingers together to find the correct grid square.

In the second method, use a ruler and pencil to draw the vertical and horizontal lines and so the precise point can be located.

A ***6 figure grid reference*** uses the 4 figures from a 4 figure grid reference, example 0667 and then adds two more, example 065675.

This allows you to find an exact point (on the diagram this is the letter **D**) in a grid square and is used in a square which has a lot of information in it, such as finding a building in the centre of a town. In finding the third and sixth figures, you have to imagine that the grid line has been split in to 10 equal parts. This means that 065 will be halfway between the 06 and 07 lines.

Again, use your fingers to keep a place on the bottom of the map and up the side, and then bring your fingers together to find the point. You might find it useful, again, to also make a pencil mark on both lines to help with the accuracy.

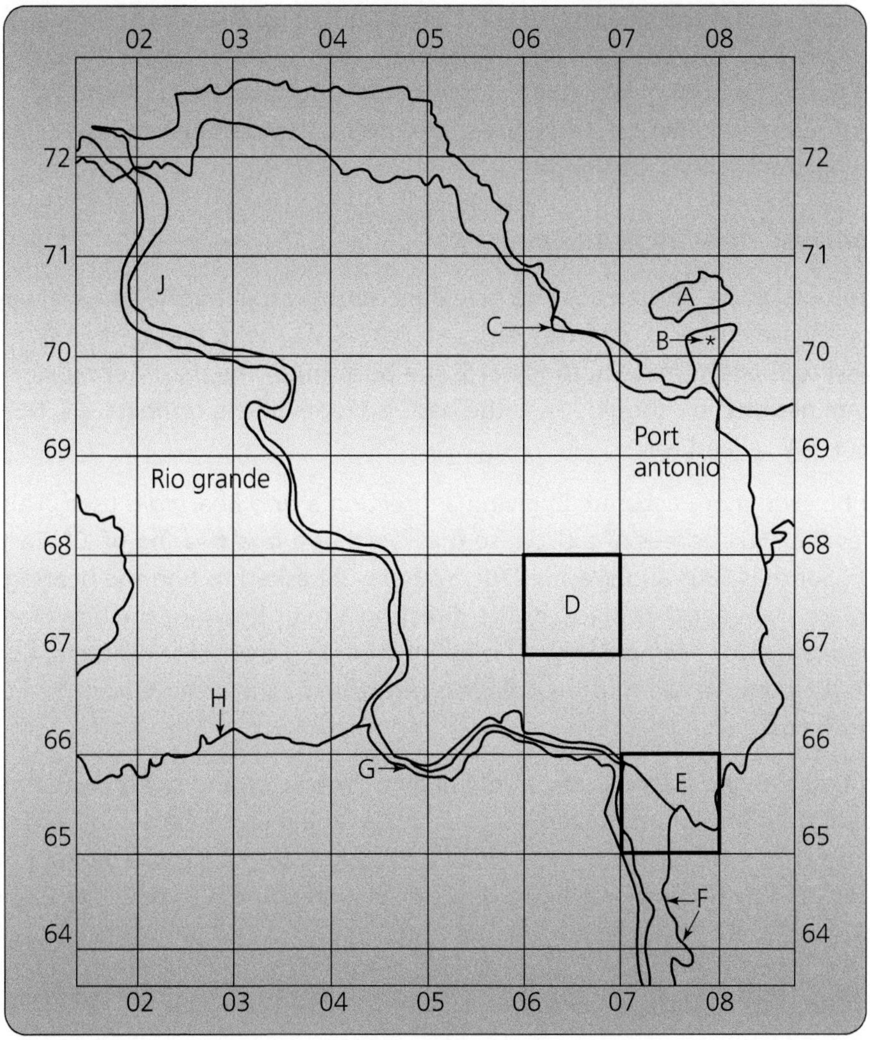

Figure 1

Cambridge 0460 Paper 2 Q1 Fig 1 June 2006

The following explanation and Figure 1 will help explain all this further.

1. On the diagram two grid squares are located – **D** (Grid Ref 0667) and **E** (Grid Ref 0765). To find **D** go **along** the bottom of the map until you find the 06 vertical line. The square we are looking for will be in the column between the 06 and 07 lines, so keep your finger here. Going **up** the side find the 67 line.
   The square we are looking for will be between the 06 and 07 lines, so keeping your finger here, bring your two fingers together and they should meet in the **D** square. Try the same exercise with the **E** square.
2. On the diagram, **B** is used to locate a point marked with an asterisk * which has a 6 figure grid reference of **079702**. To find the 6 figure grid reference we firstly go along the bottom line (*or the top line if that is nearer*) and find the 07 line and go along 9 tenths of the way between the 07 and 08 lines. Keep a finger on this location, or put a pencil mark on the line.

Then go **up** the side to find the 70 line and go **up** 2 tenths of the way between the 70 and 71 lines. Again put your finger or a pencil mark here. Then bring your fingers together and you will find the asterisk!

3. The vertical lines on a map are sometimes called ***eastings*** and the horizontal lines ***northings***.

Compass directions and bearings

The compass order can be remembered by making up a phrase such as Naughty Elephants Squirt Water!

You need to be able to use and give **directions** on the map. ***North*** is always up, towards the top, on these maps, so ***East*** is always ***to the right*** and ***West*** to the left (and ***South*** towards the bottom) of the map. For most examinations you should know the basic 8 points of the compass – N, NE, E, SE, S, SW, W and NW.

To be even more accurate in giving a direction a ***grid bearing*** is used. This uses the 360 degrees of a circle, so that North is a ***grid bearing*** of 0°, East is 90°, South is 180° and West is 270°. You may be asked to find the bearing of a place from another place, or the direction a river flows, or the direction a road takes, for example, from a road junction in a town. For example, using the diagram we can find the ***compass direction*** of the letter **E** from **D** – it is **South East**.

To find the ***grid bearing*** you would need a **Protractor** and put it on the map so that the 0° is pointing vertically, north, up the map and the centre of the protractor is on the letter **D**. You can then calculate the degree bearing of a location by finding how many degrees around from 0° is the letter **E**. It is **150°**.

Finding the height on a map

Height is shown in ***three ways*** on the topographical maps – by ***contour lines, spot heights*** and ***trigonometrical stations***.

A **contour line** is a line that joins places on the map with the same height. The **contour interval** is the height between contours. This can be either **5** or **10** metres.

A **spot height** is an exact point, or Spot, on the map with a height in metres written beside it.

A **trigonometrical station** is a small blue/black triangle with an exact height in metres written beside it.

Describing the shape and slope of the land

A lack of contour lines on a map means that the land is ***flat***. If the contour lines are very close together the land is ***very steep***, if they are further apart the land is ***gently sloping***. You may often be asked to describe how steep are the sides of valleys or hills and the contour lines allow you to describe this.

Sometimes land is so steep, or almost vertical, that they use a special sign is used, for a cliff, on a map. This can be found in the key.

Depending on the shape of the land contours take on distinct patterns. A ***hill*** will have a series of circular shaped contours; a ***valley*** will have a V shaped set of contours, usually with a river in the bottom of the valley.

You may be expected to identify basic landscape features such as river valleys and areas of uplands and to give brief descriptions of them using appropriate geographical terms such as a ***high ridge*, *or plateau*** (a high flat area), a ***scarp slope*** (another name for a steep slope), and a ***floodplain*** and simple descriptions such as ***broad, flat, steep-sided, deeply cut (by a river), gently sloping***.

You should be able to recognise differences in the ***density of drainage*** (this simply means that the length of streams, rivers or drainage channels you find in grid square if there are lots of rivers and streams in the square it has a ***high drainage density***, if it has few it has a ***low drainage density***). Th **drainage pattern** could also be described – river channels radiating out from the tops of hills produce a **radical pattern**, while in some areas a river system with all its joining tributaries may look like the veins on a leaf– producing a **dendritic pattern**.

You should be able to describe the ***physical*** features of coastlines such as ***cliffs, headlands and bays, beaches, spits, bars and tombolos***, and the shape and form of river channels as they are shown on large-scale maps – such as ***meanders and oxbow lakes and deltas.***

Measuring gradients on a map

The information gained from measuring horizontal and vertical distances allows you to calculate the drop in height, the ***gradient***, between two places. It is very useful to know how steep the land is between two places if a road or railway is to be built or even if you are just hiking or walking between the two places. Instead of saying that a road or valley side falls/drops a certain number of metres over a certain distance, for example 100 metres over 3 kilometres, a ***gradient*** converts this figure into how many metres in distance it takes to drop 1 metre in height.

In the following example, it would be 100 metres in 3 000 metres which is then converted to **1:300** using the following formula:

$$\frac{\textbf{Vertical interval (Difference in height in metres)}}{\textbf{Horizontal equivalent (Horizontal distance in metres)}}$$

This equals $\frac{100}{3000}$ which is $\frac{1}{300}$ which is the written as a **Gradient** of **1:300**.

Cross-sections

There may be use of drawn ***cross-sections***, like the one below, of parts of the map for you to mark on and describe certain places on the map. The cross sections allow you to see areas of flat, steep and gentle slopes and locate rivers and towns, etc. You may use them to analyse and describe certain areas of the map. They normally run the cross section along one of the vertical or horizontal grid lines drawn on the map between two places. The vertical lines on a map are called ***eastings*** and the horizontal lines ***northings***. On the one below the instructions said:

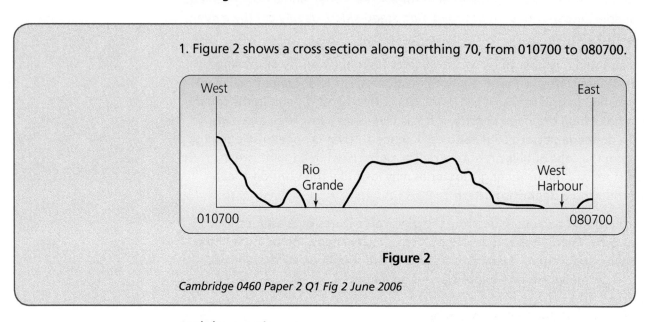

1. Figure 2 shows a cross section along northing 70, from 010700 to 080700.

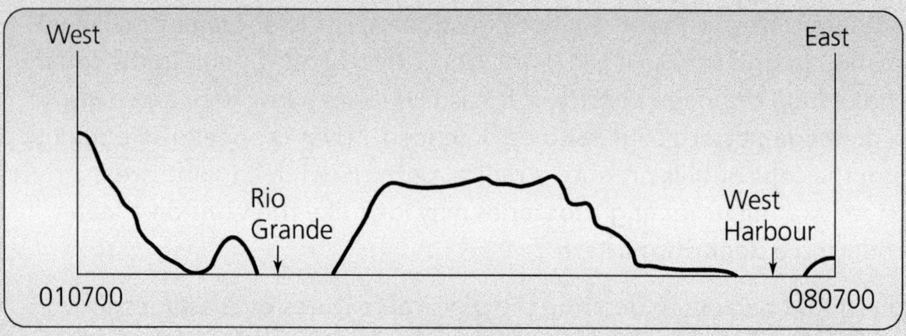

Figure 2

Cambridge 0460 Paper 2 Q1 Fig 2 June 2006

And the question was:

On Figure 2, use labelled arrows to show the positions of:

(i) The Rio Grande flood plain,
(ii) Stony Hill,
(iii) The railway line. [3 marks]

Patterns of settlement

You should be able to recognise and analyse the main patterns of settlement (***dispersed, nucleated, linear***) and be able to draw simple sketch maps illustrating these patterns.

You should be able to interpret and describe features of ***urban morphology*** (meaning urban shape) on the maps and be able to describe the ***functions*** of and ***services*** provided by settlements. You should also be able to give reasons for the ***site*** and ***growth*** of individual settlements.

Transport networks (the provision of roads, railways, ports and airports) should be recognised in terms of their type and density in relation to the physical geography (i.e. keeping to areas of flat land and valley floors, avoiding steep slopes and mountainous areas) and human geography (i.e.

linking settlements together, taking traffic around a large town or city rather than through the middle – called a by-pass) features.

Your explanations ***should be based entirely on map evidence*** showing the interaction between humans and their physical environment, example differences in land use between upland and lowland areas as a result of climate differences due to height; differences in land use within a town; differences between dense settlement on river flood plains and sparse settlement on steep upland slopes.

Questions on any of the Geography papers may be set using some or all of these resources.

The maps

- Apart from topographical maps, all the papers may contain a variety of maps in their questions.
- The maps may contain many of the answers and marks so spending time in the exam to understand, interpret and analyse them is important.
- The maps may, on purpose, be a variety of different scales.
- Many may be world/global maps, but others may show individual continents, countries, regions, cities, towns, rivers, coastlines, etc.
- The common theme for the maps is that usually they will have been carefully drawn and designed just for the question to only show the information you need to answer the question and get the marks you need.
- Usually, you will be asked to find, identify and then describe, or compare, analyse and explain important features of the human and physical landscape.
- You may be asked to recognise patterns on the maps and work out relationships.
- For example, population distribution and density – often this is on a world scale so pick out areas of high and low population density.
- You may then be asked to identify areas of:

    1. High and low population density and give reasons for their differences – hot or cold, wet or dry, long or short growing seasons, fertile or infertile land, mountainous or flat, fertile river valleys like the Nile in Egypt or the Ganges in India, natural resources like coal, oil and gas fields or other minerals like iron ore.
    2. Population migration/movements – how many people, whether it is international (between countries) or national (within a country), economic, forced or voluntary.
    3. Road and rail transport networks.
    4. Settlement sizes, shapes and patterns.
    5. Relief (the shape and height of the land).
    6. River – including floodplains, deltas (arcuate/fan or digital/birds foot), meanders, oxbow lakes and drainage pattern.

7. Coastal – including headlands and bays hard – and less resistant – soft rocks and differential erosion), spits, bars, tombolos, beaches, wave cut platforms and cliffs.
8. Volcanoes and earthquake features, etc.

The maps may have diagrams added to them such as small ***bar*** or ***line graphs***, or ***population pyramids***, to illustrate the age and sex structure of a country or contrasting countries.

Graphs and diagrams, tables of data and written material

You may be expected to be able to extract and analyse information from graphs, diagrams, tables of data and written material.

The types of graph used may include:

- Pie graphs
- Line graphs
- Triangular graphs
- Radial graphs
- Bar graphs
- Divided bar graphs
- Histograms
- Scatter graphs
- Wind roses.

In the questions that follow, you will see examples of these and how they may be used in questions. You may be asked to **describe variations** and **identify trends** in the information on the graphs. Graphs may show, for example, temperature, rainfall, birth rate, death rate, energy use, rainfall distribution, river discharge, etc. Also, you may be asked to plot information on the graphs when axes and scales are provided.

Population pyramids

You may be asked to describe the broad features of the ***population structure*** to show comparisons and contrasts between the male and female populations, the working (economically active) and non-working (non economically active) population and the young (young dependant – 15 and under) and old age (old dependant – 65 and over) groups. They can use a single pyramid of one country or they may compare the pyramids two countries – normally a typical LEDC and a typical MEDC.

There are two examples mentioned here.

2. Describe the main features of the population pyramid of a developing country, shown in Figure 3 and suggest reasons for the features. **[6]**

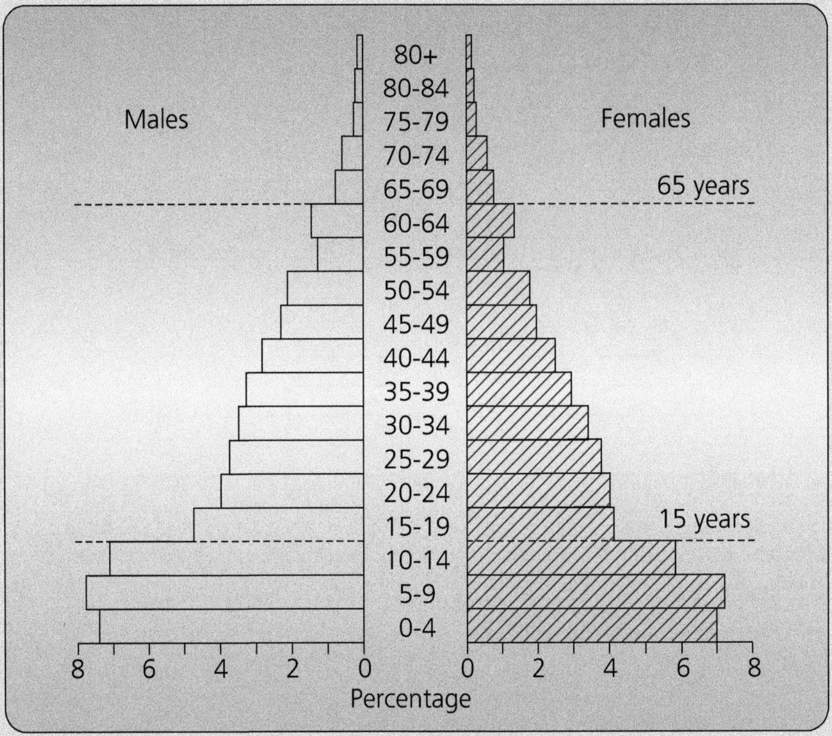

Figure 3

Cambridge 0460 Paper 2 Q1 and 2 inc Fig 2 June 2003

3. Study figures 4 and 5, population pyramids for Ethiopia (an LEDC) and the Netherlands (an MEDC).
   (a) Which age group in Ethiopia has the largest percentage of both males and females? **[1]**
   (b) What evidence in the population pyramids suggests that:
      (i) People in the Netherlands have a longer life expectancy than people in Ethiopia?
      (ii) Ethiopia has a higher birth rate than Netherlands? **[2]**
   (c) How does the dependent population of Ethiopia differ from that of the Netherlands? Support your answer with figures. **[3]**
   (d) Describe the ways in which the dependent population is supported in LEDC and MEDCs. **[4]**

Cambridge 0460 Paper 1 Q1 June 2006

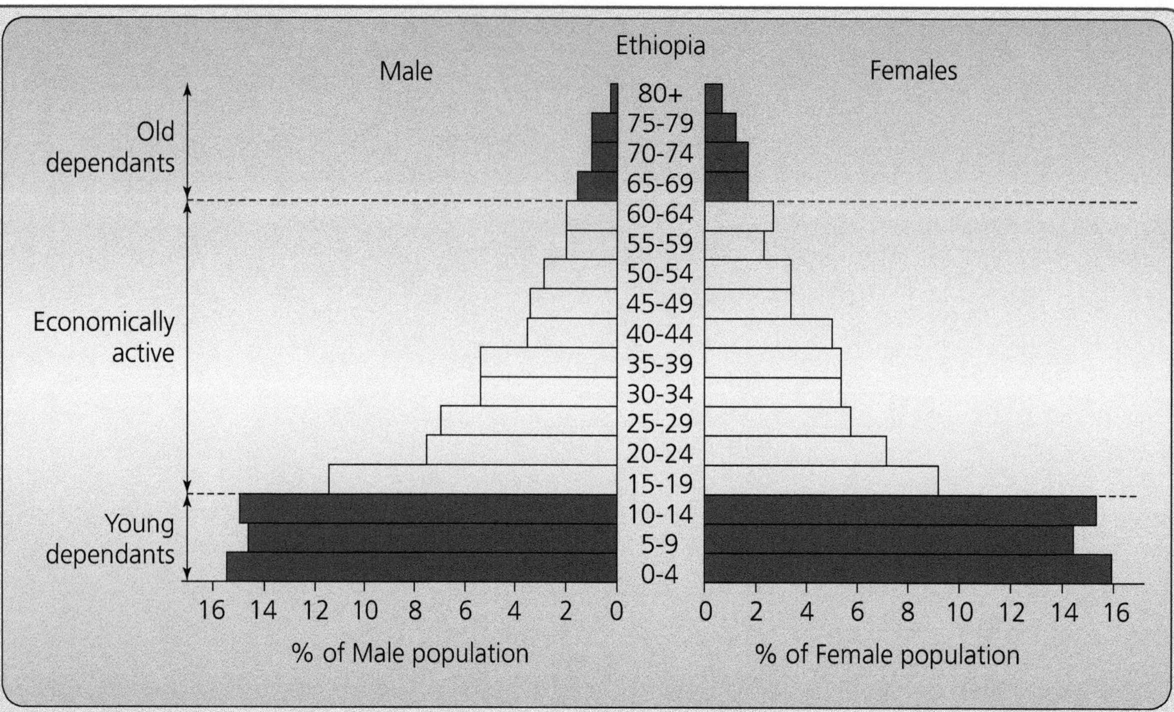

Figure 4

Cambridge 0460 Paper 1 Q1 Fig 1 June 2006

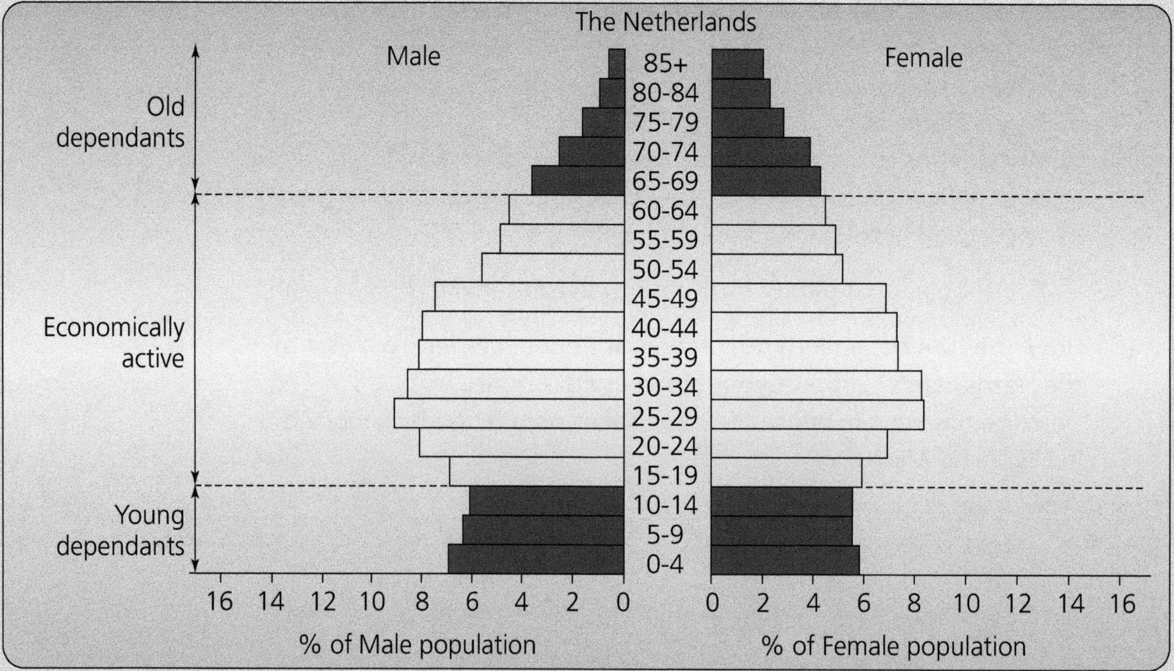

Figure 5

Cambridge 0460 Paper 1 Q1 Fig 1 June 2006

Triangular graphs

These are most commonly used to compare the percentages of people who are working in **primary, secondary** and **tertiary** industry. They have **three** axes instead of the normal two.

A typical LEDC will have a very high percentage of people working in **primary** industry – mainly poor subsistence farmers (such as Tanzania with 83% on the graph below), while an MEDC will have a very high percentage in **tertiary** (service) industries (such as USA 72%, France 67% and Japan 58% below). **NIC's** (Newly Industrialised Country) like Nigeria and Indonesia will be somewhere in between the two extremes as more of their population move into jobs in **secondary** (manufacturing and processing) and **tertiary** industries.

4. Give reasons for the differences shown on Figure 6 in the percentage employed in the three different sectors of the economy in the two groups of countries **X** and **Y**. **[5]**

Questions may not always use a triangular graph (or the term NIC – they use the term Intermediate Countries here) for this information. They may use either divided bar charts, as the following examples show.

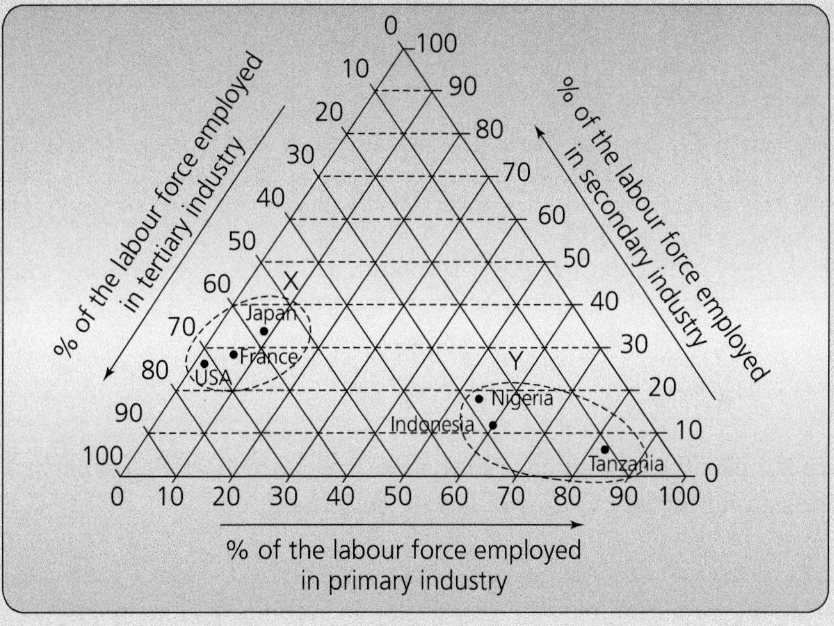

Figure 6

Cambridge 0460 Paper 2 Q5 inc Fig 8 June 2003

Divided bar charts

Figure 7 will, when completed, show the employment structure of three countries in different stages of economic development.

5. Using the information given below, complete the graph to show the employment structure of Peru. **[2]**
   Primary industry 40%
   Secondary industry 18%
   Tertiary industry 42%
6. Which country has the largest percentage of its workforce in secondary industry? **[1]**
7. Using the information in Figure 7, describe what happens to the employment structure of a country as it becomes more developed. **[3]**

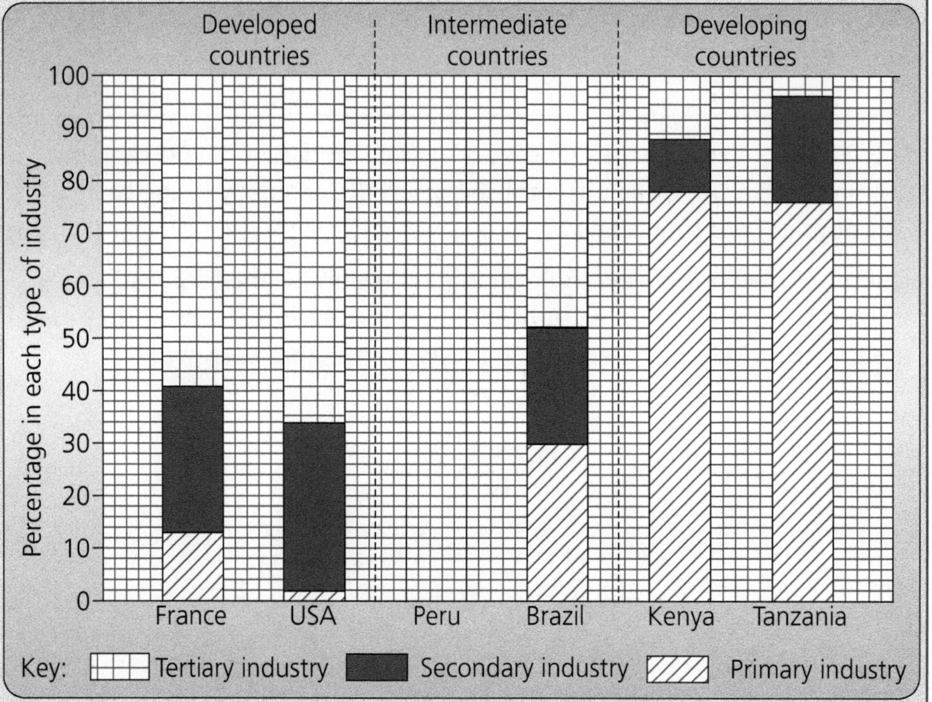

Figure 7

Cambridge 0460 Paper 2 Q6 inc Fig 5 Nov 2004

Figure 8 shows the percentages of the working population in primary, secondary and tertiary industries in four countries.

8. State the percentage of the population in secondary industry in the United Kingdom. **[1]**
9. The percentages of working population for Egypt are primary 56%, secondary 8%, and tertiary 36%.
   (a) Complete Figure 8 by adding the information for Egypt. Use the key provided. **[2]**

In the following part of this question it goes on to ask you to add some information to a triangular graph.

(b) Plot the information for Egypt on the triangular graph (Figure 9). Show the position with a labelled dot. **[2]**

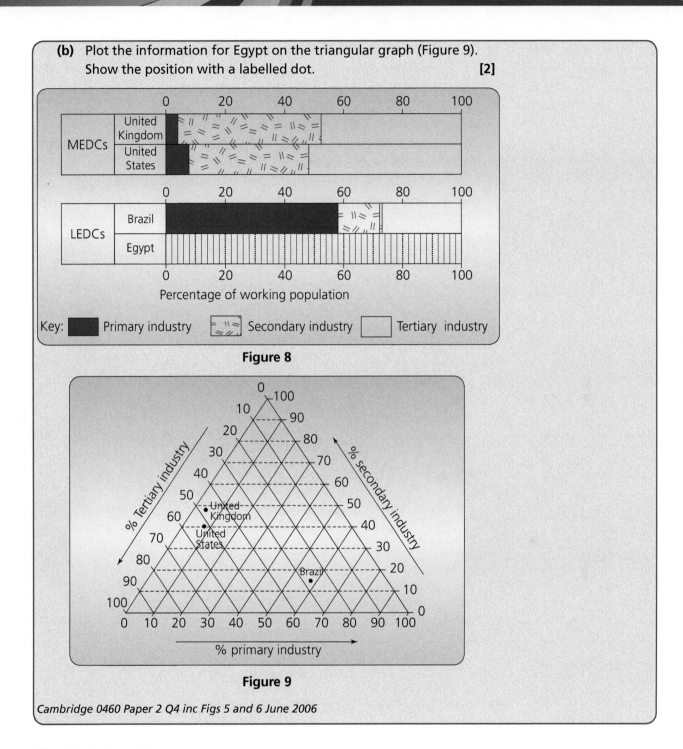

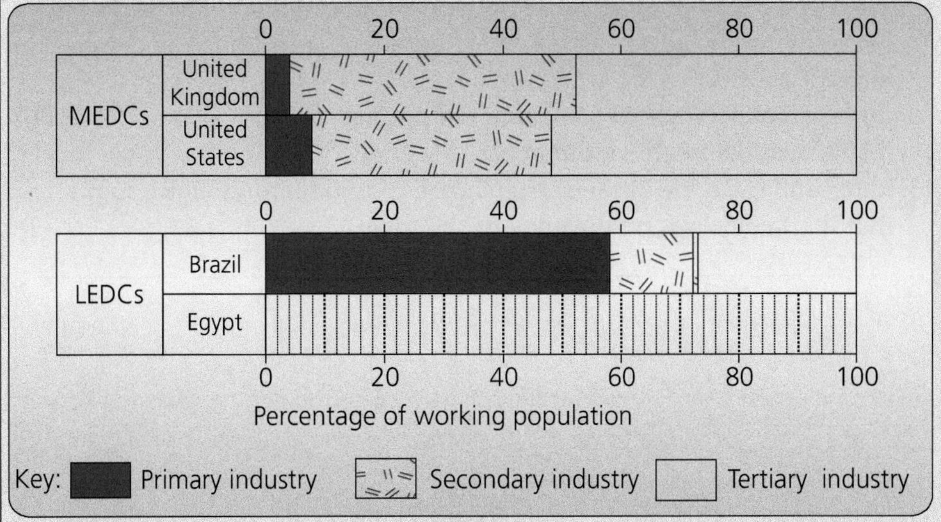

Figure 8

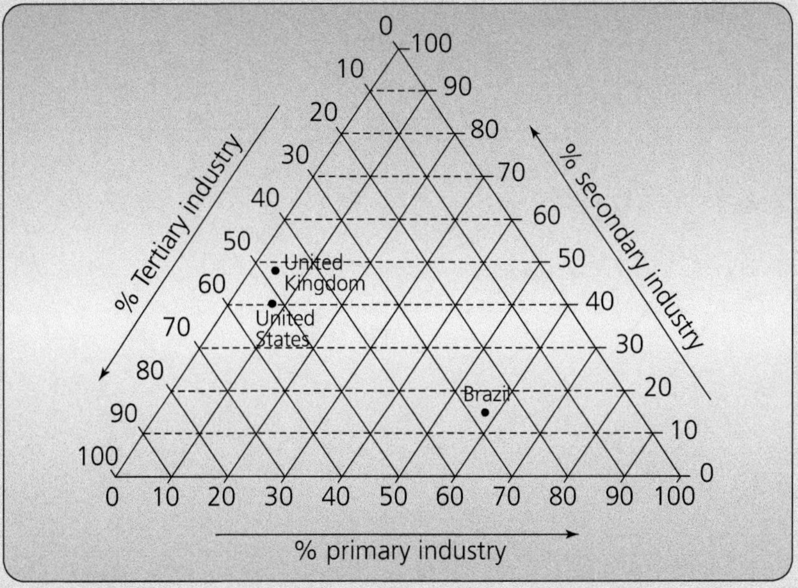

Figure 9

Cambridge 0460 Paper 2 Q4 inc Figs 5 and 6 June 2006

Radial graphs

An example of this type of graph is shown in the following question. This graph allows both direction and distance to be shown on one diagram.

Study the diagram (Figure 10). It shows how far members of a family have to travel from their home to reach different services in the town.

10. In which of the sectors shown on Figure 10 would you place a youth club? **[1]**

11. (a) How far would members of the family have to travel to visit the sports centre? **[1]**

(b) How far would a family member have to travel to the bingo hall? **[1]**

12. Place the following services on the diagram (Figure 10) in the correct sector:

(a) A secondary school 4 kilometres from home, **[1]**

(b) A bar 2 kilometres from home. **[1]**

13. Name and state the distance from home of two features which suggest that the family lives on the edge of the town. **[2]**

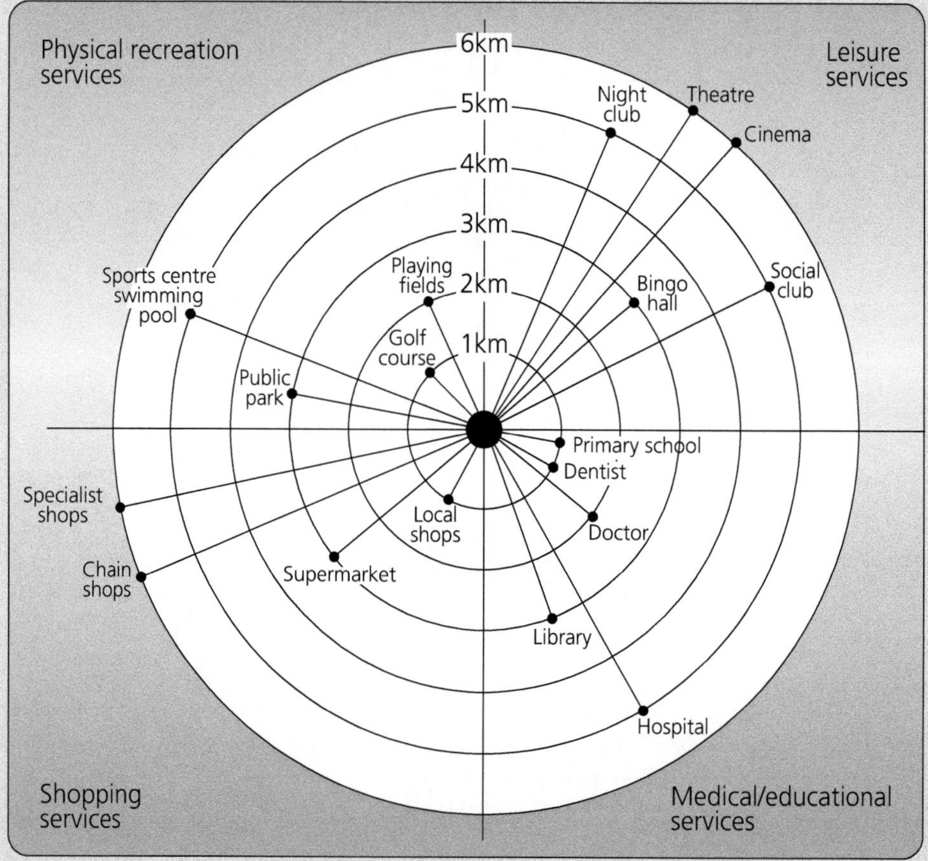

Figure 10

Cambridge 0460 Paper 2 Q2 inc Fig 2 June 2003

Line and bar graphs

These are often used for showing temperature and rainfall/precipitation, as the examples shown below.

14. (a) Describe the main features of the climate of an area of tropical rain (evergreen) forest shown in Figure 11. **[4]**

Or, a typical climate graph, on a typical climate graph, may combine both the rainfall and the temperature, as in the first example question below.

Study the climate graph (Figure 12) for a town in Nigeria, Africa.

15. (a) How much rain fell in the month of July? **[1]**

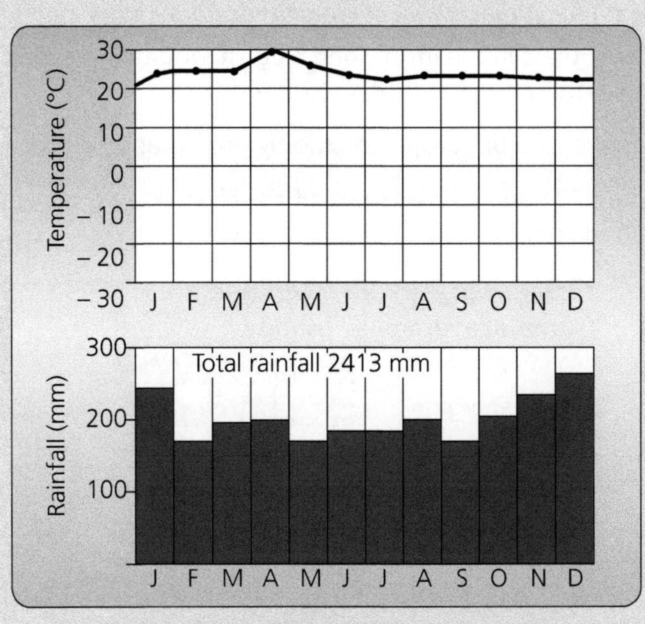

Figure 11

Cambridge 0460 Paper 2 Q4 inc Fig 5 June 2003

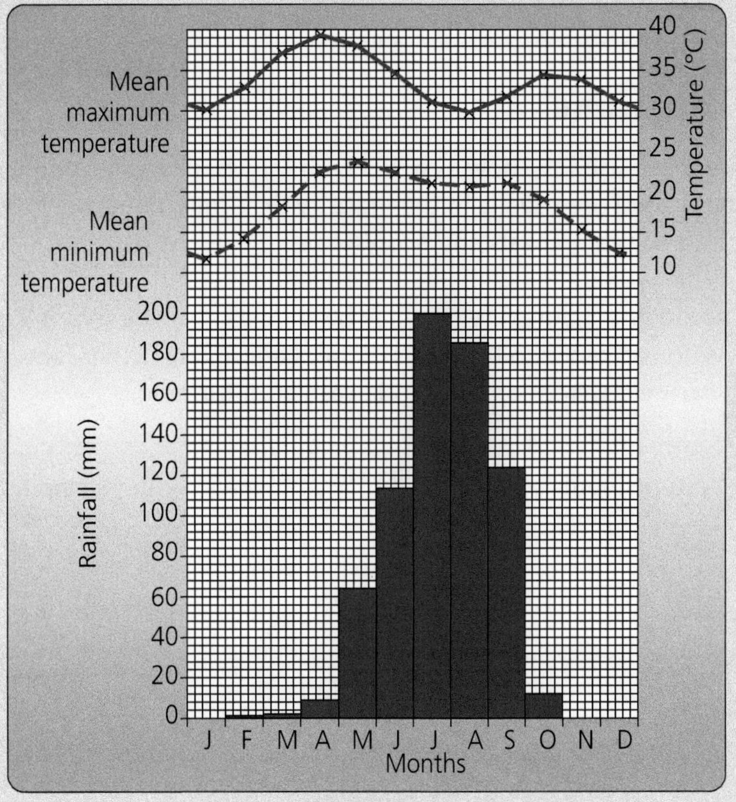

Figure 12

Cambridge 0460 Paper 2 Q4 Fig 3 June 2005

(b) What was the highest temperature reached during the year? **[1]**

(c) What was the average daily range of temperature in December? **[1]**

16. Why does the average temperature fall between May and August? **[1]**

17. Explain why the climate in July and August would be uncomfortable for people from temperate latitudes visiting this area. **[2]**

Another example of a bar graph commonly used is as follows.

18. Study Figure 13 which shows some of the changes in global energy use from 1990 to 2000.

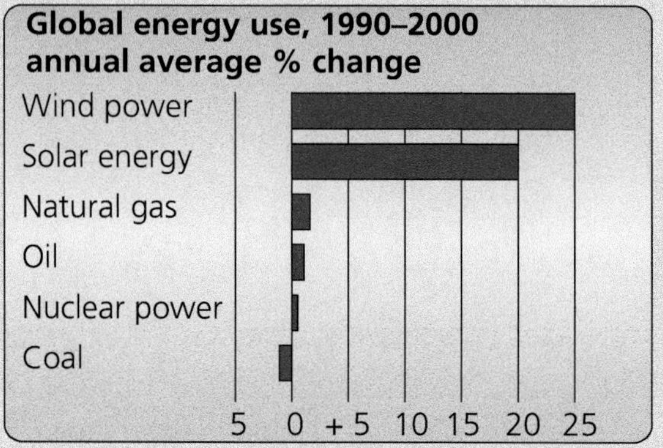

Figure 13

Cambridge 0460 Paper 2 Q6 inc Fig 10 June 2003

Flow diagrams

These are often used to show **systems** with **inputs, processes** and **outputs**. The systems used are usually in the industry or farming questions, but they can be used in rivers, coasts and ecosystems.

Mentioned here is a farming example.

Figure 14 shows a diagram which may be used to describe a farming system. With reference to the ideas in the diagram and other facts you may know, describe a system of small-scale cash-crop farming. **[10]**

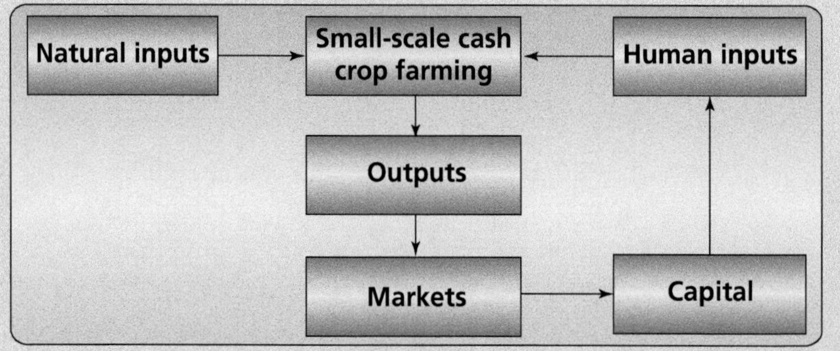

Figure 14

Cambridge 0460 Paper 2 Q 5 (c) inc Fig 9 June 2003

Scatter graphs

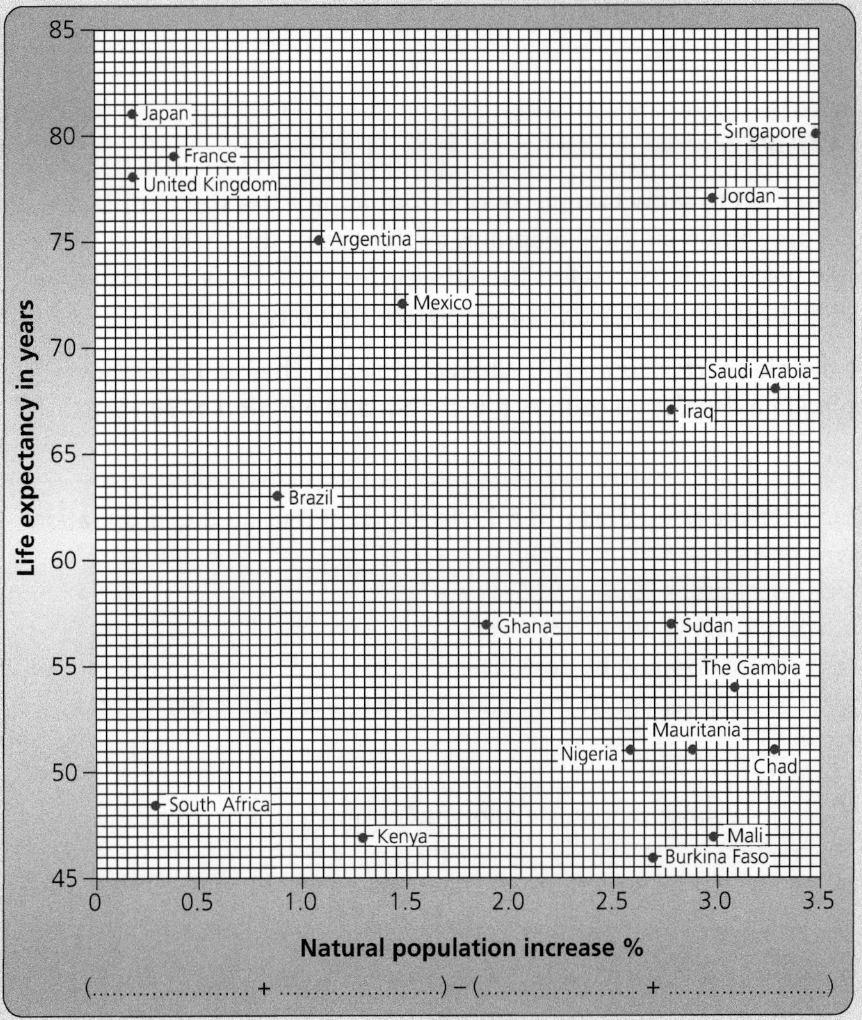

Figure 15

Cambridge 0460 Paper 2 Q6 inc Fig 6 June 2005

These are usually used to show and compare a wide range of data, as the population example here shows.

19. Figure 15 shows details of natural population increase and life expectancy in a number of selected countries in the year 2001.

(a) Which country, shown on Figure 15, has a natural population increase of 2.9% and a life expectancy of 51 years? **[1]**

(b) Which country, shown on Figure 15, has the lowest natural population increase and the highest life expectancy? **[1]**

(c) On Figure 15, mark the position of and name Pakistan, which has a natural population increase of 2.1% and a life expectancy 61 years. **[1]**

20. Explain the meaning of

(a) Life expectancy,

(b) Natural population increase. **[2]**

21. Complete the statement below Figure 15 to explain the total change of a country's population. Use the terms death rate, emigration, birth rate and immigration in your answer. **[2]**

Pie charts

These are used to show **two** pieces of information – the **size** of different samples are shown on these diagrams by the size of the circle used – in the example below, it is total sales. Then the circles themselves are divided to allow you to **compare** the types and relative amounts of sales.

Study the pie charts (Figure 16). When completed, they will show how shopping in a developed country has changed in a period of 30 years.

22. Complete the pie chart for the 1990s (Figure 16) using the information given below:
    Small, local shops 25%
    Supermarkets/hypermarkets 65%
    Mail order (Shopping by post) 5%. **[2]**
23. State the changes which took place in shopping during the 30 year period. **[4]**

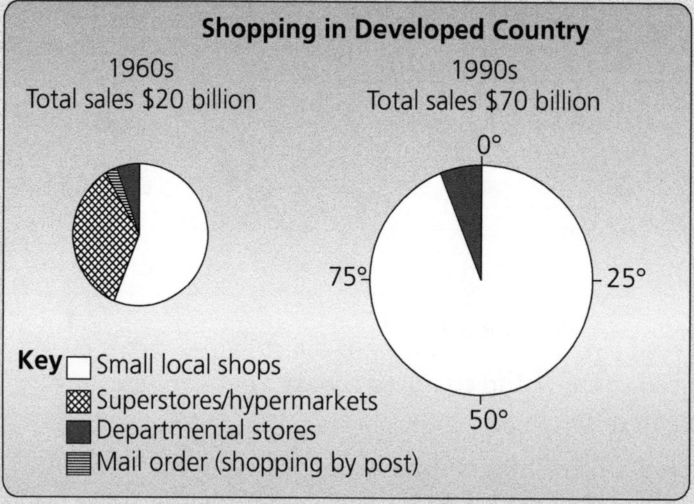

Figure 16

Cambridge 0460 Paper 2 Q3 inc Fig 2 June 2005

Tables of data

These may provide information on physical phenomena such as river discharges and flood events, size of earthquakes, on economic activities, on population/settlement, on agricultural and manufacturing output etc.

Photograph A

You may be asked to describe and analyse features and trends from the data provided, as in the example below. You may also be asked to suggest an appropriate type of graph on which you could plot the data provided.

24. What is meant by urban area?

25. Study Figure 17 which shows data about the quality of life in nine large urban areas, along with Photography A, taken in New York, USA.

(a) Use Figure 17 to name an urban area where:

(i) Housing is overcrowded,

(ii) Air quality is poor. **[2]**

26. Using information from Figure 17, identify three differences between the quality of life of people living in Shanghai and New York. **[3]**

	Socio-economic indicators			Environmental indicators		
Urban Area	**Persons per room**	**% homes with water & electricity**	**Murders per 100, 000**	**Levels of measured noise (1–10)**	**Mean traffic speed (km/h in rush hour)**	**Levels of measured air pollution (1–10)**
Tokyo	0.9	100	1.4	4	44.8	4
Mexico City	1.9	94	27.6	6	12.8	9
Sao Paulo	0.8	93	26.0	6	24.0	4
New York	0.5	99	12.8	8	13.9	5
Shanghai	2.0	95	2.5	5	24.5	4
Los Angeles	0.4	100	12.4	6	30.4	7
Kolkata	3.0	60	1.1	4	21.3	10
Mumbai	4.2	83	1.1	5	16.6	7
Beijing	1.6	89	2.5	4	41.1	10

Note: where 1–10 scale is used 1 is low and 10 is high

Figure 17

Cambridge 0460 Paper 1 Q2 inc Fig 3 June 2006

Written material

This may be extracts from books, periodicals and newspapers and you will be expected to comprehend and show an understanding of the information. Two examples are given below.

27. Study Figure 18, an extract about population growth in Japan.

(a) Suggest reasons why Japan has an ageing population. **[3]**

(b) Suggest the likely effects of this population trend on the Japanese economy by 2050. **[5]**

28. Explain why the governments of some countries may be concerned by a rapid growth of population. You may refer to examples which you have studied. **[7]**

Population crisis in Japan

Japan's population growth has slowed to the lowest rate since the 1940s. In 1999, Japan's population grew by 0.16% to reach 126.7 million. Of that number, children under 14 made up about 14.8% of the population, a record low. By comparison, the same group in 1949 represented 35.5 per cent of the population. A United Nations population report indicates that Japan's population is expected to fall to 105 million by 2050, with the average age expected to rise from 41 to 49. The proportion of the population 65 and older is expected to grow from 17 per cent to 32 per cent over the same period.

Figure 18

Cambridge 0460 Paper 1 Q1 Fig 2 June 2006

29. Study Figure 19 (a and b), based on a newspaper article about traffic in Auckland, New Zealand.

(a) How do the results of the 'rush hour challenge' reported in Figure 19 (a and b) show that there is traffic congestion in Auckland? **[3]**

(b) Explain why traffic congestion is a problem in many large urban areas. **[5]**

No Contest as bikes hit heavy traffic

Transport: Cars, buses and bikes raced to the city in rush hour challenge. **Pedal power ruled.**

Cyclist left car drivers behind yesterday as they pedalled their bikes through Auckland's slow traffic in the morning rush hour.

In the Auckland Commuter Challenge four sets of cyclists, car drivers and buses raced into the centre of Auckland.

The cyclists were quickest with an average time of 26 minutes 51 seconds. This is the latest demonstration of Auckland's traffic crisis, says Cycle Auction Auckland, which organised the event.

About 6 per cent of commuters travel by bike or foot, 7 per cent by public transport and the rest in their cars.

Traffic congestion is getting worse as 3 per cent more cars each year are using roads that have not been significantly improved.

Tuesday's announcement of a $1.6 billion funding package to improve the road network is hoped to get Auckland moving.

Figure 19 (a)

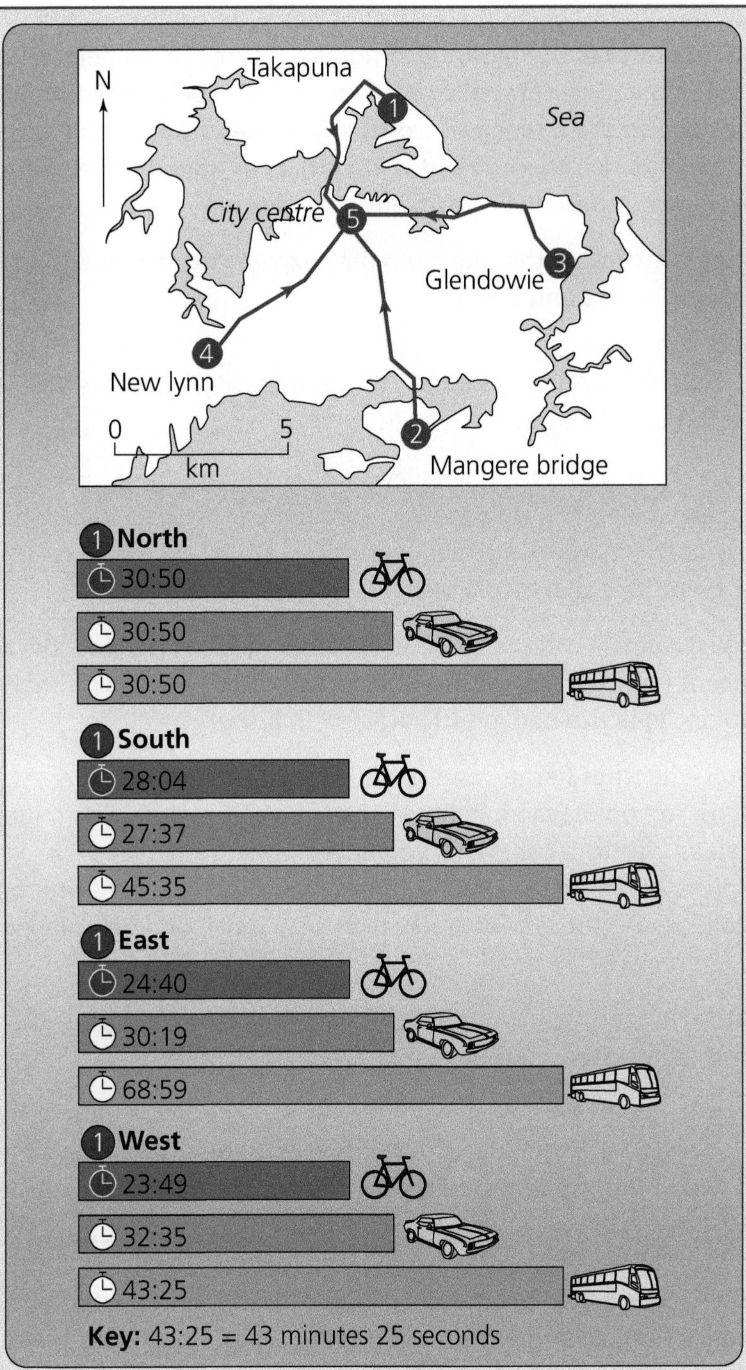

Figure 19 (b)

Cambridge 0460 Paper 1 Q2 (a and b) inc Fig 4 June 2006

Photographic and pictorial material (including field sketches)

Questions usually use ***oblique*** photographs. You should be able to describe the human and physical landscapes (landforms, natural vegetation, land-use and settlement) and other geographical features from photographs.

You may be asked to give simple descriptions. Questions may also use simple ***field sketches*** of physical and human landscapes to help in your understanding and geographical description and labelling (annotation). You may need to use a range of words in your descriptions and each of these will get marks. Therefore, it is just a matter of you remembering to look and name or describe certain obvious features.

In a ***natural landscape***, the questions may expect you to identify and use the following words and terms.

High, Low, Steep, Gently sloping, Mountains, Hills, Cliffs, vertical slopes, bare rock, Loose rock, scree.

Valleys – small valleys, large valleys, V shaped valleys – wide or narrow V shaped valleys, tributary valleys, confluence (where two or more valleys or rivers meet), gorges, waterfalls, rapids, oxbow lakes, river cliffs, point bars (slip off slopes).

Rivers, streams – wide or narrow river channels, fast or slow flowing, turbulent (white water), muddy/full of sediment, clear, lakes, ponds, reservoirs, well drained, poorly drained (marshy).

Coastal – beaches (large, long small, wide narrow), spits, bars, lagoons, tombolos, sand, pebbles, marshes (salt water),cliffs (high, low, steep, vertical, bare rock, vegetated, collapsed), wave cut platforms, caves, arches, stacks, stumps, geos (caves where the roof has collapsed), cliffs – with cracks or faults, joints, bedding planes, layers of rock.

Vegetation – forests, woods, trees (tall or small), shrubs, grass, bare ground, deforested, cleared.

Farmland – fields (large or small), arable or pastoral farming or both, crops, hedges, shelter belts (trees grown on hedges to protect land from wind erosion), fences, ditches.

In **cities and towns** you may have – shops, offices, banks, restaurants/cafes, hotels flats, apartments, residential/housing, multi storey car park, bus station, tall/high/high rise/multi-storey buildings, low rise buildings, modern/new/old buildings, flat roofs, steep roofs, high density/low density buildings, concrete/brick/glass, balconies.

In **rural areas** you may have villages, individual houses, farmhouses, single storey, two storey, etc. Farms, farm land, fields, crops orchards, woods, forests.

For streets and roads – narrow or wide, straight or winding, sealed or unsealed (sealed means covered in bitumen/tarmac, or unsealed not covered in bitumen/tarmac) pavements, motorways, roundabouts cars, lorries/trucks, buses, coaches, cycles, motorbikes.

Lastly, cartoons may be used to illustrate a geographical theme for you to interpret and analyse.

Geographical skills for Paper 4 of examination

Questions may set a series of tasks on this paper on issues relating to one or more of the topics you have covered in the Geography syllabus. You may need additional materials for this exam such as a ***ruler, protractor and calculator***.

Questions may cover the topics that could be studied by students who get the opportunity to carry out Geography fieldwork, either ***inside*** (as in a weather study), or ***outside*** (as in a river, coast or urban study) the school grounds. For the two fieldwork topics that are chosen you are expected to understand:

- The ***aims*** of the questions or hypotheses chosen
- The ***enquiry skills*** that can be used to ***collect*** data
- The ***different types of presentation techniques*** that can be used to ***display*** data.
- How the data can be **analysed**.
- How the enquiry can be **concluded** and **evaluated**.

Enquiry skills

Putting together, formulating and the aims of questions/ hypotheses

Fieldwork enquiries may be put together so that either a **question** can be answered or a **hypothesis** can be proved or disproved. A **hypothesis** is a statement that can be tested. Some people when doing a fieldwork project prefer to use either a question, or a hypothesis.

The questions or hypotheses chosen may investigate a geographical idea or concept. It is very easy to change a question into a hypothesis and vice versa depending on your preference. For example, an urban fieldwork study may choose to examine the CBD of a town or city. One of many possible topics could be a study of the types of shops, comparison or convenience, found in the CBD compared to other parts of the town or city.

A question that could be investigated is, '***Does the CBD have the highest concentration of comparison shops***?'

If a ***hypothesis*** is used, rather than a ***question***, the wording can be slightly changed so that it becomes: '***A CBD has the highest concentration of comparison shops***'. The field trip is then spent collecting relevant data, analysing it and then drawing conclusions to **either** answer the question **or** prove/disprove the hypothesis. Further examples of typical fieldwork exercises are to follow.

The enquiry skills that can be used to collect data

Questions may test your knowledge and application of the methods used in collecting data during fieldwork. The most common methods used are explained below.

Questionnaires – Questionnaires are used to gain information from people about themselves and their opinions. The questionnaires can either be completed by asking people personally or by handing them out to people to fill in. Questionnaires are most often used in the ***Human Geography*** topics. For example, in trying to find the ***sphere of influence*** of towns, the ***use of services*** such as libraries, the different ***shopping habits*** of people and where they prefer to shop for comparison and convenience goods, a farm study, a factory or industrial study, peoples preferred leisure activities, tourism – such as finding where people have travelled from and what form of transport they used, or attitudes of the public to the development of a resource like a quarry.

A typical exam question may ask you to consider the important factors influencing the successful design of questionnaires, for example the layout or format of the questions, the appropriate wording of the questions so that people can understand them easily and without you having to explain them to each person, and the number of questions – so that people do not have to spend too much time completing the questionnaire.

You may also be asked to look at the ***practical considerations*** of conducting a questionnaire. For example, the sampling methods being used – are you attempting to question everybody or are you going to attempt to cover half the population or less; or every tenth person that passes you in the street? Carrying out a quick ***pilot survey*** of perhaps 10–20 people to find out if your questions are easily understood and if you have covered all the topics and options you need to. For example, has the questionnaire listed all the possible types of transport used by people to get to a shop, town or leisure centre; and have the correct locations, days and times been chosen to conduct the survey successfully.

Observation – Careful observation is an important enquiry skill to help you collect data including the recording of the land use in an urban area – such as types of shops, offices, industry and the types, size, number of storeys and age of buildings: or observations of river or coastal features. Maps, recording sheets, and annotated/labelled field sketches or photographs may all be used to record student observations.

Counts – Pedestrian and traffic counts are two important and commonly used examples of this enquiry skill. You may be asked if appropriate methods were used for recording the counts and if the layout of recording sheets, instructions and the necessary information required in identifying the sheet when analysing the count afterwards (i.e. time, date, location and name of the person doing the recording).

Measurement – When recording measurements, you should carefully plan the layout of the recording sheet, the location of measuring equipment and instruments and the sampling methods you use to provide reliable data. Knowledge of the simple field study equipment used in measurement may be required such as the following.

- A ***quadrat*** – these are used so that you can study a small manageable area of the whole area you are investigating. They are made out of plastic, wood metal or string – or combinations of those things! They are square in shape and have sides that are normally half a metre in length. So that you do not pick a place that has lots of plants, big pebbles, etc. in it you normally throw it away from you or back over your shoulder – taking care not to hit anyone with it! You then record what is inside the area covered by the quadrat. To make it more representative of the total area you may do this several times and take an average of your readings.
- A ***clinometer*** – this is used to measure the angle of a slope – such as on a beach, a river channel or a valley side.
- A ***pebbleometer*** (a pebbleometer is a board containing measured squares of different sizes through which pebbles are passed to assess their size) or **callipers** (these are two short lengths of metal hinged together, and a ruler) are used to measure the axes of pebbles found on a beach or a river bed.
- ***Scale of roundness*** – this is used to measure the 'roundness' of a piece of rock. The longer a rock is rolled down a river bed or rolled up and down a beach by swash and backwash, the process of **attrition** will make it both rounder and smaller. It is a very common fieldwork technique. A commonly used scale is shown below.

Roundness score chart

Shape	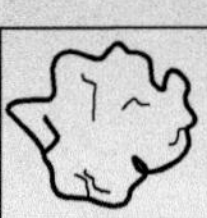			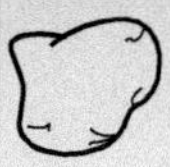	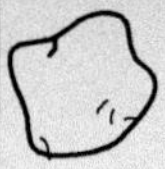	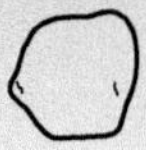
Score	**0**	**1**	**2**	**3**	**4**	**5**
Description	very angular	angular	a little angular	a little rounded	rounded	very rounded

Figure 20

Cambridge 0460 Paper 4/43 Q1 Fig 3 Nov 2011

Sampling – sampling is used because during the short period of time spent doing fieldwork it is normally impossible to measure every river channel variables at every metre from its source to its mouth, every pebble on a beach, question and interview every person in a town or CBD, etc. Sampling reduces the time taken to collect data, but sampling may miss important sites.

Types of sampling are used commonly – ***systematic, random*** and ***stratified*** sampling.

Systematic sampling involves regular/organised/orderly sampling – for example taking a sample every 50 metres down a stream or river, giving a questionnaire to every 20th person that passes you, measuring a beach profile at regular intervals across a beach, etc. The advantages of this method compared to random sampling are that there is no student bias or choice in the site location. This makes it a fairer, more representative area that is covered; it is easier to compare; and it is an easier/faster/quicker method.

Random sampling involves choosing locations at random in a study area. For example, throwing a quadrat behind you so that you do not pick out an area with nothing or everything in it; or picking people of your own age group to survey about shopping habits – random sampling may be very prone to student bias/error.

Stratified sampling can be used with either systematic or random sampling when there are significant sub groups in an area being studied. It is used to make sure that the sampling adequately covers these sub groups – such as different rock types or soil types in an area of farming. Therefore once the sub groups have been recognised the whole sample is stratified to ensure that each sub group has been sampled. Each sub group can then be sampled systematically or randomly.

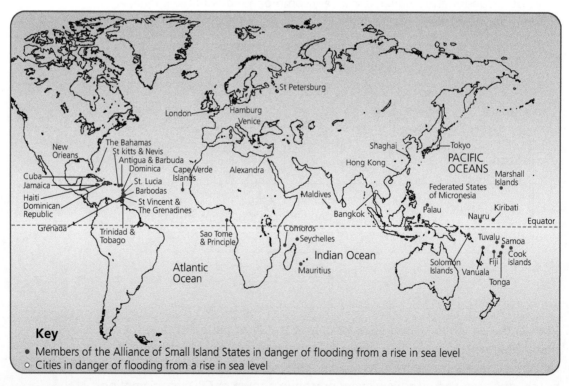

Figure 21 (a) How global warming threatens some major world cities and island nations

Cambridge 0460 Paper 2 Fig 13 Nov 2002

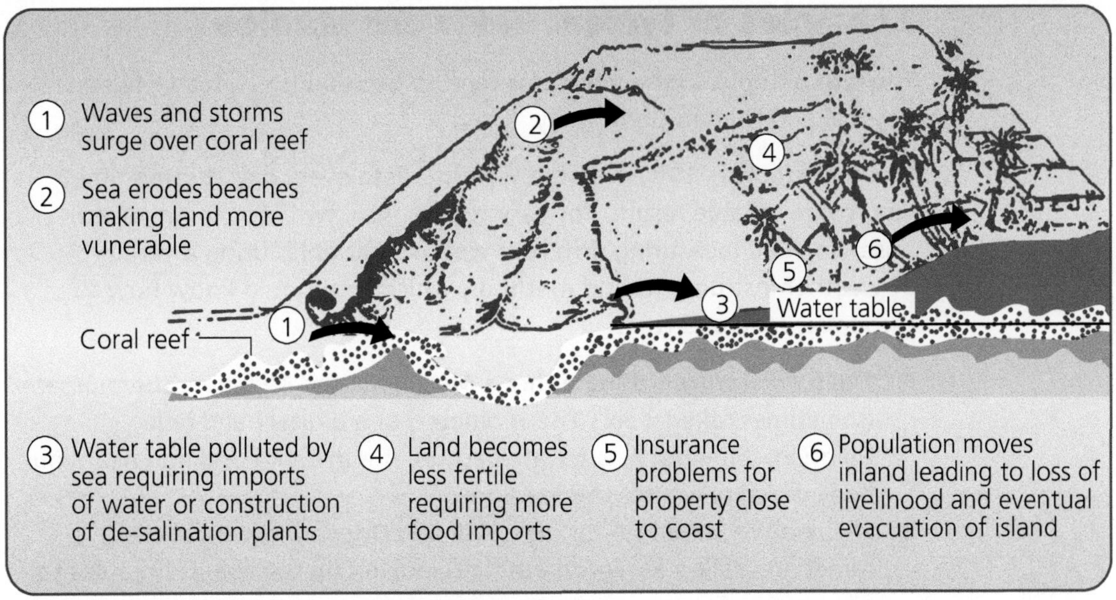

Figure 21 (b) Stages in the flooding of island States as a result of a rise in sea level

Data presentation techniques

You should be aware of the various techniques that are used to present data and if only one method has been used in a question suggest alternatives. These techniques include the following.

1. Various types of ***graphs*** – for example, line graphs, bar graphs, divided bar graphs, wind rose graphs, histograms and scatter graphs.
2. Maps – for example, isoline maps.
3. Diagrams – for example, flow diagrams.

Analysis

You should be able to describe the ***patterns*** in the data presented in graphs and tables of results – the means and modes, the extreme values found and be able to use your geographical knowledge and understanding in the simple interpretation of the data.

Formation of conclusions

Using the evidence from the data, you should be able to do the following.

- Make judgements/conclusions on how correct/valid the original hypothesis is or aims of the field study.
- Assess the reliability of the collected data.
- Give a critical evaluation of the data collection methods used in the study.
- Suggest ways in which the study could have been improved. This part will often involve you in saying that with more time and with more and/or better, equipment the study could have been improved.

Examples of typical fieldwork studies

The typical topics in the questions tend to be equally divided between Physical and Human Geography.

Weather studies – Why measure weather data every day at same time? To provide reliable results, for easy comparison, with no bias involved, observing and measuring different weather variables using a variety of weather instruments and methods, which you should know how to recognise, read and reset.

1. ***The temperature*** – using either a ***Maximum and Minimum thermometer*** (sometimes called a Six's Thermometer) or a digital hand held thermometer – not as accurate because it is in your hand and near your body which may alter the readings.
2. The ***relative humidity*** – using a ***Wet and Dry Bulb thermometer***, sometimes called a ***Hygrometer*** and looking up the results in tables to give the reading as a per cent.
3. ***Rainfall*** – using a ***Rain Gauge***.
4. ***Wind Speed*** – using a ***Cup Anemometer***.
5. ***Wind Direction*** – using a wind vane. The results can be recorded on a ***radial graph*** – a ***wind rose***. These are used to show the number of days that the wind blows from a certain compass direction. It uses 8 points of the compass – North, North East, East, etc. Each segment on the lines is one day. When completed, it allows you to see how often the wind blows from a particular direction. They are normally used to show a month of daily readings. The most common direction is called the ***prevailing wind*** (Figure 22).

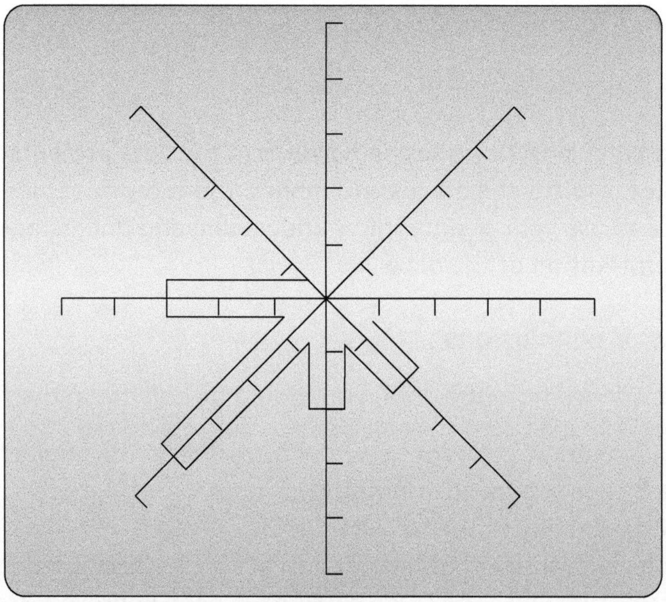

Figure 22

Cambridge 0460 Paper 4 Q2 Fig 9 Nov 2008

6. ***Atmospheric Pressure*** – using an ***Aneroid Barometer*** (often just called a Barometer).
7. How to measure and reset a barometer – after each daily reading the index pointer on the outside of the glass is moved so that it lies over the top pressure indicator pointer on the inside of the glass. By doing this it allows you to see any changes in the pressure from the previous readings.
8. ***Cloud Amount*** – calculating how many eighths of the sky is covered in cloud.

Sometimes a ***Stevenson Screen*** may be part of the study so you need to know the instruments kept in one of these (Max and Min Thermometer, Wet and Dry Bulb Thermometer and, sometimes, a Barometer). The fieldwork investigations used may include the hypothesis testing and measuring of the following.

- Rainfall using rain gauges; where they should be sited and how the data is collected and then displayed on bar and dispersion graphs.
- Wind direction looking at the siting of wind vanes and displaying data using wind roses.
- Atmospheric pressure with the use of a barometer and how to record data from it.
- Wind speed using a standard conventional, and a digital anemometer. Sample size and site locations for measuring wind speed.
- The use and siting of a Stevenson Screen; the instruments inside it – max and min thermometer and wet and dry bulb thermometer (hygrometer); the use of relative humidity tables; and use of secondary data such as previously recorded data to compare readings.
- A microclimate – such as the school grounds and the problems of siting instruments close to buildings and trees. The advantages of using a hand held digital thermometer and a digital hygrometer.
- The differences between climates of tropical rainforest and a desert. The use of scatter graphs and working out a line of best fit.

River studies – involves observing and investigating river variables (a river variable is a feature or process that changes as you travel down a river or stream from its source to its mouth).

The most common river variables studied may include the following.

1. ***Channel width*** measuring the distance from one river bank to the opposite river bank.
2. ***Channel depth*** – the depth of the water in the river; normally you measure at a quarter, half and three quarters of the way across the river channel and then take an average of the 3 readings.
3. ***River velocity*** – the speed of the river flow, normally measured in metres per second. This is usually done by timing a float, such as an easily seen orange, over a distance of 10 metres and repeating the exercise 3 times to get an average reading.

4. The ***size and the shape of the pebbles and rocks*** found on the bed of a river – called its **bedload**. The size is normally found by measuring the longest axis of a rock or pebble. It is measured using a ruler or special ***callipers*** or ***pebbleometer***, while the shape is done by observing how round or angular a rock or pebble is. A sample of at least 20–50 pebbles is taken to give a good ***representative*** sample at each site.

The type of fieldwork investigations used may include the hypothesis testing and measuring of the following.

- A study of pebble size and shape measurement in a desert wadi.
- The measurement of the river variables of width, depth, velocity/speed, channel cross sectional area and the wetted perimeter. An example of a river channel recording sheet, depth measurements are done systematically across the channel at half metre intervals is shown below.

		Depth in metres at distances from left bank													
Site	Total width (m)	0.5m	1.0m	1.5m	2.0m	2.5m	3.0m	3.5m	4.0m	4.5m	5.0m	5.5m	6.0m	Wetted perimeter (m)	Discharge (m^3/sec)
A	1.40	0.15	0.10											1.50	0.01
B	2.31	0.12	0.15	0.30	0.20									2.50	0.09
C	6.42	0.20	0.25	0.28	0.30	0.32	0.35	0.48	0.48	0.50	0.35	0.36	0.28		1.25

Figure 23

Cambridge Paper 4 Q1 Table 1 Nov 2007

- Drawing and labelling channel cross sections, including meander cross sections.
- Completing and drawing histogram/bar graphs.
- Drawing river valley long and cross profiles using distance and height data.
- The advantages and disadvantages of field sketches.
- Types of sampling – random and systematic.

An example of a river with tributaries and channel cross sections drawn is shown here (Figure 24).

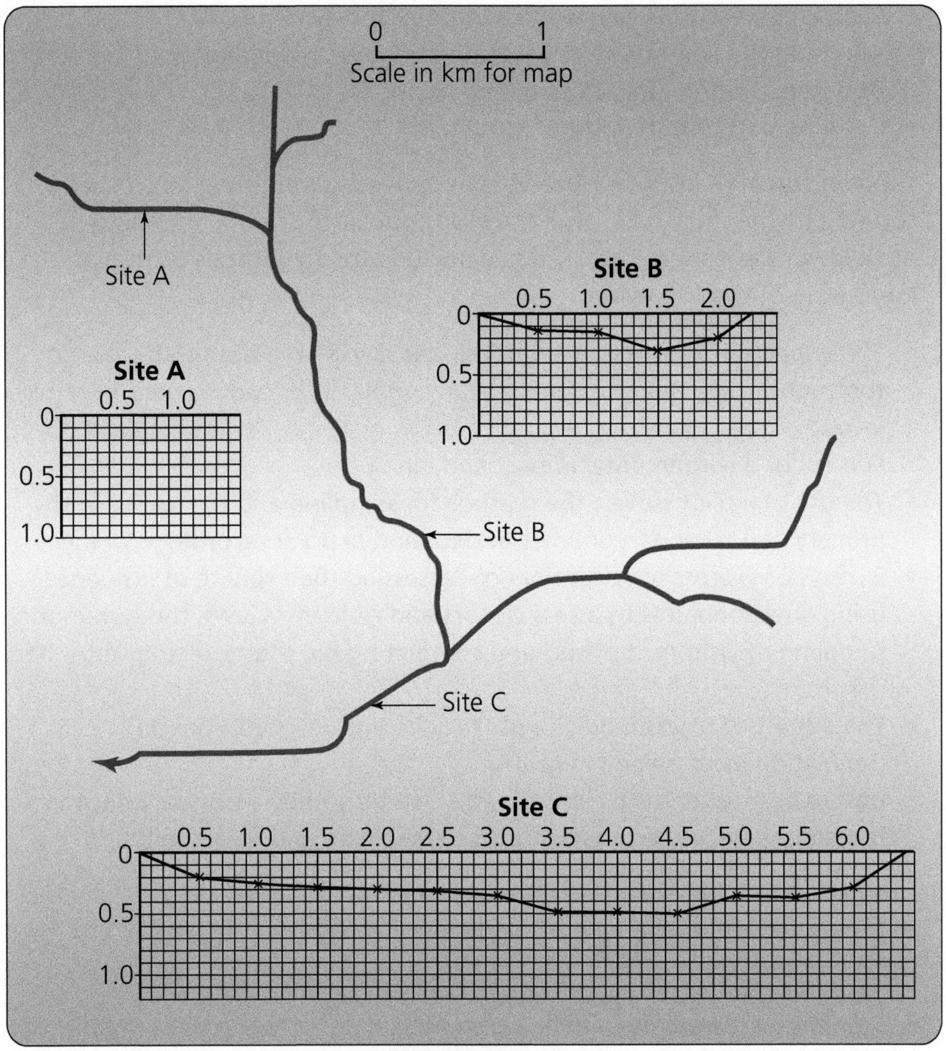

Figure 24

Cambridge 0460 Paper 4 Q1 Fig 1 Nov 2007

Coastal studies – involve observing and measuring the following.

1. The length and angle of the beach from the edge of the sea to the cliff or sea wall – called the beach profile.
2. The size and shape of pebbles – in the same method as with river pebbles.
3. The movement of pebbles and sand on a beach by waves – this is usually to see if sand and pebbles are moving along the beach by the process of Long shore drift.

The type of fieldwork investigations may include the hypothesis testing and measuring of the following.

- Coastal beach surveys investigating wave processes, the types of waves – constructive and destructive, long shore drift, measuring and drawing beach profiles.

- Sediment measuring and using a bi-polar survey.
- Assessing the limitations of data and the advantages and disadvantages of systematic and random sampling methods.
- Drawing and completing bar graphs.

Tourism studies – involves observing and investigating the impact that tourist activities may have on honeypot/popular tourist resort. The type of fieldwork investigations used may include the hypothesis testing and measuring of the following.

- The ***impacts of tourists on a natural landscape*** – measuring the size of footpaths, using quadrats, pedestrian counts, litter counts, measure noise levels.
- Surveys of environmental impact and land use.
- The use of a pilot survey, the reasons for sampling and the use of both primary and secondary sources of data and bi polar recording.
- Surveys of ***visitors*** to ***leisure parks*** – assessing their sphere of influence, using questionnaires to assess visitors and residents views, the systematic sampling of visitors, drawing and completing pie charts, pictographs, bar graphs.
- The ***impact of tourism*** on a town and the impact of tourism on population increase and migration.
- Before or after the trip, the students can try to find secondary data to research previous records of traffic flows, litter and noise pollution.

Urban CBD Studies – involves observing and investigating the central areas of towns and cities. The type of fieldwork investigations used may include the hypothesis testing and measuring of the following.

- ***Settlement hierarchies*** – building count, survey of services and traffic, best fit line,
- The characteristic features of a **CBD** – by building height, width and function, traffic and pedestrian counts, land values, pedestrian counts, shopkeeper interviews, sampling methods.
- A ***comparison of shops*** using interviews, customer counts, the measurement of shop frontages and their sphere of influence.
- Presenting the data by means of isolines (lines that join places with the same/equal value).

Urban sphere of influence studies – involves observing and delimiting the size and area of influence that a city, town, shop or service, like a hospital, has over its surrounding area. These studies involve looking at ***shopping habits*** – by means of questionnaires, systematic sampling and presenting this information in graphs and diagrams such as proportional bar graphs.

Industry studies – involves observing and investigating the impact an industry or factory has on the environment. This can be done by interviews – using systematic and random sampling, field sketches, and the use of secondary data, systems diagrams and pie charts.

Traffic studies – involves observing and measuring the impact that traffic has on an area. They can involve the use of ***traffic flow surveys*** in a town, using a land use survey and a tally system and then representing the information in flow and proportional squares diagrams.

Some important terms and points explained

Comparison shopping/goods – involves shopping for an item that is bought infrequently and is normally bought after comparing prices. They are usually high value goods with a high profit margin example TV, cars, computer, furniture/shoes/clothes.

Convenience shopping/goods – involves shopping for a low cost item that is bought frequently. They are usually cheaper, low value goods with a low profit margin and are often bought almost every day, example milk/bread/newspapers.

Questionnaires – the problems with these are usually that the people who you want to fill them in, such as shoppers or shopkeepers may be in a hurry; sometimes people cannot understand/remember what you are asking; they are often too subjective/biased/not quantitative; the results may vary with different times of the day and different days of the week.

Use more sites along a river so that you cover more sections of the river; compare the results of different rivers; do surveys at other times of the year so that you can compare winter with summer readings; increase the number of measurements you do at each site, for example, do three velocity/speed measurements instead of one, measure 20–50 pebbles instead of 5–10 at each site; use more accurate instruments, for example use a flow meter to measure velocity instead of measuring the time it takes a float to travel downstream; etc.

Using pacing as a measure of the length of a shop front, etc. – the advantages of pacing are that it is quick/easy/no equipment needed. The disadvantages of pacing are that it is not precise/gives an inaccurate measurement/pace length varies between students!

Why measure weather data every day at same time?

To provide reliable results, for easy comparison, with no bias.

How to measure and reset a barometer – after each daily reading the ***index pointer*** on the outside of the glass is moved so that it lies over the top pressure ***indicator pointer*** on the inside of the glass; By doing this it allows you to see any changes in the pressure from the previous reading.

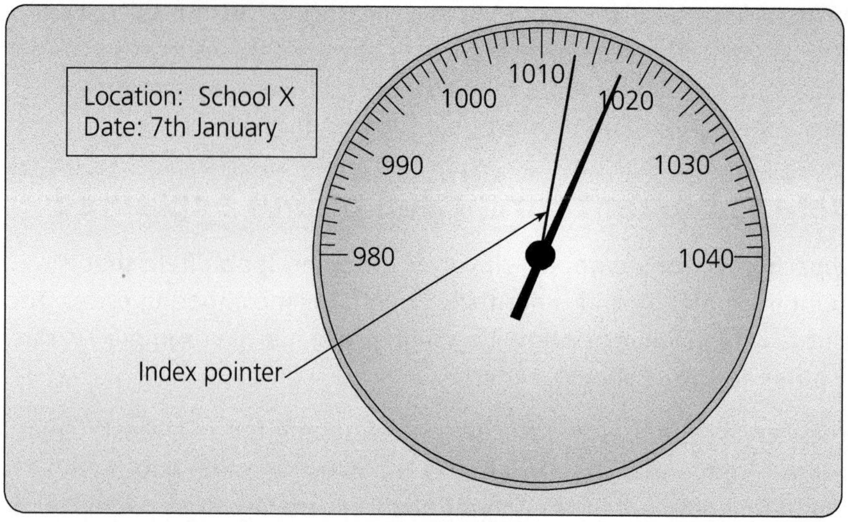

Figure 25

Cambridge 0460 Paper 4/41 Q2 Fig 8 Nov 2011

The advantages and disadvantages of using a hand held digital anemometer or flow meter?

The advantages include that they are quick and more accurate to use and it cuts down the possibility of student error.

The disadvantages include the higher costs of these instruments; they usually need batteries; they are often more likely to go wrong.

What can go wrong, and what are the problems with, data collection methods in a field study?

- Most field studies for students can only be carried out for a short period of time, often only for a few days which allows little time to compare data over a year or more; or compare winter and summer.
- Students are limited to certain locations, along a river or coastline for example – again, often due to limited time.
- The possibility of student error in the siting and use of instruments, such as thermometers or rain gauges, for example, which need to be in an open area away from buildings and trees; with their top raised off the ground so there is no water flowing in to them and no water splashing in to them; away from people and animals where the gauge can be knocked over; sunken in ground for stability and so they cannot be blown over.

Why should students repeat a survey?

The extra information that they gather from repeating a survey may help improve their analysis; they may obtain different results if they repeat a survey at a different time or location; in a survey involving people, the number of people may change during the day or a week; the type of people using a facility may change during a day.

A ***tally system***, used for example in a pedestrian survey, or in recording cars passing a particular location is a fast recording method; it is quick and easy to use, read and to total; it is more accurate than writing down numbers.

When using ***sketch maps*** there are certain essential pieces of information, other than just the location of the map, which should be included when completing a sketch. They should have the date and time added and labels and annotations to highlight important features and processes on the map.

The ***advantages*** of a sketch map is that it gives a visual representation of information and explanations can be added; the ***disadvantages*** are that it depends on the drawing skills of a student; it is sometimes difficult to work out the scale and they can be inaccurate and slow compared to taking a digital photo with a phone camera.

1. ***About the land use in a town*** – Students need to organise themselves into groups and divide the study area in the town make collection easier. This can be made even easier and quicker by doing the survey along a transect, along a road for example and doing a systematic survey. The study will involve students observing and surveying buildings to classify the buildings with regard to their function. The information and data collected should then be recorded, often on a base map. This primary data is data collected during fieldwork by students or a group of students for an investigation as first-hand information and it is not collected by other people. For example, a questionnaire, a traffic or pedestrian count, an interview with somebody; bi-polar surveys; sketches or the students own photographs. Secondary data, such as land values, can be obtained to compare with the primary data. Secondary data is information which students did not collect themselves during a fieldwork investigation. It is the data and information found out either before or after the investigation by the students doing their own research, for example from textbooks, newspapers and the Internet, or maps and censuses.
2. ***About pedestrian or traffic flows*** – Students need to select their sites carefully, possibly at road junctions. Then decide on the length of time that the count will last for – possibly 5–15 minutes. Watches need to be synchronised to make sure the surveys are started at the same time in the different locations. Cars and pedestrians can then be counted as they pass a point.

   Depending on the number of cars or pedestrians, it may be possible to tally/record the number going in different directions – but that may require two different students if there is a high number of cars or pedestrians. The count should be repeated at different times to see if there are differences in traffic or pedestrian flows at different times of the day, or to compare weekends with weekdays.

In other investigations, for example in a coastal tourist or ski resort, the time of year the investigation takes place may be very important – in winter more visitors may be skiing; fewer visitors, if any, may be camping in winter in a coastal tourist resort. Apart from the common methods of displaying data and results such as using line and bar graphs, divided circles and choropleth/shaded maps, there are a number of other simple and easy to use methods. These include the following.

Isolines – Once data has been collected for a town or part of a town the information can often be plotted on a map using isolines. These are lines that join points with the same value. This can be traffic, pedestrians or land values, as on the example that follows, where places with the same land value are joined together.

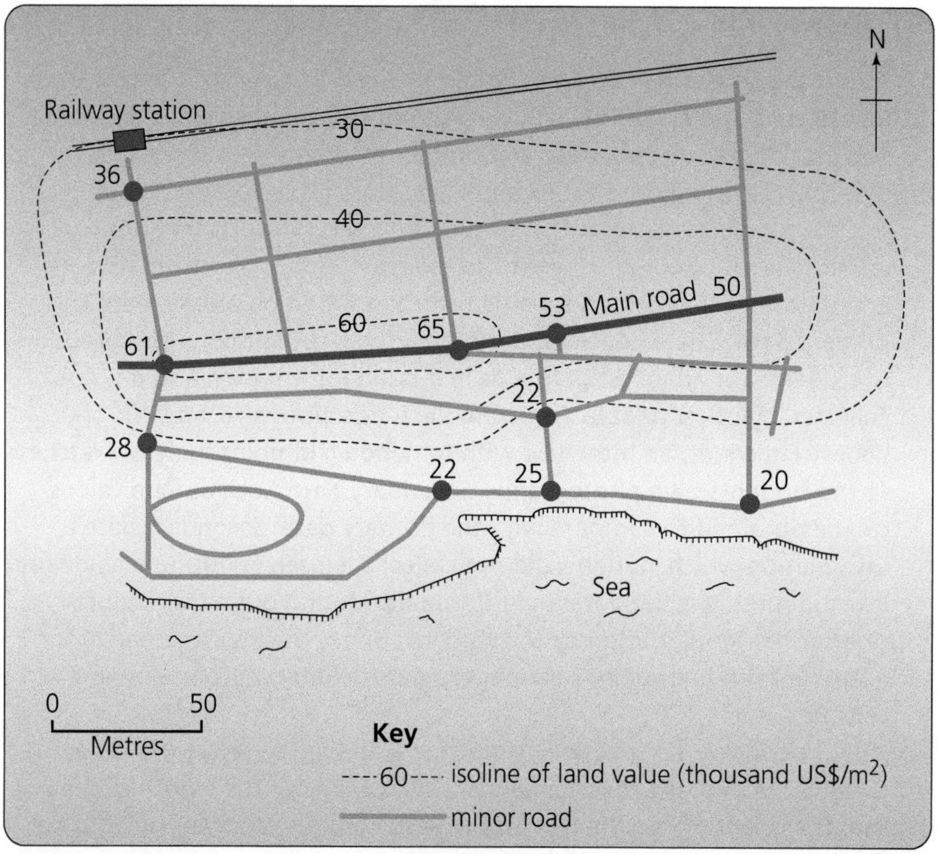

Figure 26

Cambridge 0460 Paper 4 Q1 Fig 3 June 2007

Bi-polar recording systems – The Bi-polar method allows students to assess an area – such as a street, river or beach in a subjective way. It allows students to give a score or grade to a particular location. This can be carried out to compare different locations for pollution with regard to litter, for example, on a beach, in a town, or on a road: or levels of graffiti, etc.

Its disadvantages though are that it does depend on the assessments skills of the students and it is their personal view – so it is subjective. An environmental assessment is shown below.

In a town, along a road or river, or along a beach, students should decide how far apart they wish to make their assessments and either use a tape measure or pace out these distances. They will need to design a recording sheet to score or grade, and then record their findings. At the end of their study, they should add up their scores for each location and compare and analyse their results.

In Figure 27, the students used photos and their own experiences on a field trip to a town centre to fill this in and then record the results.

Number of paces from W:						
	−2	−1	0	+1	+2	
lots of wood						no wood
lots of glass						no glass
lots of paper						no paper
lots of cigarette ends						no cigarette ends
lots of plastic						no plastic
Total for Site:						

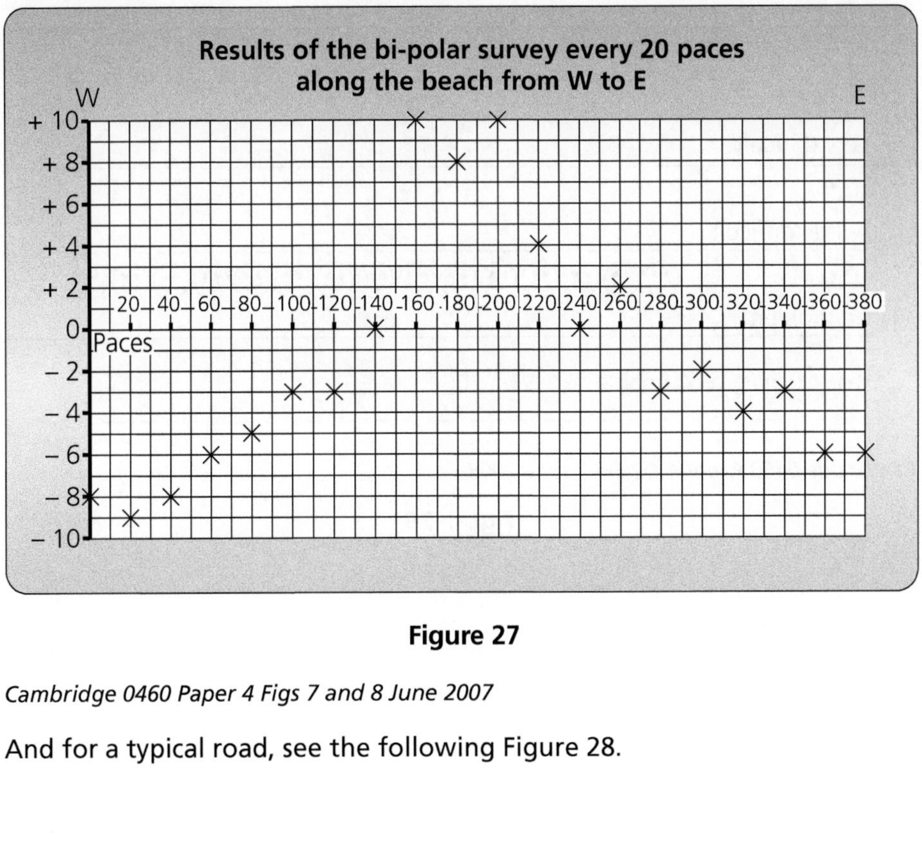

Figure 27

Cambridge 0460 Paper 4 Figs 7 and 8 June 2007

And for a typical road, see the following Figure 28.

Bi-polar scoring system

Negative variables	−2	−1	0	+1	+2	Negative variables
Dirty from litter						Clear from litter
Noise						Quiet
Unmaintained roads and pavements						Well maintained roads and pavements
Crowded						Few people
Unattractive						Attractive

Cambridge 0460 Paper 4 Q1 Table 2 Nov 2005

Figure 28

Pictographs – Displaying data using symbols, such as the example below.

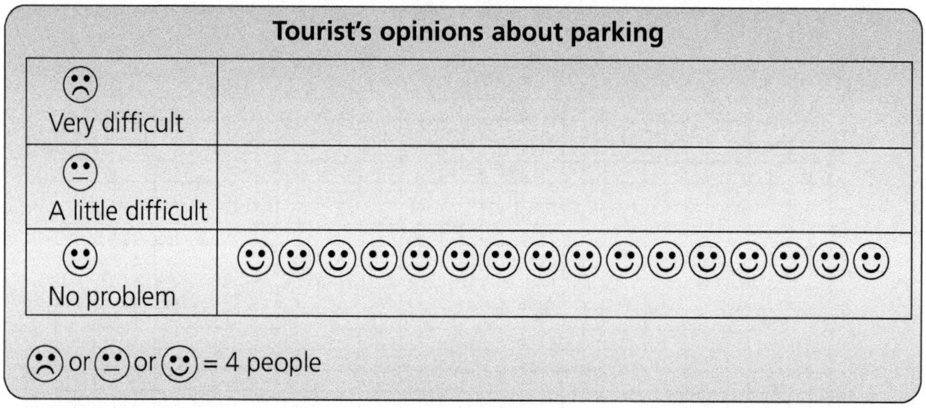

Cambridge 0460 Paper 4 Q2 Fig 9 June 2008

Figure 29

Answers to questions

The answers given in this section are not presented as sample answers but list the key points that should/could be included in your answer. These answers and the questions were written by the author; in examination the number of marks awarded to questions like these may be different.

Answers to theme 1

Chapter 1

Examination style questions for you to try

1. (i) There is little or no birth control or family planning;
More children will mean that a family will have more help to farm the land, as they cannot afford machinery; In some societies a large number of children is seen as a sign of virility;
As so many children die when they are young parents have several children to try and ensure that some will live and look after them in old age;
Religious beliefs – some religions encourage large families' example Roman Catholics.

(ii) As a response to poverty or environmental concerns;
To improve the quality of life for a society;
As a solution to overpopulation;
To improve people's lives, giving them greater control of their family size.

(iii) Improvements in the food supply brought about by higher yields due to better agricultural practices and better transportation of food which helped prevent death due to starvation.
These agricultural improvements include crop rotation, selective breeding, and seed drill technology.
Significant improvements in public health care which helped reduce death rates (mortality), particularly for children. These included medical breakthroughs (such as the development of vaccinations) and, more importantly, improvements in water supply, sewerage, food handling, and improved general personal hygiene which came from a growing scientific knowledge of the causes of disease and the improved education of mothers.

2. The positive effects include: provides more workers either a skilled labour supply such as foreign doctors into the UK from Europe, or cheap/unskilled labour on fruit/vegetable farms in the UK; it produces a multi-cultural society with increased cultural understanding; introduction of specialist amenities example restaurants and food outlets
The negative effects include: possible racial conflict; increased pressure on employment as there are extra people looking for jobs; pressure on housing as more people need to be housed; pressure on the existing amenities and infrastructure.

3. Population control across the many different societies of the world may involve one or more of the following practices:
Increasing access to contraception;
Increasing access to abortion;
Advertising campaigns putting forward the advantages of a smaller family;
Offering bonuses to those people who have smaller families;
Educating women about family planning;

Improving health care so that infant and child mortality rates drop reducing the need to have more children.

A typical case study to use is China's One Child Policy in which having more than one child is made extremely unattractive. China's 'One Child' policy caused a very significant slowing of China's population growth which had been very high before the policy was introduced. Measures included: Couples were allowed only one child; Men could not get married until they were 22 and women 20; Couples had to apply to the authorities to get married and again when they wanted a baby; Couples were rewarded for doing this by being given a salary/wage bonus – an extra 10%, free education, priority housing, family benefits; Priority in education/health facilities/employment/housing; Those who did not conform lost these benefits and were given large fines; Women who became pregnant a second time were forced to have an abortion and women who became repeatedly pregnant were sterilised; A 'workplace snooper' was employed by most factories and businesses who could grant permission for employees to have child; The government advertised the benefits of small families such as having a greater amount of disposable income available.

Chapter 2

Examination style questions for you to try

1. (i) Nucleated – buildings are close together in a group around a nucleus or central point; Linear – buildings are in a line along a road, railway or river; Dispersed – buildings are scattered/long distances apart.

(ii) Where people and employment move out of large urban areas to smaller rural areas – a process of decentralisation. It began in European cities during the Industrial Revolution with people reacting to the pollution and overcrowding of the cities.

(iii) The process of the renewal and rebuilding of older, deteriorating areas of a city accompanied by the moving in to these areas of middle-class, more affluent people into the refurbished buildings.

2. (i) People only travel short distances to use their local shops and services to get convenience goods, such as water, milk, bread, newspapers or low order services such as a post office; whereas they will travel longer distances to use a large out of town shopping centre for comparison goods such as computers, white goods such as cookers, fridges and washing machines and specialised services such as a solicitor and a bank or entertainment such as a cinema or theatre.

(ii) Examples could be from Brazil – such as Rio de Janeiro and Sao Paulo where there is huge in migration of people from the countryside which may overwhelm the existing housing supply leading to the formation of squatter settlements. Attempts which have been made to solve the problem include: the installation of mains water and sewage pipes; the building of sewage works; Infrastructural development such as the building of sealed roads, providing electricity and schools, clinics/hospitals, waste disposal; setting up Self-help schemes; providing education in building skills; the provision of low cost building materials;

(iii) Must use a named example such as London. CBD's have high order shops and services all along major streets like Oxford Street; large retailing department stores such as Harrods/ Selfridges; specialist shops such as shoe shops, jewellers; entertainment such as cinemas and theatres in the West End. Many of the buildings are likely to be high rise such as the offices of major companies; some streets may be pedestrianised such as in Covent Garden; there may be indoor malls. There will be high land and rent prices due to the intense competition for space; the central area may be congested therefore there may be a large amount of air pollution and traffic noise.

Answers to theme 2

Chapter 3

Examination style questions for you to try

1. (i) Fold Mountains – are mountains formed from the Earth's crust/rocks/strata which have been uplifted by massive movements of the crust. Examples include the Himalayas in Asia, the Rocky Mountains in North America, the Andes in South America, the Alps in Europe and the High Atlas mountains in North Africa.

(ii) Fold Mountains are formed when two plates, either two continental plates or an oceanic and a continental plate, move towards each other and collide. The material to make the Fold Mountains comes from layers of deposited sediment eroded from the land – sedimentary rock.
These sedimentary rocks get compressed by a combination of the weight of rocks lying on top of them and two plates colliding. They then become uplifted, bent and crumpled into a series of folds as the plates collide and form Fold Mountains as a result.
Fold Mountains are usually found along the edges of continents where the thickest deposits of sedimentary rock accumulate, such as the Himalayas, where the Indian and Eurasian plates are in collision. The question asks for a diagram and this is a key skill that will be required in some examination questions.

(iii) There are three main types of volcano based on their shape and what they are made of:

- Shield volcanoes – these are made from lava only and form on constructive plate boundaries or at hot spots like Mauna Loa in Hawaii, where lava appears at the surface as two plates pull apart. They form large volcanoes sometimes hundreds of kilometres across because the lava that forms these is alkaline and very runny and travels a long way on the surface before cooling and going solid.
- Dome volcanoes – these are also made from lava only but their lava is acid and thicker and cools quickly. It does not flow very far and so these volcanoes become very steep sided and high, such as Mount St. Helens in USA.
- Composite volcanoes – these are made from both lava and ash, often in alternating layers as both lava and ash come out of the vent during an eruption. They form on destructive plate boundaries where oceanic crust has melted as it is subducted. The lava forces its way up through the crust and emerges as a violent explosion – such as Mount Etna in Sicily, Italy.

2. (i) Composite volcanoes – these are made from both lava and ash, often in alternating layers as both lava and ash come out of the vent during an eruption. They have a central vent and crater and can emit explosive hot gases as well as ash and produce pyroclastic flows and lahars. All these can be labelled on a simple diagram and this is a key skill that will be required in some examination questions.

(ii) These mudflows are called lahars – a mixture of melted snow and ice from the top of the volcano, often combined with rain water, which mixes with ash and runs off the volcano flooding valleys and flatter areas with mud covering crops and settlements, choking rivers with mud and causing death and injury to people.

(iii) The Depth of the Earthquake, a shallow earthquake can be much more destructive than a deep one – many earthquakes take place deep in the crust, below 150 kms, so much of their energy is absorbed by the crust above them. The Haiti Earthquake was less than 10 kms in depth and so appeared at its Epicentre on the surface with much more energy. Other factors include:
The Geology of the rocks in the area – loose sedimentary rocks may liquefy and cause buildings and structures to sink into the ground;
While more solid harder rocks will normally provide the safest foundations for buildings;
Building construction materials and designs – steel framed buildings are better able to absorb movement than concrete framed buildings;
The Space between buildings – as buildings sway they may hit each other, if they are built too close to each other and become damaged;
Number of Storeys – in a tall, high rise building shock waves become amplified as they move up

the building which can cause them to sway and collapse;
The Density of Population living in an area – a densely populated urban area is likely to suffer many more casualties and damage than a low density rural area;
The Time of the day when the Earthquake occurs – at night in residential areas most people will be inside their homes and asleep. During working hours, people in cities and towns will be working or going to school and be inside buildings.

3. Many people live in areas where there are natural hazards such as volcanic eruptions. People live in these volcanic areas for a number of reasons:
Volcanic soils are often very fertile and yields of crops are high;
People can obtain hot water for heating and also generate electricity from the volcano using the hot steam to produce geothermal power;
Volcanoes provide raw materials such as sulphur, zinc, gold and diamonds which can be mined and sold;
Volcanoes can attract tourists and they can get jobs as tour guides;
Governments, as in Italy, can set up volcanic and earthquake prediction equipment and then local people may feel more secure in living in high risk areas;
Many people have lived near volcanoes and earthquake zones all their lives. They are close to their family and friends, they work in the area and also, many just cannot afford to move away to another area.
However, active or dormant volcanoes can always erupt with the consequences of destruction and death.

Chapter 4

Examination style questions for you to try

1. (i) Hot temperatures and high rainfall
   (ii) Either high temperature ranges for exfoliation, or alternating freezing and thawing of water in cold climates.
2. You can either use: Freeze-Thaw weathering – is most common in polar and temperate climates where freezing temperatures cause water to freeze in rocks. When water freezes, it expands its volume by 9%. It takes place when water gets into small spaces and cracks in a rock. If it then freezes and expands it can put enormous pressures of up to 2,000 kg/cm² on the rock and split the rock apart. Where bare rock is exposed on a cliff or slope fragments of rock may be forced away from the face. These fragments of rock may then fall to the bottom of the cliff or slope where they form a large pile of rocks called Scree.
Or:
Exfoliation (or onion skin weathering) is most common in hot tropical climates where the surface temperatures of rocks exposed to the sun can reach over 90°C during the day and then drop below 0°C during the night! Bare rock surfaces will expand and contract each day as temperatures rise and fall. These daily stresses can cause the surface layer of the rock to separate and peel away (called exfoliation) from the rock. Again, these fragments of rock may then fall to the bottom of the cliff or slope where they form a large pile of rocks called scree.
3. One of the processes of Solution, Carbonation and Oxidation can be used:
Solution – rainwater contains a cocktail of dilute acids. The most common is carbonic acid, formed by carbon dioxide gas, CO_2, combining with the rain water. Certain minerals are put into solution by these acids – the carbonate rocks like limestone and chalk are very susceptible to this process.
Carbonation – Carbonation occurs in rocks with a high content of calcium carbonate such as limestone and chalk. Carbon acid reacts with the calcium carbonate to form calcium bicarbonate. Calcium bicarbonate is soluble so therefore the rock is dissolved and carried away.
Oxidation – occurs when minerals combine with oxygen destroying the structure of the original mineral. Iron minerals are especially susceptible to this process.
4. The rock type, including its mineral composition and grain size, will affect the degree to which a rock will react to physical and chemical weathering. Rocks that contain calcium carbonate will be very susceptible to Solution – Carbonation. In sedimentary rocks the type of natural cement that binds together the grains of rock will be important. Those rocks with iron oxide cements will be affected by Oxidation, while those with silica cements will be very resistant to erosion.
Rocks with different grain sizes will weather at different rates. Those that are coarse grained will

weather more quickly than fine grained rocks as they absorb water more easily

The rock structure will determine the presence of lines of weakness, such as fault lines, bedding planes, joints and cracks, Such lines of weakness will increase the surface area of the rock which can be exposed to water, air and freezing; while plants will find it easier to develop their roots in rocks where lines of weakness exist.

Chapter 5

Examination style questions for you to try

1. (i) Watershed

(ii) Where two rivers join

(iii) Hydraulic action: This is where the weight and force of the water flowing in the river removes particles of rocks from the river channels bed and sides.

Abrasion (sometimes called Corrasion): This is where the river's bedload (boulders, pebbles, gravel, sand and silt) as it rolls, bounces and collides with the channel bed and sides, removes particles of rock from the channel bed and sides.

(iv) Two from: Traction: This is where the larger, heavier material that makes up the river's bedload (boulders, pebbles and gravel) is rolled along the river bed.

Saltation: This is where the lighter material that makes up the river's bedload (gravel, sand and silt) is bounced along the river bed.

Suspension: This is where the smaller, lighter material that makes up the river's suspended load (clay size) is carried/ suspended by the river.

Solution: This is where dissolved material that makes up the river's solute load is moved by the river in solution.

2. (i) Floods may destroy crops and buildings. Floods can also kill people and animals; they can be sources of water related diseases because the flood water provides a breeding ground for certain animals that spread disease, such as the mosquito which can spread malaria and dengue fever, and the Bilharzia snail. Polluted water can also spread diseases such as cholera and diarrhoea.

(ii) There are two main methods of reducing the impact of flooding. The first set of methods involves intercepting rainwater before it reaches and fills a river channel. The second set involves increasing the size/capacity of a river channel so that it can carry more flood water – this is called channel engineering.

Forests and vegetation naturally intercept rainfall but on large areas of the Earth deforestation and farming have removed the trees and vegetation so flooding now occurs where it never existed before or it is much worse than before. To solve this problem, there are several methods which involve keeping water on the valley sides, allowing it to infiltrate into the soil and not allowing it to flow quickly over the surface of the land into the river channel. By preventing this Surface Run Off/Overland flow it also prevents the loss of soil – soil erosion – from farmers' fields. The methods include:

Planting trees – called afforestation;

Leaving permanent crops, such as grass on the valley sides;

Tiered or layer cropping, where several layers of trees and crops are grown on the valley side by farmers to intercept the rain;

Contour ploughing – ploughing across a valley side rather than up and down the valley side. Each small bank of soil stops rainwater flowing down the valley side and the rainwater infiltrates into the ground and is available to the growing crops and is not lost as it flows away to the river channel;

Terracing – where large level steps are built into the side of a valley which provide areas of flat land for crops to be grown;

Tied ridging – creating a grid of raised soil embankments, taking the shape of squares, from which rainfall cannot flow away down the valley side, again the water is kept in the soil on the valley sides and the crops can make use of it;

Leaving crop stubble in the fields which both stabilises and protects the soil and stops water flowing to the river channel;

Creating natural wetlands – A natural floodplain stores a large amount of floodwater which reduces the threat of flooding further down the river. As many floodplains have now been drained and protected from flooding, the water that they would have stored is now moved further down the river putting flood defences under much greater pressure downstream and many are now not big enough to hold this extra water.

The second set of methods – channel engineering, increases channel capacity so that the river can hold more floodwater. The methods include: Dredging – where the bedload is dug out by diggers and there is greater channel capacity as a result; Wing Dykes – these are walls built out from the side of the river made out of concrete and stone on one side only of a river channel. The aim is to force the river into a smaller area which means it flows faster and carries away the bedload and alluvium and therefore does the job of dredging without the use of machines; Two stage channels – this is where the top of one side of the channel is cut away to increase the amount of room in the channel for flood water; Building embankments or Levees – these are high banks of soil, clay, sand and gravel built beside the river channel to increase the volume of the channel. Sometimes these are built further away from the river channel to make the capacity even bigger; Straightening the river channel – This involves cutting out meanders so that floodwater can flow away much more quickly; Holding dams – these dams are built in the upper sections of rivers and hold back floodwater, from melting snow or heavy rainfall from Monsoons, which they can then release after the flood threat is over; Check dams – these trap the rivers bedload as it is being transported down the river in a flood so that the Bedload does not fill up the river channel further down the river and reduce its capacity to carry water; Overflow channels or Spillways which allow water to flow away from the main river channel.

In addition to these methods, and often as a last resort, buildings and homes can be flood proofed by sealing doors and other openings or raising them up above flood level

3. The Nile or Mississippi rivers may be used, but the Ganges and Brahmaputra are also relevant examples.

   The advantages include: The alluvium that has been deposited on the Nile, for example, during floods provides extremely fertile soils which mean that they are often very important for agriculture;

   The water from the river Nile is used for irrigation, allowing arid land in Egypt that lacks water to be used for agriculture;

   Larger rivers, such as the Mississippi in the USA, are very important route ways for transport and communications (by the river and by roads and railways built on the flat land on the floodplain);

   A river, such as the Brahmaputra in Bangladesh, is an important source of food for both subsistence and for selling the fish and prawns that it contains.

   Rivers, such as the Nile flowing through an arid area, are important sources of fresh water;

   A large river, such as the Mississippi, provides a large area of flat land on its floodplain that can be used for building houses and industry.

   The disadvantages include: Rivers such as the Ganges and Brahmaputra in Bangladesh are liable to flood which destroys crops and buildings. Floods in Bangladesh can also frequently kill people and animals;

   Rivers such as the Niger in West Africa and the Mekong in Vietnam can be sources of water related diseases because they provide a breeding ground for certain animals that spread disease, such as the mosquito which can spread malaria and dengue fever. Polluted water in these rivers may also spread diseases such as cholera and diarrhoea;

   The alluvium that makes up a floodplain and delta of the Ganges and Brahmaputra in Bangladesh is not very stable for building so foundations need to be carefully constructed;

   It is often very difficult and expensive to cross or bridge a large river such as the Brahmaputra;

   Floodplains, such as around Cairo and the Nile delta on the river Nile in Egypt, are often very densely populated and so there is great competition for space.

Chapter 6

Examination style questions for you to try

1. (i) It is a harder, more resistant area of land projecting out to sea.

(ii) Bays, stacks, stumps, arches and caves.

(iii) Two taken from:

Hydraulic Action: This is where the weight (this can be up to 20 tonnes per square metre) and force of a wave crashing against a cliff removes particles of rocks from the cliff. It also includes

the process where air is trapped by a wave in a crack in the cliff and the enormous hydraulic pressure this opens up the crack further which weakens the cliff.
Abrasion (sometimes called Corrasion): This is where the boulders, pebbles, shingle and sand is picked up by a wave and thrown against the cliff. This constant collision removes particles of rock from the cliff and wave cut platform.

Solution (sometimes called Corrosion): Some minerals (mainly the Carbonate minerals found in rocks like Limestone and Chalk) are put into solution by the weak acids found in sea water.
Attrition: This process does not actually erode the cliff but it is the process that breaks up the boulders, pebbles, shingle and sand on the beach. It takes place when the rocks on the beach are rolled up and down the beach by swash and backwash. As this happens they collide with each other and become smaller and rounder as a result.

(iv) Where a coastline is made out of one type of rock and has no weaknesses it will erode back at a constant rate. However, if there are weaknesses in the coastline such as sections of softer, less resistant rock, Differential Erosion will take place.

As the softer, less resistant rock is eroded at a faster rate it will form a Bay, leaving the harder, more resistant rocks projecting out to sea as Headlands. Such a coastline is called a discordant coastline.

2. The development of coral reefs is controlled by seven limiting factors:

- Temperature – The mean annual temperature has to be over 18°C. The optimal temperatures for them are between 23 - 25°C.
- Depth of Water – Coral reefs can only grow in depths of water less than 25 metres.
- Light – The shallow water allows light for tiny photosynthesising algae – called zooxanthellae. In return for the corals providing the algae with a place to live these tiny algae provide the corals with up to 98% of their food. This is an example of a symbiotic relationship – an ecological relationship which benefits both sides.
- Salinity – Corals can only live in sea water, but they can tolerate sea water of high salinity.
- Sediment – Sediment clogs up the feeding structures and cleaning systems of corals. Cloudy water also reduces light penetration in the water reducing the light needed for photosynthesis.
- Wave action – Coral reefs prefer areas of high energy wave action. This ensures freshly oxygenated water. It helps to clean out any trapped sediment. It brings in microscopic plankton – a food source for the corals. In areas that are too exposed though, corals may be too easily destroyed.
- Exposure to air – Corals die if they are exposed to air for too long. They can only survive and grow therefore at the level of the lowest tides.

3. For sand dunes to form in a coastal area such as Hayle in Cornwall, England or St Petersburg in Florida, USA, there needs to be: A large, sand beach to supply the sand;
A strong, onshore wind to firstly dry out the sand and then transport it inland; An obstruction to trap the sand, such as seaweed at the top of the beach – the strand line;
The sand will accumulate (build up) in to a small dune, about one metre high, called an embryo dune;
Pioneer species of plants, such as Marram Grass, will colonise the small dune. The roots and stems of these plants will trap more sand and speed up the process of deposition so that the sand builds up in to bigger mobile or yellow dunes;
As this process continues the sand dune will increase in size and height to become fixed or grey dunes.

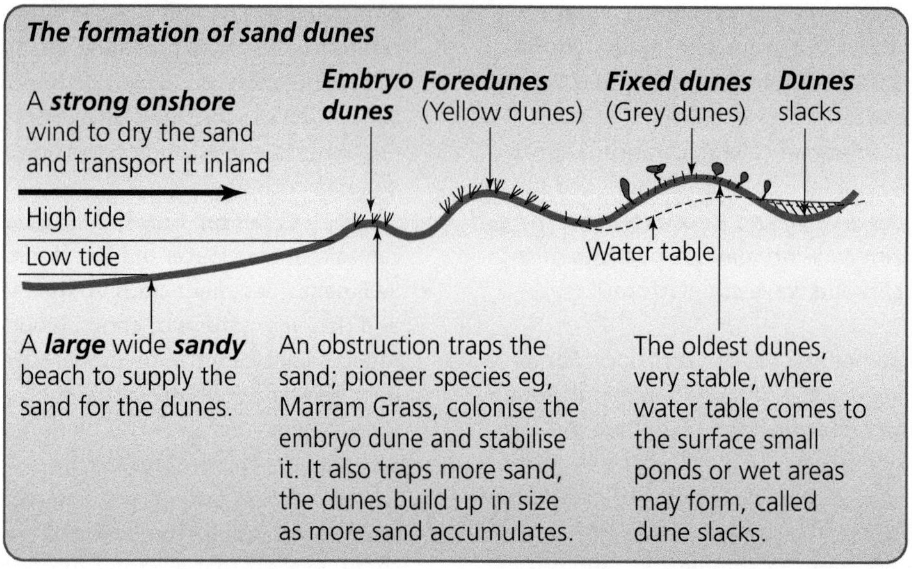
The formation of sand dunes
Embryo dunes
Foredunes (Yellow dunes)
Fixed dunes (Grey dunes)
Dunes slacks
A strong onshore wind to dry the sand and transport it inland
High tide
Low tide
Water table
A large wide sandy beach to supply the sand for the dunes.
An obstruction traps the sand; pioneer species eg, Marram Grass, colonise the embryo dune and stabilise it. It also traps more sand, the dunes build up in size as more sand accumulates.
The oldest dunes, very stable, where water table comes to the surface small ponds or wet areas may form, called dune slacks.

Chapter 7

Examination style questions for you to try

1. (i) The trees, plants and animals have many special adaptations to living in this wet tropical environment. Due to constant high temperatures and high rainfall plants are found in all stages of growth. Tropical Rain Forests has distinct layers each with its own characteristic features and adaptations to the climatic conditions:

- The emergent layer contains a small number of very tall, large trees which grow above the general canopy. Their trunks are straight and, in their lower sections, branchless as they attempt to get to the light above the canopy. The trees need to be able to withstand hot temperatures and strong winds. As a result many have large buttress roots for support. They often have many other plants growing on them like lianas (which are like vines and they use the tall trees to get up to the light above the canopy) and Epiphytes (which grow on the trunks and branches of the trees and trap water and dead leaves falling from the tree or running down their trunks).
- The canopy layer forms a roof over the three remaining layers. Most canopy trees have smooth, oval leaves that come to a point, called a Drip Tip, to get rid of the rain that falls on the leaf.
- The under canopy layer has little light reaching it so the plants have to grow larger leaves to catch the sunlight.
- Shrub layer is very dark– only about 5 % of the sunlight shining on the rainforest reaches down to this layer. Tree ferns and small shrubs grow here able to grow in low light conditions. Many have large leaves to catch the little light that gets down to this layer.

(ii) These high towering clouds form as a result of the high temperatures experienced in the tropical rainforest. As the forest heats up during the day it warms the moist air above it which expands and rises quickly to form a very high cloud. The warm moist air cools and condenses as it rises and then forms and releases very heavy rain.

2. (i) Cloud cover is estimated by how many eighths of the sky is covered by cloud. One eighth is one OKTA, four eighths four Oktas, etc. It is shown on a map by the division of a circle.

(ii) The instrument is made up of two thermometers, one of which is a Dry bulb thermometer, which measures the temperature of the air, and the other of which is a Wet bulb thermometer. This bulb is kept wet by being covered by an absorbent muslin wick which is kept wet by its end being kept in a container of distilled water. It measures the temperature of the air if there was 100% humidity – called Absolute Humidity.

If the humidity of the air is 100% the readings on both thermometers will be the same – it will normally be raining or there will be mist or fog surrounding the instrument. If it is less than 100% the Wet bulb reading will be lower than the Dry bulb reading.

By recording the temperatures of both thermometers, it is possible to work out the Relative Humidity, as a %, of the air surrounding the instrument.

This is done by:

- Recording the temperatures of both the Wet and Dry bulb thermometers.
- Recording the difference between the two readings.
- Looking up the results in a Relative Humidity table.

(iii) They are mainly found in tropical areas which experience hot temperatures; with high atmospheric pressure; where the air is usually descending; and therefore warming (to make the water vapour in air condense into water droplets and rain the air needs to be cooled – which is what happens when air is forced to rise); so that there is little opportunity for precipitation to form. They may also form in areas of rain shadow, or in areas which are a long distance from the sea, or where there is a cold ocean current offshore as in the Namib desert in south west Africa.

3. The Amazon, Central African or Indo-Malaysian forest can be named.

There are many activities that can be used to illustrate the impact on the TRF's they include:

Deforestation – where the rainforest is logged for its valuable timber, the habitat for thousands of species of plants and animals is removed and destroys delicate food webs and food chains and the animals disappear, often to become extinct. As mentioned it also takes away the habitat for the indigenous peoples. As well as loss of natural habitat, soil erosion may be increased and species of plants and animals lost.

Plantation agriculture where the forest is cleared it destroys the natural environment to create huge farms for the growing of plantation crops such as sugar cane and oil palms – both now in great demand as Biofuels.

Land cleared for cattle ranching will lead to loss of natural habitat and increased soil erosion.

New settlements to provide land for small scale farmers will lead to loss of natural habitat for plants and animals.

Mining – Many of the mines are some of the biggest in the world and are open cast – where the soil and forest are removed (called the overburden) and the minerals removed. Often the mines are then abandoned when the minerals are removed and the natural environment is totally destroyed by the mining activities and soil erosion may be increased and species of plants and animals lost

Dams and Reservoirs – destroy the ecology of the areas they have flooded and drown existing settlements and communities, forcing people to migrate.

Cultivated foods and spices – many are grown on plantations in cleared areas of rainforest. However, as the forest is no longer supplying the soil nutrients many of these crops rely on the heavy use of artificial chemical fertilisers which can pollute rivers and lakes.

Answers to theme 3

Chapter 8

Examination style questions for you to try

1. (i) Nomadic farming is where farmers move from one area to another. Sedentary is where the farming is located in a permanent location

(ii) Irrigation is the artificial application of water to the soil which assists in growing crops. In crop production it is mainly used in dry areas and in periods of rainfall shortfalls, but also it helps to protect plants against frost. Additionally irrigation helps to suppress weed growing in rice fields.

Drainage – land needs to be well drained to allow most plants to grow and not find their roots waterlogged.

2. (i) Ways include:

- The building of small Earth dams and wells to provide water for basic irrigation projects.
- Simple methods of Soil Conservation, such as planting trees to make shelter belts to protect soil from wind erosion in dry periods, or building low stone walls along the contours of a slope to stop the run off of rain water and allow it time to enter the soil helping to prevent soil erosion and increasing the amount of water in the soil and making it available for crops. Tied Ridging where low walls of soil are built in a grid of small squares which stops rainfall run off and again allows water to be drained into the soil. Crops such as potatoes and cassava are grown on the soil walls.
- Strip or Inter Cropping which has alternate strips of crops being grown, at different stages of growth, across a slope to limit rainfall run off as there is always a strip of crops to trap water and soil moving down the slope.
- Tier or layer cropping where several types and sizes of crops are grown in one field to provide protection from rainfall and increase food and crop yields. For example, the top tier, or layer, may be coconut trees, below this may be a tier of coffee or fruit trees, and, at ground level, vegetables or pineapples.
- Improved food storage which allows food to kept fresh and edible for longer periods of time and protected from being eaten by rats and insects and affected by diseases.

(ii) The Natural Factors include:

Drought and Unreliable Rainfall – Crop yields can be drastically reduced without adequate rainfall.
Tropical /Hurricanes/Cyclones/Typhoons – when these storms hit, with their high winds, torrential rainfall and storm surges (where sea levels are raised by the high winds and then surge inland flooding low lying areas like southern Bangladesh), they can devastate farm land and crops. Subsistence farmers have very little resources to recover from such events, a situation made even worse if the storm is repeated within short periods of time.

Floods – though often associated with Tropical Hurricanes, they usually result from heavy rainfall, often associated with Monsoons or El Nino events. Crops can be destroyed by flooding, as well as the effect on whole communities who may lose their houses, belongings, animals, roads, etc.

Pests and diseases – there are many pests and diseases which can prey on crops, for example, locusts and diseases, such as mildew. Without the expensive pesticides and sprays to deal with them poor rural communities may suffer severe crop losses.

Soil Erosion and loss of Soil Fertility – land that has been cleared of its natural protective cover of vegetation is much more easily eroded by rainfall. Soil Fertility will be lost as land is eroded and soil minerals washed out of the soil. Also, overgrazing by grazing herds of domestic animals can remove the protective vegetation cover. Without applying either natural fertiliser, dung, or expensive artificial chemical fertilisers, or allowing the soil to rest and recover (leaving the land fallow), will lead to a loss of fertility and lower crop yields.

Rural Poverty in many LEDC's means that there is a lack of money to invest in irrigation or buy expensive fertilisers. Many farmers are still using traditional farming practices such as ploughing up and down slopes which increases soil erosion.

The ***human Factors*** include:

War – people have to leave their homes and farms and it is impossible for farmers to grow crops and rear animals. Those that do may find their crops and animals destroyed or stolen.

Increasing population – as a result of rising population more land is having to be cleared of forest, less fertile, marginal land brought in to use, and farms divided into much smaller units amongst farmer's children as they grow up and have their own families to feed. As less land becomes available food shortages result.

Inability to invest capital and improve infrastructure – the lack of capital available in LEDC's, particularly in rural areas, means that schemes to improve agricultural production, improve food storage, improve roads and transportation for distributing farm products are very hard to initiate and develop.

Rising Food Prices – between 2001 and 2012 the price of many globally important crops rose dramatically.

3. There are several types of large scale commercial farming. Plantation farming is one of the most common and involves the growing of one crop (called Monoculture), often over very large areas. Examples include sugar cane, bananas, rubber, tea, coffee and pineapples. Other types of large scale commercial farming include the growing of cereals, such as wheat, maize and barley and the rearing of livestock animals such as cattle and sheep.

   An example of commercial farming is sheep farming in Australia. Sheep are raised either as lambs for meat or as older sheep for wool. It is found on very large farms in marginal areas – areas where other animals and crops would not be as successful or as profitable due to physical and human factors. Therefore they are often found in areas of low rainfall, high temperatures and poor quality grazing where they are left to graze on grass or small bushes. Such land is also cheaper to buy.
   Inputs – per hectare, sheep farming has very low Inputs of capital – much of the land that is used is of relatively small value as it cannot often be used for arable farming, so it is cheap to buy. Farms may need up to 25 hectares of grazing land per animal as grazing land is so poor. Rearing animals in these areas produces the smallest profits per hectare of any type of commercial farming. However, Australia has very large areas of land available for this activity, though, so is suited to this type of farming.
   Labour – it takes very few people to both look after large numbers of sheep – as they can be left out in the fields all year round.
   Processes – gathering the sheep together for shearing, applying any pesticide to their fleece and antibiotics to overcome any pests.
   The Outputs are meat and wool.

Chapter 9

Examination style questions for you to try

1. (i) Primary – mining, farming, fishing, forestry
Tertiary – transport, retailing, healthcare, education

(ii) A Footloose industry is one which is not dependent on a particular location, unlike many other types of industry which need to be beside their raw materials, ports, fast and easy transport, etc. The reasons being that they: Use small light component parts; Their products tend to be small and light; They use electricity as their power source; They need a small skilled labour force; They are non-polluting and so can locate in or near residential areas.

2. People – More people will be in employment; they will receive higher wages than in their existing work; It will bring an improvement in skill levels; Bring about a rise in the standard of living.

Economy – the money from taxes and income can be used for improvements in transport infrastructure - to roads and railways; Improvements in service infrastructure example electricity, water supply, and sanitation; Improvements in public services such as health care and education.
The multiplier effect/cumulative causation – there will be positive effects on other areas of the economy – people will be able to buy more goods in the shops; they may want to extend and improve their houses, they can afford to send their children to school.

(i) Examples could include Nissan in Washington in NE England, LG in South Wales.
The government may offer:
- Financial incentives to attract a factory to economically weaker areas
- Help with training costs
- Rent free premises
- Building of essential infrastructure, such as upgrading roads and power supplies
- Tax free profits.

(ii) There may be various forms of pollution:
Air – gases and dust from the industrial processes
Water – waste and hot water may be put into rivers and the sea
Noise – noise levels may increase
Roads may have increased traffic on them from the works, increasing congestion and increasing wear on the roads themselves and increasing pollution
Destruction of natural habitat and ecologies.

Chapter 10

Examination style questions for you to try

1. (i)

- A rise in incomes which gave people, after they had paid for their basic needs, spare 'disposable' money which they could spend on leisure activities and tourism.
- Increased leisure time caused by a shorter working week, flexitime, paid annual holidays, earlier retirement with a pension.
- Increased mobility as a result of a decrease in the cost of air travel combined with greater numbers of airports and flights, the expansion of budget airlines, like Air Asia, Ryanair, Jazeera, Jet, Air Dubai and Easy jet and the increased numbers of flights to a wider range of destinations.
- Increased media coverage by television, magazines and the internet of different holiday destinations and types of holiday.

(ii)

- Restricting tourist numbers to certain areas.
- Having tourist firms which are licensed and their activities are regulated in several ways.
- Limiting or preventing the destruction of natural vegetation and habitat that is cleared for tourist development.
- Ensure that any building developments are low level and made out of local materials and in local styles.
- Use local labour in as many activities as possible and provide training for local people.
- Educating tourists with regard to the environmental and conservation issues.
- Restricting access to sensitive areas and at certain times of the year.
- Employing local people to check and to clear up any tourist rubbish regularly.
- Ban tourists from any hunting activities.

2. (i)

- Farmers and fishermen can greatly increase the income, fishermen by using their boats to take people on trips to see and dive on the reefs and farmers will have a whole new market for their crops in the new hotels and restaurants.
- The hotels, restaurants and other facilities also provide hundreds of new jobs, from building to maintenance, cleaning and cooking, making furniture, etc. The restaurants and cafes provide many new job and career opportunities.
- The jobs in cleaning and looking after tourists can add enormously to the local people's incomes.
- Local crafts people also have a much bigger market for their goods.
- Transport also provides many jobs with coach and bus companies needing drivers, engineers and cleaners.

(ii)

- The local people may have different cultures, traditions and religions. This can lead to problems when tourists are unaware of the local culture, customs and values and can offend local people by their dress and activities. Young local people can be influenced by the behaviour of tourists and copy them, such as in their clothes – in the worst cases by drinking alcohol and taking drugs – the Demonstration Effect.
- At the worst level contact with the tourists has led to prostitution and the introduction of diseases like HIV/Aids.
- Young people may truant from school to work in the informal tourist industry and earn money as unofficial guides or selling souvenirs.
- People leave family farms to work in the tourist industry and this makes it more difficult to run the farms without their help.
- People may be moved from their houses and land to make way for tourist developments. Local landowners may sell large areas of land and coastline to non-local or foreign buyers who may then deny access to local people.
- House and land prices may rise as non-locals buy them and put them out of the reach of local people.
- The natural environment and ecosystems may be sensitive to any form of development and pollution and this may lead to the destruction and degradation of the environment which may lead to the loss of tourists and their income to other, better managed areas. This can be managed with guidelines, rules and regulation. Numbers of visitors and how they conduct themselves can be regulated to ensure that the natural environments provide a long term income for local people and businesses.

3. For this answer look at the examples used in the Tourism section of this guide – for example, Kenya in East Africa or a National Park.

Chapter 11

Examination style questions for you to try

1. **(i)** A fossil fuel is a non-renewable energy resource that is either finite or non-sustainable and their use will eventually lead to them running out and their exhaustion. Coal, oil, natural gas and peat are examples.

   (ii) A major river with a large, reliable discharge for most, if not all, the year to fill the reservoir created by the dam;

   A relatively narrow steep sided valley made of hard, impermeable rock to provide a solid foundation for the building of a large dam;
   A large upstream area, with few people that need to be moved, which can be flooded to provide the reservoir of water;
   Access to electricity transmission lines to transmit the electricity to centres of population and industry.

   (iii) HEP is renewable, clean and non-polluting;

   Cheap (after the initial cost of the dam);
   Dams also help with flood control;
   Provide water for the local population and for farming (irrigation) and industry;
   They can also be stocked with fish and support a local fishery;
   They can be used for recreation and to attract tourists.

2. On the positive side it has: Allowed the development of major agriculture and industrial projects in a semi desert area; allowed the development of large urban areas – such as Phoenix and Tucson.
   On the negative side it has:
   Large costs – the CAP cost $4 billion and providing the money to pay for this heavily subsidised water;
   Now that Arizona is taking more water California has to find a way to make up for the shortfall between what it is now allowed and what it used to take;
   Salinisation of soils as the irrigation water brings salts to the surface of the soil making them too salty to grow crops in; the water is no longer available for projects further downstream.

3. Many EU countries such as the UK, France, Germany, Spain and Italy, plus Japan, USA and Canada are developing all forms of renewable energy so the EU can be used as an area or a state like California – all these are examples that can be used. The question mainly wants a brief description of the ways and the reasons of how different types of renewable energy are developed. In the UK, HEP is being developed in the high rainfall and mountainous areas of Scotland, wind farms off the coast of England and in counties like Cornwall, solar energy in southern UK, wave energy off Cornwall and Scotland, etc.

Index

A
abiotic living thing, 108
abrasion (corrasion), 69, 73, 87
absolute humidity, 101
Action Aid, 132
active volcanoes, 58
afforestation, 83
ageing population, problems of, 18–19
age pyramid, 16
alluvial fans, 117
alluvium, 77, 79
altostratus clouds, 107
Amazonia, 108
Amazon River basin, 128–129
anemometers, 104–105, 208, 214
aneroid barometer, 102–103
appropriate technology, 132
arable farm, 125
arcuate deltas, 79
arresting factors of corals, 94
ash from volcanoes, 57
atolls, 95
attrition, 69, 87, 205

B
backwash, 87
Bangalore, 149
bankfull discharge, 77, 81
Barchan dunes, 117
barograph, 103
barometers, 102–103, 209, 213
Barra de Tijuca, 43
barrier reefs, 95
bars, 92–93
bay, 92
beaches, 92–93
bedload, 70
beriberi, 132
biodiversity, 114
biofuels, 173
biomass, 172
biotic living thing, 108
bi-polar recording systems, 216–217
bird's foot deltas, 79
birth rate, 4, 13–14
birth rates, 12–13
blowhole, 91
bottom-set beds, 78
bridging point, 32
'Bright lights' syndrome, 20, 36
Burgess Concentric model, 37
business parks, 148
buttress roots, 110

C
calcareous rocks, 70
calcium bicarbonate, 66
California State Water Project, 177
callipers, 205
canopy layer, 111
capital, 126
carbonation, 66
carbonic acid, 69
carried/suspended by the river, 70
carrying capacity of the region or country, 4
cattle ranching, 113
caves, 91
Central Africa, 108
Central Arizona Project (CAP), 177
Central Business District (CBD), 37
channel capacity, 83–84
channel engineering, 82–83
check dams, 84
China's 'One Child' policy, 27–28
cirrus clouds, 107
cliff notch, 90–91
cliffs, 90–91
climate
    of tropical rainforests, 109
climate, defined, 97
climate and population changes, 6
climate zones, 6
clinometer, 205
cloud, types of, 106–108
cloud cover, 106
coal, 166–167
coastal deposition, features of, 92–93
coastal erosion
    features of, 90–92
    processes of, 87
coastal studies, 211–212
collecting funnel, 103
collision boundaries/margins, 51
Colorado River Compact, 177
community housing projects, 42
comparison goods, 35
composite model, 37
composite volcanoes, 58

confluence, 71, 141
congestion charging, 44
conservative boundaries/margins, 52
constant high temperatures, 109
constructive boundaries/margins, 51
constructive wave action, 89
continental crust, 49
contour ploughing, 83
convection currents, 50
convenience goods, 35
coral reefs, 93–95
corrasion, 69
corrosion, 87
corticos, 42
counter-urbanisation, 22
crop stubble, 83
cross profile of river, 71–72
crust, 49
cryptobiotic soil, 118
cultivated foods and spices, 113–114
cumecs, 71
cumulative causation, 8, 145
cumulonimbus clouds, 107
cumulus clouds, 107
cyclones, 130

D
dams, 80–81, 113, 132
death rate, 4, 12, 13–15, 18
deaths, 3
deep water anchorage, 33
deep water estuary, 33
deforestation, 82, 111–113
deindustrialisation, 17
deltas, 78–80
Demographic Transition Model (DTM), 11–18
dependency ratio, 18
deposition, processes of, 70–71, 90
desalination plants, 178
deserts, 116–117
  human life in, 118–119
  lakes, 118
  vegetation, 117–118
destructive boundaries/margins, 51
destructive wave action, 89–90
differential erosion, 73–74, 92
digital deltas, 79
digital electronic devices, 102
discharge of the river, 72
discordant coastline, 92
discounted travel tickets, 44
dispersed settlement, 32
distributaries, 78
dome volcanoes, 58
do-nut effect, 22, 38
dormant volcanoes, 58
dredging, 84
drip irrigation, 145
drip tip, 111
drought, 130
dry bulb thermometer (hygrometer), 100–102, 208–209
dry point site, 31

E
Earth
  layers of, 49–51
  population, 10
  resources, 178–179
earthquake, 52–53
  aftershocks, 53
  amount of damage caused by, 53–54
  depth of, 53
  epicentre of, 52
  impact on humans, 55
  intensity of shaking, 53
  living in an earthquake or active volcanic zone, 54–55
  reasons for, 53
  shaking of the crust, 52
  shallow, 52
  Sichuan province, China, 2008, 55–56
  size of, 53
  slipping of crust, 52
  strength of, 53
Earthquake Early Warning system, 62
economically active population, 18
economically active portion of population, 13
economically inactive population, 18
economic factors and population changes, 8
ecotourism, 161
'edge towns or cities,' 43
embankments, 78
embryo dune, 88
emigrants, 19
employment, formal and informal, 140
energy resources
  non-renewable, 166–168
  renewable, 168–174
epicentre, 52
epiphytes, 110
erg, 117
erosion
  defined, 65
evaporation, 177
exfoliation (onion skin weathering), 65, 117
extinct volcanoes, 58

F
farming/agriculture
  classification, 123
  commercial, 125–128
  inputs in, 124–125
  outputs in, 125
  processes in, 125
  subsistence, 125, 128–129
  as a system, 124–125
Favela Bairro project (the Favela Neighbourhood Project), 42–43

fertigation, 145
fertile land, 31
fertility decline, 17
fixed or grey dunes, 88
flash floods, 81
flat or gently sloping land, 31
flocculation, 78
flood hydrographs, 81–82
flood irrigation, 144
floodplains, 77
flood prevention, 82–84
floods, 130
Fold Mountains, 50–51
Food and Agriculture Organisation (FAO), 132
'Food for Work' programme, 132
food shortages, 129
  human factors, 130–131
  impact of, 132
  natural factors, 130
  possible solutions, 132–133
footloose industry, 146–148
fore-set beds, 78
fossil fuels, 166
freeze-thaw weathering, 65
fringing reefs, 95
fuel wood, 174

G
gas sensors, 58
gauging station, 71
gene pool, 114
gentler slope, 124
gentrification, 38
Geo, 91
geographical skills for examination
  aims of questions/hypotheses, 203
  cities and towns, 202
  compass directions and bearings, 184
  contour lines on a map, 184–185
  counts, 204
  cross sections, 186
  data analysis, 207
  data collection, 204
  data presentation techniques, 207
  dendritic pattern, 185
  density of drainage, 185
  divided bar charts, 191–193
  eastings, 184
  enquiry skills, 203–207
  field sketches of physical and human landscapes, 202
  fieldwork studies, examples, 208–213
  finding height on a map, 184
  flow diagrams, 196
  formation of conclusions, 207
  graphs, diagrams, tables of data and written material, 188
  grid references, 182–184
  hill pattern, 185
  important terms and points explained, 213–218
  landscape features, 185
  line and bar graphs, 194–195
  measuring gradients on a map, 185
  measuring 'roundness' of a piece, 205
  natural landscape, 202
  northings, 184
  observation, 204
  for paper 4 of examination, 203
  photographic and pictorial material, features of, 201–203
  physical features of coastlines, 185
  pie charts, 198
  population structure, 188–190
  questionnaires, 204
  radial graphs, 193
  random sampling, 206
  recording measurements, 205
  rural areas, 202
  sampling, 205–206
  scale of maps and measuring distances, 181
  scatter graphs, 197
  settlements, mapping, 186–187
  shape and slope of the land, 184–185
  stratified sampling, 206
  systematic sampling, 206
  tables of data, 198–199
  topographical maps, 187–188
  transport networks, mapping, 186
  triangular graphs, 191
  written material, 199–201
geosynclines, 50
geothermal energy, 170
GM crops, 125
good defence site, 31
gorge, 75
Green Revolution, 133
growing population, problems of, 26
groynes, 88
Gulf wives, 21

H
Haiti earthquake, 2010, 53
headland coastlines, 92
hierarchy of services, 33
high order services, 34
high order settlement, 34–35
high population density, 6
high rainfall, 109
High Yielding Varieties (HYV's), 133
hinterland, 33
Hi tech industries, 146, 149
HIV/AIDS, impact of, 25–26
  strategies to reduce spread of, 26
holding dams, 84
holiday lets, 163
hot spots, 57
housing, 39
Hoyt Sector model, 37
humidity, 109

hunter-gatherers, 112
hydraulic action, 69, 73, 75, 87
Hydro Electric power (HEP), 114, 141, 166, 169–170
stations, 175

I
immigrants, 19
indigenous people, 112
indigenous population, 114
Indo-Malaysia, 108
industry, 212
  access to cheap sources of power, effect of, 141
  capital availability, effect of, 141–142
  changes in technology, 143
  changing location and nature of, 143–144
  economies of scale, 142
  employment structure, 138
  factors affecting the location of, 140–143
  government policies affecting, 142
  human and economic factors affecting, 141–143
  iron and steel industry in South Wales, UK, 144–145
  land availability, effect of, 141
  physical factors affecting, 140–141
  primary, 138
  quaternary, 138
  secondary, 138
  size and the location of a market, 142
  suburban and rural environments, 143
  as a system, 140
  tertiary, 138
  transportation and, 142
inner core of Earth, 49
inter cropping, 132
irrigation, 144–145
Island Arcs, 51
isohyets, 104
isolines, 216

K
Kenyan coast, 159–161
Kuwait, 21
Kwashiorkor, 132

L
labour, 126
lagoon, 93
lahars, 57
landforms associated with processes, 71
land-use zones of urban areas, 36–39
layer cropping, 132
less-developed countries (LEDC's), 11, 15, 25, 36, 85, 131
levées, 77–78, 84
lianas, 110
linear settlement, 32
liquefaction, 53
Liverpool, 33
London Docklands Development Corporation
  (LDDC), 39
longitudinal or seif dunes, 117
long profile of river, 71–72
longshore drift, 88
long term food aid, 132
low humidity, 115
low order services, 34
low order settlement, 34–35

M
Macau, 10
magma, 51
malnutrition, 132
mantle, 49
marginal areas, 126
Marram Grass, 88
mass transit systems, 44
maximum and minimum thermometer, 99–100
meanders, 75–77
Mercalli Scale, 53
mercury barometer, 102
Merseyside Development Corporation - (MDC), 39
Mexico, 21
microelectronics industry, 138
Mid Atlantic Ridge, 51
migration, 18–24
  external, 19
  forced, 19, 22
  internal, 19
  permanent, 19
  problems of migrants, 21
  push and pull factors, 19–20, 36
  rural to urban, 20
  temporary, 19
  voluntary, 20
minerals, 114
mining, 113
monoculture, 126
most developed countries (MEDCs), 11, 21–22, 36, 85, 176–177
  problems of urban areas in, 41–44
Multinational or Transnational Companies (TNCs), 145

N
National Parks, 162–163
  footpath erosion, issue of, 163
  traffic congestion and, 162
native people, 112
natural decrease, 4
natural increase, 4
natural resources, 7
natural wetlands, 83
Newly Industrialised Countries (NIC's), 138
nimbostratus clouds, 107
nodal point, 32
nomadic people, 126
Non Government Organisations (NGOs), 132
non-renewable energy resources, 166–168
nuclear energy, 166
nuclear power stations, 175
nucleated settlement, 32

O
oases, 117
oceanic crust, 49
oil and natural gas, 166, 168
Oktas cloud cover, 106
optimum population, 4
outer core of Earth, 49
out of town shopping centres, 38
overflow channels, 84
overpopulation, 4
oxbow lakes, 75–77
Oxfam, 132
oxidation, 66

P
Pacific Ring of Fire, 52
padi-fields, 129
park and ride schemes, 44
parking charges, 44
pastoral farm, 125
pebbleometer, 205
periodic droughts, 127
pests and diseases, 130
pioneer species of salt tolerant plants, 93
plantation agriculture, 113, 127–128
plate boundary/margin
  collision boundaries/margins, 51
  conservative boundaries/margins, 52
  constructive boundaries/margins, 51
  destructive boundaries/margins, 51
plate margins, 50
plate tectonics, 49–50
political factors and population changes, 8
population control, 26–27
  China's 'One Child' policy, 27–28
population density, 4, 85
  countries showing variations, 9–10
  human factors affecting, 5, 8
  physical (natural) factors affecting, 5–7
population distribution, 4
  factors affecting, 5
  human factors affecting, 5, 8
  physical (natural) factors affecting, 5–7
population pyramid, 11, 16
population structure, 11–18
potholes, 73
precipitation, 124
prevailing wind, 208
protein and vitamin deficiency diseases, 132
public transport, 44–45
pyroclastic flows, 57, 60

Q
quadrat, 205
quaternary industry, 138
quotas, 125

R
rain-fed farming, 144
rain gauges, 103–104
range of services, 34
rank order, 34
rapids, 74
recycle of water, 178
refugees, 22
regeneration schemes, 38
regs, 117
relative humidity, 100–101, 208
relief and topography, 7, 124
renewable energy resources, 168–174
reservoirs, 113
retirement homes, 163
reurbanisation, 38
rice farming, 128–129
Richter scale, 53
rickets, 132
Rio de Janeiro, 42
river basin/drainage basin, 71, 209–210
river catchment, 71
river cliff, 75–76
river erosion
  processes of, 69
river floods, 81–83
River Nile Agreement, 1929, 176
river transportation, processes of, 70
river valleys, forms of, 71–72
road and rail communications, 33
rock pedestals/mushroom rocks, 117
rocks, 67
rubber plantation, 127
rural poverty, 131
rural-urban fringe, 39–41

S
salination, 135–136
saltation, 70
salt marshes, 93
sand dunes, 88–89, 117
satellites, 58
saturated ground, 81
science parks, 148
scree, 65
scurvy, 132
sea routes, 33
second homes, 163
seismometer /seismograph, 53, 58
self help schemes, 42
service or skill based industries, 139
settlement hierarchy, 34–35, 212
settlements, 119
  factors affecting, 31–32
  function of a, 33
  site of a, 31
  situation of the, 31
shallow earthquake, 52
sheep farming in Australia, 126–127
sheltered anchorage, 33
sheltered site, 32

shield volcanoes, 57
shifting cultivation, 126
short term food aid, 132
Silicon strip, UK, 148–149
Silicon Valley, USA, 147
sketch maps, 215
slash and burn agriculture, 112, 128
slave trade, 22
slip off slope, 76
Snowdonia, 21
social factors and population changes, 8–10
soil erosion, 131
soil fertility
  loss of, 131
soil fertility and population changes, 7
solar power, 172
solute load, 70
speedometer, 104
sphere of influence, 35–36
spillways, 84
spits, 92–93
squatter settlements, 42–43
stack, 91
'staff of life,' 174
star dunes, 117
starvation, 132
steep slope, 124
Stevenson, Robert Louis, 98
Stevenson screen, 97–98, 209
stratocumulus clouds, 107
stratus clouds, 107
strip cropping, 132
stump, 91
subduction, 49
subduction zone, 51
subsurface drip irrigation (SDI), 145
supply of fuel, 31
surface irrigation systems, 144
sustainable tourism, 161
swash, 87, 93

T
tally system, 215
tectonic plates, 50
terracing, 83
thermal power stations, 175
thermometers, 58
Thompson, Warren, 11
threshold population, 33, 36
tidal currents, 90
tied ridging, 83, 132
tier cropping, 132
tiered or layer cropping, 83
tilt meters, 58
tipping rain gauges, 104
Tombolo, 93
top-set beds, 78
tourism, 212
  defined, 153
  economic, social and cultural advantages, 155
  economic, social and cultural disadvantages, 156–157
  growth of leisure facilities and, 154–155
  in island nations, 154
  in Kenya, 157–161
  as popular global leisure activity, 153
  sustainable, 161
traction, 70
traffics, 162, 213, 215
transportation, processes of, 88–89
transverse dunes, 117
tributaries, 71
trickle irrigation, 145
tropical deserts, 115
tropical hurricanes, 130
tropical rainforest ecosystems (TRFs), 108–114
  importance of, 112–114
  structure, 110–111
  threats to, 112–114
tsunami, 52
  Asian, 2004, 61
  Japanese, 2011, 61–62
typhoons, 130

U
undercut, 75
underpopulation, 4
United Nations, 132
Urban Development Corporations (UDCs), 39
urbanisation, 20, 36
  impact on environment, 44–45
urban land use, models, 37–39
urban regeneration, 39
urban studies, 212
U.S. Historical Climatology Network, 98

V
very low population densities, 6
volcanic bombs, 57
Volcanic Explosivity Index, 59
volcanoes, 57–61
  active, 58
  areas for a number of reasons, 58–59
  composite, 58
  dome, 58
  dormant, 58
  extinct, 58
  Krakatoa eruption, 1883, 59
  Mauna Loa in Hawaii eruption, 61
  Mount St Helens eruption, 1980, 59–60
  predicting, 58–59
  shield, 57

W
wadis, 117
war, 131
waterfalls, 74–75
water resources, 84–85

and impact of water shortages, 176–178
watershed, 71
water supply and population changes, 6
wave cut platforms, 90–91
weather, defined, 97
weathering
biological, 66
chemical, 66
defined, 65
factors influencing the type and rate of, 66–67
physical/mechanical, 65–66
weather stations, 97–98
weather studies, 208–209
weed infestation, 127
wells, 132
wet bulb thermometer (hygrometer), 100–102, 208–209
wet point site, 31
wind abrasion, 117
wind deflation, 117
wind power, 171
wind vanes, 105–106
wing dykes, 84
world births, 3
World Food Programme (WFP), 132
world's largest pharmacy, 114
world's population, 3

X

xerophytes, 118

Y

yellow dunes, 88

Z

zooxanthellae, 94